Vocational Astrology

Judith A. Hill

Copyright 1997 by Judith A. Hill. All rights reserved.

No part of this book may be reproduced or transmitted in any form or by any means, electronic or mechanical, including photocopying or recording, or by any information storage and retrieval system, without written permission from the author and publisher. Requests and inquiries may be mailed to: American Federation of Astrologers, Inc., 6535 S. Rural Road, Tempe, AZ 85283.

ISBN-10: 0-86690-502-2
ISBN-13: 978-0-86690-502-2

First Printing: 2000
Current Printing: 2015

Cover Design: Jack Cipolla

Published by:
American Federation of Astrologers, Inc.
6535 S. Rural Road
Tempe, AZ 85283

www.astrologers.com

Dedication

This book is dedicated to my grandmother, Rozann, who generously encouraged my serious childhood studies in astrology, and to all students of astrology everywhere who are committed to excellence in their practice.

Acknowledgements

Gratitude is due all persons whose birth charts, and the professional accomplishments they represent, have contributed to the collection of vocational charts included in this book.

Contents

Introduction — vii
What Is Vocational Astrology/How It Works/History/ Research/The Three Vocational Houses/Role of the Midheaven

Chapter 1: The Zodiacal Signs and Vocation — 1
Sign Character/Vocational Rulership by Sign/Work Faults of the Signs

Chapter 2: Temperament and Profession — 17
The Role of the Sun/The Role of the Moon/The Twelve Moon Signs/The Role of the Ascendant/The Twelve Ascendant Signs

Chapter 3: The Four Elements and Three Modes — 27
Introduction to Elements and Modes/Vocational Rulerships

Chapter 4: Vocational Rulerships: The Planets and Nodes — 37
Vocational Listings by Planet/People and Products/Planetary Families

Chapter 5: Vocational Supplements of the Birth Chart — 49
The North and South Lunar Nodes/Planetary Combinations that Nullify or Reverse the South Node/The Part of Fortune/ Zodiacal Degrees/Fixed Stars/Vedic Nakshatras

Chapter 6: Planetary Strength and Weakness — 61
Planetary Dignity and Debility/Vocational Strength for Planets/Vocational Avoids: Planetary Weakness

Chapter 7: House Rulerships in Vocational Astrology — 69
What House System to Use/How to Interpret the House Placement of the Midheaven Ruler and other Vocational Planets/House Rulerships

Chapter 8: The Three Vocational Houses — 75
The Midheaven, Tenth, Second and Sixth House Rulers Through the Houses

Chapter 9: Reading the Vocational Horoscope   89
*What It Takes/The Best Planets/Beginning Synthesis/
Example Reading*

Chapter 10: Vocational Time Clocks   101
Saturn's Role/Important Transits and Progressions/Eclipses

Appendix A: A-Z Vocational Listings   113
Planet/Sign/House Combinations, Rulerships

Appendix B: Glossary of Vocational Terms   137

Appendix C: Collection of Vocational Horoscopes   141
*About the Data/How to Study the Collection/Vocational
Chart Collection Listing/The Vocational Chart Collection*

Bibliography   201

Introduction

And he shall be like a tree planted by the rivers of the Water, that bringeth forth his fruit in his season; his leaf also shall not wither; and whatsoever he goeth shall prosper.—Psalm 1:3

Everyone has his/her place in this world. No one exists who does not fulfill some particular role upon the stage of life and it is to this role that the art of vocational astrology directs itself. Astrology assigns each career a planet, a sign and sometimes even a special start. Our familiar expression, "it was in his stars ... " stems from the ancient concept that the life one leads is written in the stars at birth. In many societies, vocation is an inherited affair and the son or daughter continue the work their father and mother have done. Western cultures, on the other hand, present their high school graduates with an almost infinite and often confusing array of choices. To facilitate such choices is the work of vocational consultants who decipher various aptitude test scores in hopes of suggesting suitable careers for their clients. The vocational astrologer performs this same task with the assistance of a planetary birth map accurately calculated from the exact minute, day, month, year and place of birth.

Roots

Vocational astrology is not new. English astrologer William Lilly, a "latecomer," writing in 1647 addresses "the employment of which any one is capable." The simplistic vocational astrology of his day was appropriate to his time and culture. Each career was allotted a sign and planet, a practice well described in Ptolemy's Tetrabiblos (140 A.D.) and probably ancient at that time! We must remember that Ptolemy copied much of his material from ancient sources at the Library of Alexandria, which was later burned. Furthermore, the four astrological elements (fire, earth, air, water) were quite literally associated with like careers.

Lilly comments: "As fiery Signs shew worker at the Fire, whether goldsmiths, & c., so Earthy Signs shew occupations connected with the Earth, as potters, ditchers, brick makers, gardeners & c.; Airy Signs import singers, game keepers, actors, & c., and Watery, sailors, fishermen, watermen, laundresses, waiters in taverns, & c."

The Three Vocational Houses

Each chart possesses three vocational houses related to livelihood (see Figure 1). An astrological house is created by spherically dividing the celestial sphere that surrounds the infant at birth. Houses also imply directional meaning because they exist directionally (east, west, north, south, above, below) in relation to the birth site. A planet's house position is directionally placed above or below your birth place, east or west, north or south, etc.

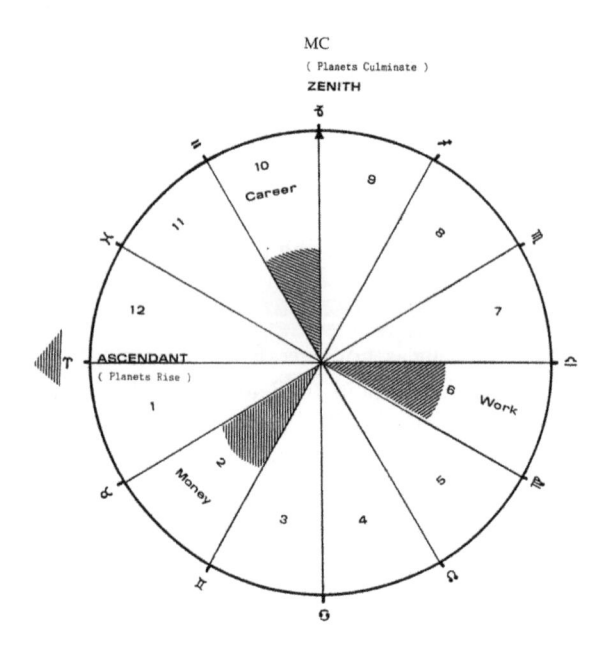

Figure 1 THE THREE VOCATIONAL HOUSES
Primary Vocational Regions of the Planetary Birth Map.

All ancient traditions attach qualitative meaning to each spatial direction, and it is this special quality of received light that in part gives the astrological houses their interpretive meanings. There are many ways to divide the celestial sphere, producing an array of house systems quite bewildering to the novice astrologer. I suggest using the system of your choice in combination with the system of "whole sign houses" described in Chapter 7. With a few exceptions, most house systems include twelve houses. Collectively, and in order of importance, the tenth, sixth and second houses form the triad of "artha" houses, a Hindu term implying materially oriented affairs. The tenth house governs position, reputation, career and life work, whereas the sixth house governs jobs, useful work for hire, skills, coworkers and the work environment. The second house refers to one's earning power, money and sources of income.

The Midheaven

The Midheaven, also known as the Mid Celestial or Zenith, represents the intersection of the great meridian (north-south circle) with the ecliptic (circle of Earth's orbit around the Sun). In northern latitudes, this point will be above your head, a bit south, at your birth. More precisely, it is always where the Sun peaks, i.e. culminates at high noon.

Although your entire chart plays a part in vocational analysis, the planet(s) nearest the Midheaven and also the *planetary ruler of the sign on the Midheaven,* may satisfactorily describe your career (see Figure]).

Claudius Ptolemy, writing his *Tetrabiblos* near 140 A.D., stated: "The dominion of the employment or profession, is claimed in two quarters, viz. by the Sun, and by the Sign on the Midheaven. It is, therefore, necessary to observe whether any planet may be making its oriental appearance nearest to the Sun, and whether any be posited in the Midheaven; especially also receiving the application of the Moon. . . ."

For vocational purposes, modern astrologers pay scarce attention to the planets placed oriental to the Sun, probably because finding a consistent meaning for the word "oriental" is next to impossible. Ptolemy was probably describing the planet positioned so as to first rise before the Sun, also known as the "doryphory" or spear bearer. Although I strongly encourage students to study the vocational implications of this oriental planet, this book emphasizes the Midheaven sign and degree, the nearest planets in proximity to the Midheaven and the Midheaven ruler.

The planets culminating or nearest the Midheaven, and also sometimes rising (Ascendant), have long been thought to describe the work of the individual. For instance, Mars near the Zenith (Midheaven), or alternatively near the Ascendant (Figure 1) denotes the fighting careers-lawyers, soldiers and athletes. All "careers of the sword" also come under Mars, which rules sharp tools. Mechanics, engineers and acupuncturists also come under its beams. Chapter 4 provides a thorough listing of vocational rulerships according to each sign, planet and house.

The planet highest in the sky at birth, and therefore closest to the Zenith, is said to testify to the life work of the native, further qualified by its sign and degree placement, as well as its aspects. This culminating planet is thought by astrologers to say something of the general fortune, position, reputation and rank attainable by the individual.

When we say that one is at the zenith of his career, we reflect the old astrological idea. Shakespeare's plays give voice to these beliefs with statements such as one found in *The Tempest* when Prospero says, "I find my Zenith doth depend upon a most auspicious star; whose influence, if I now court not, but omit, my fortunes will ever after droop." (Act 1, Sc. 2).

Many astrologers today prefer an outlook quite different from that of Shakespeare's England. The Zenith planet may best be thought to symbolize the career potentials instead of ruling same. Should one have no Zenith planet, one can alternatively use the ruler of the sign at the Midheaven. This view places all responsibility for success or failure on ourselves rather than passing blame on the hapless planet!

Scientific Research of Vocational Astrology

A great body of scientific research lends support to the doctrine of the Zenith planet. In the 1950s, French scientists Michel and Francoise Gauquelin statistically tested and compared the planetary positions at birth for eminent physicians, scientists, athletes, writers, military generals, actors and politicians. The groups tested were quite large—14,409 actors, 3,547 eminent physicians and scientists, 13,522 writers, etc. What the Gauquelins found amazed them and sparked a decades-long controversy between the Gauquelin results and astrology's opponents.

The Gauquelins discovered that planets near the Ascendant and Zenith were not the same for eminent people of different professions. Instead of being born when the planets were randomly and, therefore, semi-uniformly, distributed (accounting for the natural human birth rhythm, which is not uniform because more babies are born in the morning hours), the planetary distributions were very unusual and differed dramatically for each professional group. Athletes, for instance, preferred birth when Mars was near one of these two vocational hotspots. Physicians and scientists preferred birth when Mars and Saturn were near one of these two vocational hotspots, *always peaking just before the actual point,* i.e. rising or culminating. (They also discovered two other lesser peaks opposite these first two, although these do not substantiate the Zenith-Ascendant tradition.) Writers preferred the Moon, whereas actors and politicians were disposed to birth when Jupiter was prominent. Military leaders were inclined to be born when both Jupiter and, appropriately, Mars, the war planet, were prominent in these key angles.

Not only were the results extremely statistically significant, but in most respects correlated nicely with astrological tradition with regard to the character or qualities necessary for the various vocational groups. However, Gauquelin's findings depart slightly from modern astrological tradition in one curious way: Astrologers today feel that the strongest planet should be located near the Zenith (correlating with Gauquelin's findings), but within the tenth house, or just prior to culmination (see Figure 1).

The Gauquelins' findings instead reveal the statistical peak of vocational planets to be just following culmination. This is why I always suggest using the closest planet to the Midheaven, on either side, but with preference for the Gauquelins' peak, after culmination.

The same holds true for planets rising near the Ascendant. The statistical peak for specific vocational planets was shared by an area just after rising and not before, as modern astrologers are more prone to asset. Curiously, this agrees with a comment made by the great psychic Edgar Cayce, who said that planets within seven degrees above the Ascendant (rising into eastern visibility) would be extremely influential in the life of the native.

The Gauquelin findings have been challenged by others and successfully replicated. Although they denied it, their findings lend considerable support to the relevance of ancient astrological practice. There is ample evidence that the early Egyptian and Babylonian astrologers placed great importance on the eastern rising (or late twelfth house) position of the planets and stars, this being the region of first visible appearance near the eastern horizon following their long sojourn underneath the Earth. This is one example of how scientific research and statistics can assist astrologers in the refinement of their art.

The Gauquelins' breakthrough research is made especially credible owing to the fact that it has been exhaustively reanalyzed, retested and successfully replicated by more than one outside scientist. Despite all attempts of skeptical scientists to invalidate the Gauquelin results, they remain undefeated and all studies conducted to disprove them have only ended up replicating the results! The early history of the Gauquelin replications can be found in Michel Gauquelin's *Birth Times*.

The work of the Gauquelins stands today as one of the greatest contributions to both science and astrology, although the prevailing anti-astrology bias among some scientists (not all!) has restricted the impact and application of these discoveries.

Usefulness of Vocational Astrology

People seek vocational guidance from astrologers for many reasons. They commonly feel confused about their work and need a fresh overview of their abilities or clues for increased financial profit.

The vocational horoscope is a planetary birth map used exclusively for the purpose of answering vocational concerns. Much of the information obtained will be similar to that acquired through other methods, i.e. vocational tests and counseling. However, there are major differences. A vocational test might say you will make a fine electrician but it can't predict your success in the field. Neither can such aptitude tests predict your financial potential or emotional well-being in the suggested occupations. What if an electrical career were dangerous for you because you had a weird predilection to electrocution? An aptitude test can't tell you that, but your vocational horoscope can!

Sometimes clients need to choose between two different lines of work or two positions offered. A medical student might be contemplating the best field of medicine to enter. In the first case, the astrologer works in much the same manner as any vocational counselor, sans all those expensive tests. And the medical student can be greatly helped if the astrologer is familiar with the body part rulerships as given by medical astrology. If "luck in the nose" is indicated, the intern would be well advised to become a sinus specialist or perhaps a cosmetic surgeon!

A vocational chart reading can give a good overview of abilities. Talents are assessed and needs described. Should the client freelance or hold a secure position under someone else? Work alone or with others? Be the boss or the secretary? It is important to define areas of interest, such as whether the client should work with figures, machines or people, or whether he or she would be happiest outdoors or behind a desk. Specific careers can be suggested that are compatible with the temperament and best vocational planets of the individual.

A really good vocational astrologer often surprises clients by accurately describing their precise occupations. The author has witnessed one vocational astrologer accurately assess the occupations of five people before meeting them and with no previous knowledge of their activities! In the case of confusion between two different careers, the vocational astrologer can be particularly valuable. Should the client's quandary be whether to become a lawyer or remain in the computer field, the astrologer carefully studies the planetary rulers of each field and may the best planet win.

A choice between two job offers in the same field requires another approach. Planetary charts are drawn for the exact moment each position was first offered and, if possible, for the company's birth date. These charts can be compared with the questioner's own birth chart for compatibility. Unfortunately, obtaining the prospective company's birth time can be difficult or embarrassing for the client, a situation limiting to conscientious astrological practice.

Western people are generally free today to try their hand at whatever enterprise they desire, and yet it remains true that there is work for which an individual is most fit. Vocational astrology has survived today not as a relic of bygone eras but as a rich and growing tradition in the service of our twenty-first century humanity.

Chapter 1

The Zodiacal Signs and Vocation

Aries, a Sign of Mars: Action

Aries excels at independent motivation, originality, impulse. A surprising number of teachers, jazz singers, producers and creative artists are born with the Sun in this sign. Aries types are original and are full of energy and passion. If a strong front runner is needed, look for a prominent Aries element in the chart. Aries loves to prove itself and to be out in the lead. This is a positive, upbeat and confident sign. Experiencing and inspiring, Aries makes an excellent teacher and motivational speaker. A positive Aries person is a joy to be around, full of warmth and life. Aries types are fun loving and always ready for a good laugh. This is a straight ahead, straightforward person who won't hide what he/she feels. What you see is what you get! Count on Aries for honesty, directness, physical toughness and psychological resilience. Aries people are excellent in start-up ventures, self-employment and commission-based work.

Faults: Poor follow-through. Dislikes routine and subordinate roles. Aries types possess an unfortunate inclination to act without thought, sometimes to their own detriment. The Arian urge to "just do it" overpowers the more contemplative faculties, and awareness of cause and effect is minimal. Aries is a childlike sign and displays behavioral problems such as poor discipline, brash stupidity, hyperactivity and irritability. These people are highly prone to quitting a job when pressured or when someone talks down to them. Aries may be a fighter, but it is not a strategist, having the foolish tendency to jump into battle without either a battle plan or armor. And although a strong beginner, Aries is not always at the finish line.

Taurus, a Sign of Venus: Stabilization, Endurance

Taurus is a builder, slow, steady and reliable. Natural designers, Taureans excel in both fine and technical art. This sign can be counted on for follow-through and possesses excellent common sense. Easygoing and unflappable, Taurus types are well liked and bring a calming influence to any work environment. Their appreciation for beauty and comfort is unrivaled. They typically have an excellent sense of how things are put together and the best ability to see things exactly as they are without projection. Taureans are excellent artists, chefs, heavyweight fighters, masseurs, bakers, gardeners, movers, builders, musicians (especially of mouth instruments), composers, landscapers, bankers, football players and singers.

Faults: A Taurus type makes an excellent employee with few faults. If they enjoy their work environment and are well compensated, a long-term or lifetime job commitment can be expected. However, Taurus types incline toward inertia, inflexibility, overweight and lack of speed. Taurus types can remain in ruts, jobs, homes or relationships that they should have left long ago. Also, they have a tendency to allow themselves to be used and manipulated, seemingly enjoying being a helpful resource for others. As can be seen, their faults tend to hurt themselves more than anyone else.

Persons with this Ascendant are better at follow-through (where they excel) than leadership or initiation. Fast-paced, unpredictable, risky and changeable occupations are unsuitable for security-loving Taurus unless other signs prevail. They prefer nice music in the background, a comfy chair, a satisfying lunch and good benefits, and thrive on the "same old, same old." In return they will fulfill beautifully all that is expected of them, but seldom more. Do not expect the great humanitarians, theorists and social saviors of the zodiac to line up in this season of birth!

Natives of this sign can become too laid back and comfortable on the job. As dedicated family people, Taureans should never be placed in positions requiring overtime. Getting pleasure-loving Taurus to accept critical, highly challenging or uncomfortable work may take some doing. However, their physical toughness enables them to handle physically demanding work better than perhaps any other sign except Scorpio! Like their icon the bull, once moving in any direction they are difficult to stop. As long as this direction is positive, no problem. In reverse, the bad habits of a Taurus type may be nearly impossible to break!

A self-indulgent sign, Taurus is inclined to excessive self-interest (eats too many of the office donuts and expects top pay). However, this dependable and pleasant sign takes orders beautifully, gives no lip and possesses an agreeable work ethic.

Gemini, a Sign of Mercury: Communication, Personal Coordination

Gemini gives the light touch, possessing a dexterity and coordinated speed useful in occupations requiring flexibility, dexterity and surface activity. This sign excels at all trades requiring personal coordination. Communication is key, and Gemini types love to talk and talk, making them ideal for telephone operations, news journalism and other fast communication fields. As much as they like to talk, they like to walk and window shop their way through life. They prefer a job environment with a high level of variety.

Acrobatic, lingual and "juggling" skills are common to natives of this remarkably playful sign. Planetary emphasis in Gemini suggests good hand-eye coordination. The Gemini influence produces many of the best jugglers, telephone operators, sign language workers, taxi drivers, writers of light material, columnists, disk jockeys, messengers, circus performers, mimics, mimes, thieves, instrumentalists, jazz musicians, handymen, reporters. Improvisation is a forte.

Faults: Complete lack of staying power. Gemini tires of a project if rewards are not nearly immediate. This sign demonstrates poor motivation and a short attention span. (Note: Attention deficit disorder, learning disabilities, stuttering and dyslexia are related to poorly aspected planets in Gemini or Pisces.) Gemini types have an unfortunate fault for thinking the word is the deed and the book is the knowledge. Typically, they collect books and never read them!

While on the job they write songs, scribble in notebooks or work on puzzles, and require too many coffee breaks. The more negative natives of this mischievous sign are infamous for saying one thing and doing another. While their noncommittal devil's advocacy is ideal for a lawyer, it is unsuitable for jobs where a passionate, one-sided commitment is essential. Usually they chatter incessantly, make puns and tell bad jokes. Smoking, doodling, gum chewing, finger drumming, whistling and other nervous ticks are additional bad habits of this sign. Negative Gemini frequently produces drifters and "starving students."

Cancer, the Sign of the Moon: Small Area Focus, Intimacy, Security, Organization of Immediate Environment

Cancer is the quintessential shopkeeper. These individuals do well in highly personal, family-like environments where they can play an organizational or nurturing/fostering role. A great many career and office wives are born with the Sun in this sign, which is good for all manner of emotional work, and often is psychic and musical. Small focus, sensitivity and personal contact are keynotes.

Cancerian careers include pet sitters, nannies, herb gardeners, butlers, manservants, interior decorators, musicians, nurses, child care workers, shopkeepers, groundskeepers, tavern owners, family business owners, ma and pa operations, bed and breakfast managers, cottage industries, estate keepers, shepherds, treasurers, potters, tarot readers and any parenting occupations. Cancerians are extremely loyal to the household, the boss and the company.

Faults: Shortsightedness. Persons of this sign type tend to get fixated on themselves and their feelings. There is a peculiarly Cancerian tendency to talk endlessly about personal and, often, trivial issues. Cancer is a timid and defensive sign whose natives can be fearful of change and new environments. The security instinct is usually working overtime in Cancer individuals. When devoted, however, they can be counted on to stay in one job for a lifetime.

Negative Cancerians crumble under the slightest criticism, react poorly to trivial disagreements and can brood over tiny emotional issues for days. This is a moody sign that has difficulty concealing those moods. Sometimes it really is best for the whole office when they call in sick and take a day off work (as they are quite prone to do).

However, no sign can beat the tenderness of heart and true devotion of Cancer (Princess Diana was born with a Cancer Sun and an Aquarius Moon). Trust this sign to remember birthdays, favorite flower colors, the name of a friend's dog and all those little things in life that are so important.

Leo, the Sign of the Sun: Self-Importance, Kingship, Pleasure, Power

Count on Leo type personalities for personal style, charisma and the ability (and love of) attracting attention to themselves. Work as we know it does not suit Leo people. They must rule and have lots of time for recreation. Theater and acting are natural to

Leo. However, they also excel at management and business development, especially in the pleasure and recreational industries, and possess a love of color and life matched only by the other fire signs, Sagittarius and Aries. Leos are warm and, although royal, have an excellent common touch, great smile and love of people. Usually they become entrepreneurs and enjoy owning theaters, nightclubs and restaurants. A lot of popular chefs and bartenders are born with the Sun in this sign. As one might suspect, a statistically significant number of the great band leaders in jazz music history were born with the Sun in Leo-sixty percent to be exact! Many Leos enjoy the sense of importance a uniform can bring. Police officers and guards often have strong planetary placements in this sign.

Faults: Negative Leos dislike working for others because they prefer to be the boss. They dislike routine work and petty details. If they are not having fun, entertaining, giving orders or making a splash, they become arrogant and inattentive. Leos cannot bear subordinate positions. Egotism and attitude can make Leos a real pain to be around. A really negative Leo throws tantrums when displeased. Leos never question themselves because they are always right. They do not apologize or admit error because it is not their problem; it is someone else's. Unfortunately, it is nearly impossible to get Leo individuals to change bad habits.

Virgo, a Sign of Mercury: Perfection and Preparation of the Physical Plane, Data Filing, Service, Usefulness, Technicality, Skill

A strong Virgo type is intensely focused on the useful improvements to be made within the physical world and beyond. This sign governs facts and their orderly filing. It specializes in the care and healing of the physical body. All subordinate medical professions and secretarial occupations are ideal. Virgo is the best editor, accountant, bookkeeper, file clerk and nurse, and also makes a gifted administrator, especially in the social services. Psychologists, hatha yogis, secretaries and veterinarians invariably have a large dose of this sign in their birth charts. Virgo often makes a natural social worker and these natives are found in large numbers throughout that profession. A statistically significant number of nursing administrators in *Who's Who* were born with the Sun in Virgo. Mother Teresa and Jane Adams, two women who won the Nobel Peace Prize for their work with the poor, were Virgos.

Gardening, farming, horticulture, bass playing and many technical trades are highly appealing to natives of this sign. In combination with a more creative sign, Virgo produces excellent skilled craftspersons.

This sign also governs the most humble and servile of occupations, especially those involving cleaning and service. Gas station attendants, janitors, food preparation workers and maids typically have this modest sign quite prominent in their birth charts. This is a physically tough and resilient sign. Highly compassionate, if a bit dry, this dutiful sign deserves more praise than it normally receives from astrological texts. Natives of this sign can be depended upon for the long haul. The donkey would be a more suitable icon for this birth season than the virgin!

Faults: It is difficult to find vocational faults with Virgo, the ruling sign of the worker. However, they lack imagination and also the ability to relax and just let it flow. Virgos are therefore unsuited for occupations that depend on a loose, unstructured type of mind. Virgo needs to be of use, needs tasks and needs to get things done. A do-nothing job would be intolerable for natives of this useful sign. Virgo can be shy and overly reserved. This is the assistant and the conveyor belt worker, *not* the front runner or initiator!

True Virgos loathe disorder and have an annoying habit of pointing out the trivial offenses of coworkers. Virgos at their worst can obsess about the care and precise placement of their tools, clothing and other objects. In seeing the trees, Virgo fails to see the forest. One can, after all, be too practical.

Libra, a Sign of Venus: Impartiality, Observation, Compromise

The scales are an apt symbol for the sign so concerned with the balance of "I" and "thou." In response to Aries, its opposite sign, there is the warrior side of Libra, always fighting for justice. Therefore, Libra is the quintessential sign of the lawyer (Libra combined with Scorpio and Aries makes the best lawyer), and a surprising number of military generals also have been born with the Sun in this sign.

The Libra ability to listen and observe is marked. Reasoning ability, comparative judgment and intellectual logic are highly developed in many of this sign. Counselors, diplomats, scientists and representatives and advisors of all kinds do well to have a strong Libra component in their chart. Libra can also be depended on for tastefulness, charm, sociability, wisdom and good manners.

Faults: Overly Venusian Librans can suffer from laziness, fussiness, TV addiction, weak discipline and lack of personal motivation. They need too much outer stimulus and seek to be continually entertained. A surprising number of Libra natives have drug and alcohol problems.

This sign type does poorly in solitude when there is little verbal contact with fellow human beings, and can be finicky about dirt, blood, insects, etc. Sometimes they display the curious trait of being fanatically devoted to some idealistic point of view, becoming irrational and argumentative. "Counterphobia," that curious habit of always holding an opinion opposite from that of a discussion partner, seems uniquely Libran. However, this behavior is only displayed by the negative warrior Librans and not the diplomatic Venusian Libra types.

Work faults include impracticality, indecisiveness, romantic idolization of favorite people, gossiping and absolute emotional objectivity and cold detachment just when a friend expects them to be there for him/her (never expect fair Libra to support anyone automatically, right or wrong). These, of course, are the more difficult tendencies of an otherwise charming, wise and refined nature.

Scorpio, a Sign of Mars and Pluto, Power and Knowledge over Matter, Dissection, Transformation, Concentrated Emotion

Scorpios need high intensity focus. Danger and death are interesting to Scorpio, the quintessential sign of surgeons. Paralegals, lawyers, generals, exterminators, chemists, emergency room technicians, criminal investigators, sewage workers, investigators, hypnotherapists, parapsychologists, psychologists, spies, sex workers and colonic therapists all come under the auspices of this truly courageous sign. Nothing is too foul or dirty for Scorpio to handle! Trust Scorpio when something really important needs to be accomplished.

The natural secrecy of this sign is ideal for occupations requiring strategy, subterfuge and confidentiality. No sign understands politics like Scorpio! This is an alert, dependable an extremely energetic sign that misses nothing and is capable of absolute dedication. The physical, mental and emotional stamina tops that of any other sign.

Scorpio enjoys critical, concentrated focus and high impact work. When the need arises to perform something dangerous or there is a long-term battle, hire a Scorpio type. Scorpios are crazy about dogs, with whom they have much in common-loyalty intense affection for favorite people and a willingness to give their all in battle.

Faults: The intensely heavy, brooding nature of negative Scorpios makes them unpopular, as they always have an axe to grind. They typically engage in power struggles or serious quarrels, which unfortunately can be with coworkers. Scorpios can lack social graces, be rudely blunt, scathingly sarcastic, authoritarian and dislike the silly fun that lighter types such as Gemini enjoy. Everything is taken seriously. Beware of firing Scorpio postal employees.

However, unlike some other sign types, Scorpios do admit their faults, being as brutally honest with themselves as with everyone else. And no sign is as absolutely dependable in a crisis as is Scorpio.

Sagittarius, a Sign of Jupiter: Self-extension, Universal Coordination, The Quest, Aiming

Sagittarians must have room, literally and figuratively. Distance occupations requiring travel are excellent. This is a large focus sign that understands future projections and is unafraid of risk. A great many compulsive gamblers come under the beams of Sagittarius. Intuitive, they are also lucky enough for that intuition to pay off. This is the sign of publicity, advertising and promotion.

Teachers, pilots, advertisers and "cheerleaders" in any occupation are typical of this sign. Careers are ballplayer, sharpshooter, drummer, bus driver, motivational speaker, firefighter, wilderness guide, "frontiersman" in any field, adventurer, hunter, corporate level salesperson, importer-exporter, train conductor and those who must aim, shoot or run for a living. Sagittarians are comfortable in foreign lands and cultures.

At its best, Sagittarius is a remarkably cheerful sign, uplifting and energizing to all provided they aren't also making them nervous. Most of all, Sagittarians have a spectacular gift for *coordinating* diverse people, interests or functions into one working organism. Remember, Sagittarius governs the sciatic nerve, the great coordinator of neurological connections. Similarly, Sagittarius is the sign of the orchestral conductor.

Faults: This is a careless sign, prone to great risk and foolishness. Sagittarians like the quick buck. Plunging into things, they can be accident prone. Sagittarians enjoy a good gamble or a horse race. They suffer from an excess of generosity and overly expanded mental states. Therefore, it is not always the best policy to trust a Sagittarian type with lots of important tiny details or large sums of money (unless there is a strong Virgo counterbalance).

Excitement can become an important motivation for negative Sagittarians who quickly become bored with the everyday work environment. A tendency to nervously fidget, tap their fingers, slam doors, pace and talk or laugh loudly or excessively can irritate coworkers and disturb office concentration.

Loving freedom too much, Sagittarian types cannot tolerate emotionally mushy occupations or jobs where personal attachment and bonding occur.

Many Sagittarians are compulsive travelers. Job staying power is therefore limited, as Sagittarians tend to be ever onward to greener pastures, at least in their minds. However, this unfortunate scattering tendency is less marked than in Gemini, its opposing sign, and Sagittarians can indeed stick to a job if they believe in what they are doing and can get away from it frequently. Beloved office sparkplugs, they are missed by all when they move on.

Claustrophobia, hyperactivity, excessive talking, hysteria, rambling, nervousness and fanaticism are negative traits. Negative Sagittarians get carried away with themselves and with philosophical ideas. (My apologies for listing so many faults; however, this wonderfully optimistic and uplifting sign could use a little criticism once in a while!)

Capricorn, a Sign of Saturn: Achievement, Perfection, Control of the Larger Environment

The goat needs to climb, and this is the quintessential sign of the empire builder. People who start from scratch and end up on top of a huge financial or spiritual kingdom display much of the Capricorn temperament. (Some examples of this Capricornian "sow's ear to silk purse" phenomenon are Elvis Presley, Helena Rubenstein, Madame W.C. Walker and the great guru Paramahansa Yogananda.) Determined, ruthlessly ambitious and authoritative, the natives of this sign are frequently found at the top as presidents of corporations.

Saturn gives the Capricorn a sense of importance, protocol and order. These people are good architects, police officers, physicians, school administrators, bureaucrats, teachers, politicians, organizers and real estate developers.

Austere and introverted, the quieter type of Capricorn is content with the simplest of lives and makes an excellent priest, hermit, monk or nun. The orderly Capricorn excels above all other signs in the graphic arts and printing trades.

Capricorn is the true sign of the capitalist. The natives of Capricorn earn their positions through patient planning and meticulous social climbing and rarely the luck and happenstance of some other signs. They know to whom to give their respect, and also expect to be respected.

Faults: Inflexibility, rigidity, insensitivity. Beware of the Capricornian tendency to step on anyone's head on the way to the top! A really bad Capricorn can be a control freak. People of this sign, when negative, tend to be authoritative old fogies, resistant to change. This is the unbending bureaucrat one hates to encounter. There also exists the reserved monk Capricorn.

Negative Capricorns lack warmth and have very little in the way of the common touch. Because of this failing, they should not be expected to participate in sing-alongs, hold hands in a circle or give spontaneous hugs. (The occasional friendly Capricorn will have lots of planets in neighboring Sagittarius or Aquarius.) However, they do like to conform, and will do what they can to fit in with the group, eventually leading it.

Aquarius, a Sign of Saturn and Uranus: Individuality, Interest in Humanity, Creative Intellect

The Aquarian is the type that most often turns up in the vocational astrologer's office. This is not due to a lack of potential. Heavens, no! This is one of the most brilliant signs of the zodiac. Frequently they harbor true genius in any number of fields, but do not know how to market themselves. Sometimes an Aquarian's talents are so wide that he/she doesn't know where to begin. Confidence and ego commonly are weak.

Natives of this sign are idealistic and love to work to better the planet. Satisfying this philanthropic need is essential to their vocational happiness, more so than making money. Aquarians excel at any work utilizing their wonderful imaginations. Abstract intellectual work and invention are natural capacities of Aquarius. Cartoonists, astrologers, scientists, high tech, sports, electricians, computer experts, jazz musicians, anthropologists, aviators, theorists and inventors are the typical occupations of this sign.

Often there is a deep interest in humanity, people, justice and character building. Aquarians, therefore, make the best mentors, ministers and coaches. (A statistically significant number of coaches in both baseball and football were born in Aquarius.) Hire Aquarian types for positions demanding a high level of creative thought, intuition and originality. A wonderful sense of the absurd and a gift for fellowship is classic to Aquarian employees.

Faults: The Aquarian birth month is peopled with impractical dreamers. Aquarian types have difficulty conforming, dressing normally and being on time. There is an unfortunate tendency to begin projects at strangely inappropriate moments-when the mood strikes-such as a plumbing project ten minutes before dinner guests are expected to arrive or pruning the hedges at midnight. Aquarians have an especially irritating tendency to fiddle with what "ain't broke," creating worse problems in so doing.

Many Aquarians are know-it-alls and natural teachers, compulsively doling out unasked advice and fine points on everything, including subjects about which they know nothing.

Excessively trusting, Aquarians are natural "marks" for the con artist. Rarely are material goods of top priority, and they can lose money for an organization by "giving away the store."

Warning: Aquarius, while easygoing, is the most stubborn of all the fixed family of signs. Aquarius type employees will always do what they believe best, regardless of what they are told. They might refuse to perform duties that go against their moral sentiments, a trait that's rather commendable.

Pisces, a Sign of Jupiter and Neptune: Synthesis, Universal Love, Universality, Impressions, Escape

Pisces is the greatest synthesizer of the zodiac. Think of the ocean, which is accepting of everything. Persons of this sign excel at the personal interpretation of universal feelings. Many great ballet dancers, composers, poets, impressionist painters and photographers are born with the Sun in this sign. The psychic nature of Pisces is legendary. Pisceans also have a natural gift for acquiring skills and language quickly, stunning their employers with their versatility. However, unless more alert signs like Virgo and Gemini are present, their mentality is diffusive and poor with practical details.

Note: This rule is not without exception. Some Pisceans can, in polarity to their opposite sign Virgo, be surprisingly adept at details in an almost psychic sort of way. Many of the best researchers are representatives of this kind of "Virgoan" Pisces.

The Pisces mind is fluid and absorbent, not intellectual. Indeed, Pisceans are so absorbent of thoughts, feelings and atmosphere that they require solitude and peaceful quiet to recharge themselves. A lot of room for mental "drift" is therefore a necessity.

Pisceans are prone to eccentric and off-beat careers such as selling balloons, folk singing on street corners and handwriting analysis. They love old things, fantasy, whimsy and collecting books and records. This is a gentle sign that prefers to be well out of the limelight. Pisces is the chameleon, quickly taking on the color of its environment. Atmosphere and environment can make or break a Piscean. A positive and soothing work environment is imperative for natives of this sensitive sign.

Piscean careers include antique dealer, used record vendor, clown, musician, circus worker, impressionist artist, photographer, poet, fairy tale writer or illustrator, researcher, astrologer, psychic, sleep disorder therapist, cartoonist, animator, zookeeper, animal communications expert, audiologist, worker with the autistic or deaf or blind, parapsychologist, yogi, toy seller, film editor, light show producer, sound mixer, actor, dancer, singer, sailor, boating instructor, archivist, museum worker, marijuana grower, charity worker and monk.

Faults: Excessive impressionability and shyness makes Pisces a poor choice for occupations requiring firmness, toughness or a commanding personality. Crowds, noise and chaos affect their sensitive nerves adversely because they incline to delicacy on all levels.

Because they love and require leisure, negative Pisceans become depressed when holding almost any kind of routine nine-to-five job. Depression, fatigue, character weakness and low self-esteem can become real problems on any job. Remember, there are two classes of Pisceans: the tired and depressed and the extremely cheerful and jolly.

People of this sign have trouble with boundaries. Emotionally, sexually and often in their work relationships, they get too close to the boss or, worse, a client. Pisceans can be very untidy, impractical and disorderly. (Yet they be surprising too because some Pisceans are neater than Virgo!)

Another curious work fault of Pisceans is their effect on equipment. Machinery tends to break down around Pisces type individuals. Seldom are Pisceans high on material values, and they cannot be expected to excel in purely capitalistic professions. Watch out for excessive borrowing and misplacing of everything from chewing gum to car keys.

Many Pisceans prefer dependency to work, and a surprising number are successful at attracting inheritances, gifts, wealthy spouses or strange financial luck. Unfortunately, they just don't comprehend the concept of sustained effort. This is, after all, the sign that rules sleep. (It also governs spiritual work.)

The proverbial sweetness of Pisces people makes up for all their shortcomings in the workplace. Probably their biggest fault is their seeming inability to either say or understand the word "no."

Chapter 2

Temperament and Profession

Vocational Effects of Sun, Moon and Ascendant

Every horoscope contains two kinds of vocational "significators" (see Glossary): *vocational significators* and *temperamental indicators*—the Sun, Moon and ascending signs. The former show our distinct talents and occupational affinities. These can and often do describe the exact profession of the individual. *However, it is the Sun, Moon and Ascendant that reveal our true interest and emotional suitability for particular careers.* It is not uncommon for highly successful people to be perfectly miserable in their successful careers. Invariably, their unhappiness can be traced to a temperamental unsuitability. Have you ever been bored doing something you are good at?

In the reverse, some folks love their work but enjoy little success. In such cases we find that the temperamental indicators (Sun, Moon and Ascendant) are compatible with their work, whereas the *planetary career ruler* (planet that rules the said career) is poorly placed, weak or besieged in such a way than the hoped-for success is prohibited.

There are three *temperamental indicators* of prime importance: the *Sun sign* and house position, the *Moon sign* and house position and the *ascending sign*.

For professional happiness our center values as symbolized by the *Sun's* sign and house position must not be ignored. After all, the Sun is the center of our solar system. The words "central values" refer to what is most important to us at base. What do we revolve around? If our innermost nature as shown by our Sun sign and house is not satisfied, we may feel unfulfilled.

Maybe it is the *Moon's* position that fails to agree with the planet describing the career, producing a state of emotional disenchantment and dislike of the chosen career.

Or perhaps the *ascending sign* describes an outlook on life that is incompatible with the current field of employment. We might feel "all thumbs" in the work role, a misfit.

Temperamental Indicators

The Sun, the Sun Sign and House—Inner Purpose

(In locating the Sun's house, be sure to include a whole sign house count from the Ascendant as described in Chapter 7.)

The Sun is not necessarily of itself a vocational indicator unless one of the three vocational houses (Chapter 7) falls under Leo and the Sun's rulership. However the Sun symbolizes our purpose and what we revolve around, much in the same way as it acts as the center of the solar system. Therefore, a good career astrologer seeks to discover this central value, this most essential and important ideal. Few are inwardly happy in a career that does not bring the Sun sign and house *as a central interest or value* into play in some fashion. To interpret the role of the Sun, locate its sign and house position. Chapters 7 and 8 provide house meanings and how to use them. Chapter 1 is entirely devoted to the twelve zodiacal signs, their vocational aptitudes and their vocational faults. (Apply these qualities to the Moon and ascending signs as well as the Sun sign.) An understanding of the esoteric meanings of the signs is helpful and is provided in my article, "Esoteric Astrology, 1 and 2," listed in the Bibliography.

The Moon, the Moon Sign and House—Likes and Needs, Natural Interest and Inclination

(In locating the Moon's house, be sure to include a whole sign house count from the Ascendant as described in Chapter 7.)

The Moon is not necessarily of itself a vocational indicator unless one of the three vocational houses falls under Cancer and the Moon's rulership. However, the Moon indicates our emotional needs and natural area of comprehension. We must take the client's emotional type into very strong consideration before recommending a career. Remember, should the Moon square (ninety degrees) or quincunx (150 degrees) a vocational planet, the native will never be happy in a career represented by that planet, no matter how strong that planet is.

Study the personality qualities of the twelve zodiacal signs. In the Moon's case, vocationally speaking, think of these sign attributes as emotional needs and likes. Below is a listing for the Moon through the twelve zodiacal signs.

The Moon Sign: Likes and Needs

Aries—Needs and likes excitement, newness, activity, pizzazz, color. Enjoys an honest fight. The emotional nature is flammable, immediately responsive and very expressive. Creative. Enjoys performance. Dislikes boredom.

Taurus—Needs and likes stability, comfort, beauty, money, food, regularity, slow motion, calm, physical comforts. Dislikes fast-paced jobs, poverty, excessive change or unpredictability, discomfort.

Gemini—Needs and likes play fun, humor, versatility, change, mental stimulation, talking, new interests, talent development, light focus, fads, communication, new things, motion. Requires novelty, diversion and frequent coffee breaks. Dislikes deadly regimen, routine and predictable environments.

Cancer—Needs and likes homey and intimate environments,

maturing, parental figures (the boss?), devotion, family feeling, personal contact, security, protection, predictable environments. Dislikes impersonal environments insensitive people, shock, intrusion, change, unfamiliar people or situations.

Leo—Needs and likes attention, importance, power, drama, color, warmth, fun. Dislikes unglamorous, low drama environments and strong subordinate positions.

Virgo—Needs and likes boundaries, rules, clear duties, effectiveness, skillfulness, animals, tasks, rules, processing, facts, detail, work, someone to help, teamwork, perfecting and preparing the physical world, editing, patience with matter, being useful, serving, order. Dislikes disorganized, intrusive, unclear, sloppy or "hang loose" environments.

Libra—Needs and likes people, one-on-one discussion, conversation, listening, elegance, courtesies, pleasant times, partners, etiquette, balance, harmony, beauty. Dislikes contentious, dirty, ugly or foul smelling environments or solitary jobs.

Scorpio—Needs and likes emotional intensity, concentration, emotional bonding, strategy, intrigue, danger, commitment, devotion, dogs, impact, crises, transformation, depth-intensive intimacy. Dislikes silly work, low impact jobs, detachment, impersonal contact.

Sagittarius—Needs and likes freedom, views, animals, goals, excitement, quests, big focuses, ideas, knowledge, traveling, muscular motion, self-extension, learning. Dislikes routine, busy work, detail focuses, small views, enclosed rooms, sedentary desk jobs, dull people and small town environments.

Capricorn—Needs and likes order, responsibility, burdens, protocol, hierarchy, boundaries, order, definite social roles, titles, pecking order, control of environment, sense of achievement, social importance, authority, practical accomplishments, challenges. Dislikes unexpected intrusions, disorder, intimacy, mushy emotional situations, positions without potential for advancement, risk, egalitarianism, spontaneity, socialism.

Aquarius—Needs and likes freedom, imagination, humor, social ideals, character building, humanity, equality, no rules, individuality, multiple interests, wildness, wilderness. Needs to utilize the higher intuitive and imaginative faculties. Dislikes feeling controlled, conformist requirements, dress codes, work environments devoid of altruistic impulses or spontaneity, most nine-to-five jobs, hierarchy, the "system."

Pisces—Needs and likes escape, fantasy, music, slow pace, ease, dreams, emotional sensations, music, spiritual ideals, pleasure, romance, sweetness, imagination, love, childlike things, quiet, solitude, diffusion, rest and sleep, non-application, feeling, the hidden side of life, emotional pleasure, intellectual diffusion. Dislikes the limelight, fast-paced jobs, stress, crowds, materialism, greed, power games, demands or situations requiring exceptional mental alertness, prolonged attention to detail or self-discipline.

Ascending Sign, The Approach to Life, Vocational Role and General Outlook

The ascending sign describes our basic approach to life, our outlook, our given life role. Some people are kings wherever they go and others are servants! Old texts describe the ascending sign as "how others see us." This is very true to some extent. However, the Ascendant also shows us "who we get to be," our "life role," in all life situations, regardless of the career. We all must step into life on a first foot, and this manner of *first meeting the world* around us is represented by our ascending sign.

Observe the Ascendant to find the *approach* to the career. This cannot be understated. While not necessarily tagging the exact profession, the Ascendant hints loudly as to *what field* of a particular profession might be most *natural* to the individual. Below are some helpful tips for vocational analysis of the ascending sign. Never, never, never neglect the Ascendant in a vocational analysis. Its sign will suggest the manner in which a person moves out into the world around him/her.

Aries, Experiential Approach—Within any chosen field, an Aries Ascendant should be on the job or in the field experientially, blazing the trail, the first, the leader, a discoverer, an inspired one, the energizer or promoter. The Aries approach is energetic, positive, physical, assertive and loves to "just do it," to venture forth along new paths.

Taurus, Physical, Sensual and Stable Approach—Within any chosen field, the Taurus Ascendant functions as a stabilizing force for all, something like the great oak tree. Taurus approaches life physically and is highly tactile and pragmatic. Taurus can be "the body" of an enterprise. The Taurus Ascendant is often seen as the resource, as in the guy or gal who has the money or owns the business. The Taurean approach is slow, soothing, calming, unflappable, enduring and artistic. The outlook is always realistic, making this an excellent ascending sign for business, building and natural science occupations. Artistic taste and sexual magnetism are strong.

Gemini, Communicative, Mental, Versatile Approach—Gemini risings are always in motion, in their cars, between destinations and about town. Their approach is curious, mental and outwardly directed. Best suited for high variety and stimulating occupations with lots of talk and walk, these people are open-minded, easygoing, flexible and chatty. Freelance communications work and taxi driving seem typical of this ascending sign. They are interested in everything and everybody. Predictable routines are impossible for them.

Cancer, Small Focus, Organizing, Personal, Feeling, Nurturing and Responsive Approach—Persons with a Cancer Ascendant flourish in the highly intimate end of any occupation. Personal feeling is the modus operandi of the Cancer Ascendant, and is ideal for small focus tasks to be accomplished within the immediate environment: the home, the terrarium, the microscope.

Nurturing Cancerians must know everyone personally, and familiarize each item on their desks and each plant in their beloved gardens. This sensitive and somewhat timid ascending sign is normally unsuited for large focus, high risk or impersonal work.

Leo, Commanding, Ruling, Impacting and Entrepreneurial Approach—As the performer, Leo risings shine best where they can be either the center of attention or telling others what to do. Always the entrepreneur, the approach is "I impact." Generally speaking, this sign abhors routine detail work and subordinate jobs unless several planets are in Virgo. This ascending sign has considerable warmth and personality and must never be backwatered. Leo rising always prefers to own or manage the business.

Virgo, Factual, Physical, Patient and Specializing Approach— Virgo Ascendants should seek to specialize in technical, clerical and editorial aspects of their chosen work. Because Virgo is an earth sign, they are often physically tough and, like their elemental brother Taurus, can be good at the more physical side of the job. A Virgo Ascendant often prefers the modest and more subordinate side of any career and makes a better assistant than boss. Not uncommonly, they find themselves in the humblest end of a business, excelling in all service and cleaning professions. Both the technical and blue collar trade professions are natural to this ascending sign. Virgo rising suggests the skilled and service fields within any profession, and these people are seen by others as workers and useful servants.

Libra, Diplomatic, Intelligent, Wise and Artistic Approach—The diplomatic side of any profession is best for the Libra Ascendant, and is typical of counselors, lawyers and consultants. People-oriented and people-stimulated, this ascending sign is never happy in solitary professions or those requiring exclusive self-initiative. Count on persons with this Ascendant for charm, charisma and a friendly, relaxed and considerate manner that subtly influences all around them for the better. Their downside is laziness, waffling, dispassion and lack of backbone. The balancing, listening, observing and socializing side of all careers is suitable for the Libra Ascendant. Conflict resolution and calming down intractable people are their fortes. Libra Ascendants are seen by others as mediators and partners.

Scorpio, Surgical, Power Over Others' Lives or Bodies, Strategic, Secretive Approach—The Scorpio Ascendant approaches life as a great chess player. This Ascendant is always best for long term efforts requiring confidentiality, danger, concentration and strategy. This sign is very tough, extremely alert and possesses legendary stamina. Scorpio rising excels in all high intensity fields where it can exercise power over things, money, substances, people's lives or bodies. Scorpio is the surgeon and the chemist (see Chapter 1). This fearless ascending sign makes a good wrestler and long-term battler. Scorpio Ascendants are excellent in all occupations that require exceptional patience and waiting for the perfect moment, revenge, courage, politics, scrutiny, toughness and the ability to poison an enemy's drink.

Sagittarius, Outward Moving, Seeking, Coordinating Approach—Sagittarius rising is the traveler, and ideal for the promotional side of any occupation. This ascending sign is claustrophobic and needs plenty of leg room, literally and figuratively. Excitement, new horizons, speed, athletics and distance traveling are keywords to keep in mind for field selection. The Sagittarius Ascendant approaches life with the long view and naturally understands how to coordinate people, ideas and nations. The publicity, educational and foreign sides of professional life are preferred. Persons with this ascending sign will often be bicultural, bilingual or biracial, or find themselves seen as foreigners. Enthusiastic, positive, hyperactive and stimulating, Sagittarius ascending functions well as the group sparkplug. These people make powerful motivational speakers and trainers in many fields. Frequently they are pilots and drivers, always in motion. Sagittarius Ascendants are seen by others as travelers and teachers.

Capricorn, Control and Achievement Approach—Capricorn is concerned with controlling the outer environment (opposite Cancer, so concerned with the intimate and internal environment). This is the condominium builder, the capitalist. Capricorn risings appreciate authority and order, preferring the executive, contracting or presidential side of their careers. People with this Ascendant understand the process of building in time and know how to rise in their careers, usually to the top. There is always the tendency toward authoritarianism, bureaucracy and insensitivity. Capricorn loves to plan large building and business schemes and, generally speaking, will see them through. They will be seen as authorities in whatever occupation they choose.

Aquarius, Friendly, Idealistic, Impersonal, Detached, Imaginative and Eclectic Approach—Aquarius gives the "air plane" view of life. This Ascendant provides a wonderful sense of overview, and a large soul. Consequently, these people are not overly concerned with self or the trivial; instead they are focused on the good of the whole. Count on this Ascendant for intellectual gifts and friendliness, but never closeness. The Aquarius Ascendant is eclectic and intellectual, with a great many interests. As much as Virgo is the specialist, Aquarius is the great generalist of the zodiac. Intensely idealistic, the spirit of the work performed by folks with Aquarius rising seems more important than their occupation. The adage "who you are is more important than what you do" suits the Aquarian approach to life. Plenty of free time is essential. The philanthropic, scientific or imaginative, and even humorous, sides of professional life are best for them. Persons born with Aquarius rising have trouble with conformity, dress codes and tight leashes. Aquarius Ascendants greatly enjoy being part of a group, mentoring and coaching (they always know best) and participating in social causes. They enjoy activities and projects that benefit their fellow humans or the planet. As wise, brilliant well-meaning, goodly and peace-loving as this sign can be, Aquarius is also foolish regarding everyday affairs and cannot always be relied upon for common sense or a detail focus.

Being detached in consciousness and a freedom freak, Aquarius is poorly suited for most kinds of highly dutiful work, or changing diapers. The Aquarius Ascendant is a natural candidate for the think tank, and many film producers, scientists and other assorted geniuses have this sign rising. Always they are seen as a friend in the largest sense of the word.

Pisces, the Chameleon, Sensitive, Anonymous, Diffuse, Interpreting, Compassionate Approach —Pisces rising prefers to be either the nobody or, rather, somebody else. This easygoing ascending sign can fit in anywhere, with anybody, quickly absorbing their mannerisms and offering little resistance. The Pisces Ascendant adopts a channeling approach to life, always reliant on psychic feelings. Pisces risings gravitate toward soft-touch work and also excel at research. They enjoy solitary occupations. However, Pisces Ascendants are equally at home in the more whimsical careers of music, children's books, toy shops, antiques, poetry, photography and used books and clothes. Sensitivity is key. This dreamy, sleepy and diffuse sign stands polar opposite from Virgo, the genius of detail, producing a curious Piscean relationship with detail work-either terrible or absolutely brilliant. The Pisces Ascendant also can display more versatility than Gemini as it is able to handle extremely diverse activities with the greatest of ease. Seldom, however, is ambition much in evidence, as ego and self-interest are rather weak in this sign. The Pisces Ascendant is happiest in low key, quiet, peaceful work environments where it can let its consciousness flow. These people often prefer anonymity. Pisces rising folks are most at home where their hearts are, not their heads, and prefer the shadow to the limelight and the spiritual to the material.

Chapter 3

The Four Elements and Three Modes

The Four Elements

The four elements of antiquity can be seen as a structural thread running through theoretical realms as diverse as physiognomy and Jungian psychology. However, it is in Western medical astrology that the four elements stand alone in purest form, unencumbered by abstractions and theories imposed by the less physically oriented sciences. To acquaint the reader with these four elements and their use in early medical and vocational astrology is the purpose of this chapter. First we must introduce a few basics.

The four elements represent four planes of matter (and much more, as will be described later). Classical astrology assigns each of the twelve zodiacal signs to one of the four elements—fire, air, earth or water. The fiery, airy, watery and earthy signs form our first and simplest description of zodiacal types useful to the early physicians. At birth the weight of planetary distribution within each of the elements paints a portrait of the elemental balance within both psyche and body. An observation of the planetary birth map allows us to discover the weakest elements in our physical and psychological makeup and also the most dominant.

We frequently emotionally feel and physically see the dominant element of a friend before perhaps guessing the more particular zodiacal sign type.

What exactly are these four elements? They can be viewed esoterically, spiritually, psychologically and physically. Fire, earth, air and water describe four levels of concretization of matter, four states of awareness, four temperaments and four types of matter within the chemical-molecular universe. This explains why astrologers, Jungian psychologists and medieval physicians have each defined the four elements variously and utilized their knowledge of them for quite separate purposes.

The Elements as Levels of the Concretization of Matter

In the most arcane sense, the elements refer to four levels of increasing concretization of matter: photon, particle, atom and molecule. One can think of this concretization process as the journey of light (the photon, as the fire element) from complete freedom (fire) into gradually denser and more predictable forms. This is represented first by air and then water, and finally the photon finds itself trapped in the densest plane of the molecule, symbolized as the stodgy earth element. As the photon journeys from creation toward material expression (particle, atom, molecule), it gathers weight, experience and form while sacrificing the playfulness and freedom of the photon and particle.

Four Elements and Four Worlds

The four levels of concretization of matter directly correspond to the four planes, or worlds, of the Cabalists: the spiritual world, *atziluth*, is the world of emanations and archetypes. *Atziluth* corresponds best with the photon and with the fire element.

The second plane, *briah*, constitutes the world of thought and creation. *Briah* belongs to the world of particles and to the thinking element air.

Similarly, the malleable astral world, known to the Cabalists as *yetzirah*, the world of formations, corresponds to the atom and the receptive, impressionable and feeling-oriented water element.

The physical plane (or chemical-molecular plane) is the realm of the molecule and is represented by the densest element, earth. Cabalists know this fourth world as *assiah*, the world of action and the world of dense matter. As denizens of *assiah*, we find ourselves at present to be largely confined to the Jaws of this material plane.

Four Elements as Four Types of Consciousness

The four elements are also commonly described as four types of consciousness. Jung, who studied astrology and read horoscopes, adopted these traditional four awarenesses as his famous four psychological types. However, these four types are neither Jung's invention nor anything new to astrologers who have used them for millennia.

Fire symbolizes pure being, the sense of "I," and the life force. It is direct experience. Jung made this his famous "intuitive" type. Air represents the intellect. This is the world of thought, language and abstraction. Its mode of consciousness is detached observation. Jung named air his "thinking" type.

Our receptive feeling function is water. Emotions and instincts arise from this level. Water is a responsive and subjective experience. A person with this type of awareness was termed by Jung as a "feeling" type. Earth represents sensation and the body. This is the densest of the four levels and corresponds to body consciousness, materiality, survival and the structuring body building function. Jung christened earth as his "sensate" type.

Four Temperaments

Medieval physicians classified four humors of the body and associated these with four physiognomical and temperamental types termed choleric (fire), sanguine (air), phlegmatic (water) and melancholic (earth). We do not have space here to include a discussion of these four humors and temperaments. It is enough to say that the four temperaments roughly correspond to Jung's four astrologically-based psychological types, although in some writings the melancholic or earth type is viewed as entirely negative, which is inaccurate.

In this medical paradigm, a balance of the four humors produced a balanced temperament and a state of good health. Disease was a manifestation of an imbalance of these humors. A similar idea continues today in modern Ayurvedic practice with one exception. The four humors of the body have been grouped into just three *doshas*. Air becomes *vata*, fire is *pitta* and water and earth combine in a single heavy humor known as *kapha*. The description of the *kapha* type appears to combine the qualities of both the traditional Western phlegmatic and melancholic psychological temperaments. Fruits, vegetables, medicines and activities are also classed according to *dosha*. Healing is assisted by subscribing to a regimen that balances the *dos has*. If you are too hot, you must cool off; if you are too damp, then you must dry out; and so forth.

The Four Elements as Four Types of Matter

This is very simple. The element fire manifests as fire. The element air as air. Water is water and earth is earth. However, their correspondences to the physical body are a bit more complex.

Fire is the Chinese *chi*, or life force, as well as our motive energy and the digestive force. Fire releases energy; therefore, all combustion and fuel burning activities of the body take place through activation of the fire element. The action of fire is hot, light and dry.

Air governs the little-known electrical forces and electrical connections within the body, neurotransmission, motion, oxygenation of the blood, breath, language and motion. Its action is cold, light and moist (some texts say cold, light and dry).

Water rules the waters of the body-phlegm, lymph, semen and all other secretions and fluids. The moist and protective mucous membranes of the body are a function of the water element. Memory function is related to water because water is the most impressionable of elements. The action of water upon the body is cold, heavy and wet.

Earth governs the minerals within the body, the bones and the building up of a bodily structure. Earth also holds in energy and has much to do with stamina, food storage, body building and longevity. Earth is warm, heavy and dry.

Note: The earth sign Taurus may be an exception, producing more of a warm and moist condition. Natives of Taurus, the preeminent earth sign, are noted for being human greenhouses, always maintaining a warm body temperature.

The Four Elements: Occupational Listing

Fire (combined effect of Aries, Leo, Sagittarius)

Hot: metallurgists, blacksmiths, workers with kilns and ovens, glass blowers, firefighters, explosives dealers and workers, solar power, outdoors work in sunny climates.

Energetic: athletes (large muscle and speed sports), advocates, sales people, gamblers, entrepreneurs, dancers, energy workers, energy healers, body workers, physicists, experimental scientists, race car drivers, stunt people, sharpshooters, hunters.

Stimulating: brass instrument soloists, singers, rock musicians, bluegrass musicians, actors, dancers, team energizers, producers, directors, advertisers, teachers, preachers, proselytizers, fighters.

Air (combined effect of Gemini, Libra, Aquarius)

Intellectual, electrical: brain work, computer programmers, inventors, mathematicians, theorists, electricians, electrical engineers, high tech industry, video industry, computer game designers, book store workers, cartoonists.

Ideas, idealistic: social workers, volunteer work, diplomats, legislators, senators, representatives, balloon pilots, aviators, astronomers, astrologers, humorists.

Communication: orators, reporters, taxi drivers, journalists, phone company employees, telephone operators, "people" people, writers, announcers, disk jockeys, radio industry personnel, computer programmers.

Water (combined effect of Cancer, Scorpio, Pisces)

Wet: beverage dealers, wine merchants, chemists, chemical and paint manufacturers, swimmers, ointment and oil dealers, perfumers, bathroom suppliers, plumbers, bath attendants, laundry workers, fishermen, sewage workers, hydrologists, recyclers, dyers.

Motherly: child care workers, social workers, nurses, cooks, guardians, herbalists, family or home business, pet care, personal care attendants, hospice workers.

Feelings, soothing: musicians (of the romantic and folk genres), psychics, ice cream dealers, magnetic healers, empaths, mothers.

Introverted, secretive, escaping: hypnotists, anesthesiologists, drug dealers, smugglers, spies, detectives, mystery writers, romance novelists, sex industry workers.

The hidden, the past: psychologists, detectives, researchers, museum workers, archaeologists, curators, archivists, antique dealers, used item dealers, psychics.

Earth (combined effect of Taurus, Virgo, Capricorn)

Earthy, form building, physical: farmers, land developers, landscapers, miners, diggers, massage therapists, bakers, cooks, sculptors, stone masons, tile setters, construction workers, road maintenance workers, movers, soldiers, potters, truckers, loggers, heavyweight fighters, building suppliers, hardware, potters, police officers, guards, long distance and high stamina sports, mountaineers, survivalists, jewelers, gem dealers, nurses, body workers, janitors, dirty work, meat packers, football defense, work requiring patience.

Note: Curiously, airline pilots often display a strong earth element as well as the expected air. Earth provides the rock solid dependability and pragmatic, unflappable qualities required of pilots.

Practicality, realism: bankers, accountants, editors, bureaucrats, business people, economists, file clerks, realtors, construction, builders.

The Three Modes

Rate of Matter in Motion

In the simplest context, the four elements previously described are four states of matter—light, liquid, gaseous and mineral. Each of the twelve zodiacal signs is assigned to one of the four elements. This elemental classification is accomplished in the following manner: fire—Aries, Leo, Sagittarius; air—Gemini, Libra, Aquarius; water—Cancer, Scorpio, Pisces; earth—Taurus, Virgo, Capricorn.

However, there is a further sign classification of great importance. Because matter moves, we must subdesignate each element according to the *rate of matter in motion*. There are three classifications or rates of motion known as the three modes or quadruplicities of classical Western astrology. Again, it is these modes that describe the rate of matter in motion. These three rates are known as the cardinal, mutable and fixed modes.

For example, fire igniting is cardinal, concentrated fire is found in an oven and is fixed in action. A wild fire would be mutable, or moving, fire. Cardinal always begins each season. Fixed always occurs in mid-season, such as midsummer when fixed fire (heat, dryness) is most concentrated. Mutable disperses the seasonal energy and always occur at the end of one season and the transition into the next.

The cardinal signs are those that mark the two solstice and equinox points-Aries, Cancer, Libra and Capricorn. They are active and initiating in nature. (One might argue the reverse in the case of indecisive Libra if one fails to reason that Libra initiates the air qualities of abstract contemplation and detached observation.)

The fixed signs are the stubborn four-Taurus, Leo, Scorpio and Aquarius. These signs possess strength and endurance. They are inflexible.

Mutable signs are noted for their versatile, flexible and sometimes unstable natures. They are Gemini, Virgo, Sagittarius and Pisces.

The Three Modes: Occupational Effects

Cardinal (combined effect of Aries, Cancer, Libra, Capricorn)

Initiating: The combined effect of the cardinal quartet gives the proclivity for self-starting, independent action and leadership. An emphasis in the cardinal mode is generally necessary for those who must work alone under their own volition and for business owners. Organizational gifts are shown. Follow-through may be lacking (unless the earth signs and Saturn are in prominence). Self-made artists and the self-employed in a wide variety of business activities are likely to have a preponderance of cardinal signs in the their birth charts. For best results, cardinality should be supported by fixed signs.

Remember, the above traits are produced through a combination and predominance of the four cardinal signs. Singly, both Cancer and Libra are the two more reluctant cardinals and must always be assessed on their own as independent signs.

Fixed (combined effect of Taurus, Leo, Scorpio and Aquarius)

Sustaining: A fixed person has follow-through and is well suited to carry to fruition projects begun by others. With the singular exception of Aquarius, the management of people and business is natural to the fixed signs, as is the control of money and resources. These signs bring stability and endurance to any job. However, fixed people are not recommended for positions requiring flexibility, subordination or speed. Bankers, managers and business owners are frequently of the fixed type personality.

Remember, the fixed qualities occur as a result of a combination of the four fixed signs. Aquarius, viewed singly, is too unpredictable and eccentric to match the above description and must be individually considered.

Mutable (combined effect of Gemini, Virgo, Sagittarius, Pisces)

Dispersing: As a rule, prominently mutable people neither lead nor sustain business. They are best suited in subordinate and/or freelance positions. As with the willow tree, flexibility is their gift. And like the willow tree, while appearing delicate, they can handle a surprising amount of emotional stress and come bouncing back again. Therefore, this is a good combination for public service jobs. Fluidity and the ability to quickly handle a variety of tasks are additional talents.

Mutable people are excellent in transitory jobs, part-time work and in occupations requiring the proverbial wearing of many "hats." Translators, secretaries, handymen/women, street musicians, delivery workers, taxi drivers and messengers are typically of the mutable type.

Too much mutability gives poor ambition, worse follow-through and the inability to hold down jobs. Wandering "starving students," runaways and transients can suffer from an excess of mutable signs. However, mutable is the preferred mode for airline attendants and similar occupations where one must encounter dislocation of personal routine, sleep, eating habits, etc. Mutable types go with the flow better than anyone and, incapable of structuring themselves, prefer direction as supplied by the job. Naval officers, sailors, soldiers, merchant marines, etc. frequently are of the mutable type.

Remember, mutability is a combined effect of all four mutable signs. Virgo, viewed singly, has few of the negative work traits described above and must be individually considered.

Vocation and the Four Elements/Three Modes

The reader will hopefully now possess a deeper understanding of the four elements and the three modes according to their energetic, psychological and physical aspects. How then can we incorporate this understanding into our vocational analysis? The elements and modes become useful in vocational diagnosis only when one or another occurs in excess or as a dominant theme in the horoscope. This is judged by ascertaining the element and mode of the Sun, Moon and Ascendant.

Rule: If two of three (Sun, Moon and Ascendant) share either one element or one mode, we then foresee a temperamental trend in the direction of that same element or mode. Should the Sun, Moon and Ascendant all be in one element or mode, then we may speculate that this strongly accented element or mode will be temperamentally dominant in the individual and therefore highly useful for vocational suggestions as given in this chapter.

Chapter 4

Vocational Rulerships: The Planets and Nodes

Understanding the Intermingling of Planetary and Sign Influence

This chapter contains a large listing of occupations governed by each of the ten planets (inclusive of the two lights, the Sun and Moon) and the two lunar Nodes.

The planets are primary to all vocational interpretation. Each planet has its very necessary own vibration, tone and color, made apparent to us as *quality*. All objects, people, events and vocations that align themselves vibrationally with the special quality of a particular planet are said to be "ruled" by that planet through means of this vibrational affinity.

These planetary affinities run through all levels of our existence. Venusian types are physically soft and beautiful, possess a charming personality and probably enjoy eating sweets a little too much (see *The Astrological Body Types* by Judith Hill).

Some astrologers prefer to think of the planets as representatives of the great universal principles. For instance, the force of attraction that binds all molecules together is also Venus, the planet of love. Keywords for these universal principles are listed for each planet below.

However, planets must live in one of the twelve zodiacal signs. The quality of the planet will be very pure when in its home sign of rulership. Many of the remaining signs will alter the planet's pure expression. All planets are able to readily express their best qualities in their sign of exaltation. However, we find an enormous alteration of a planet's character when posited in a sign of its fall or detriment. This occurs because these fall and detriment signs are the least adapted to furthering the essential quality of the planet. To get the idea, think of a planet as an instrument and the sign as a type of room. Each sign represents a unique acoustical quality, or vibrational character, of the sign. The element of the sign gives the right feeling for this acoustical quality (see Chapter 3).

Every sign is vibrationally composed of one of four elements (fire, earth air water) and one of three modes (cardinal, fixed, mutable), and possesses a planetary ruler or special association with one or two planets. A second or third planet will add its supportive qualities through the status of exaltation within the particular sign. It is the combination of these four forces that provides the astrological character (Chapter 1) and physical appearance of each zodiacal sign (see *The Astrological Body Types* by Judith Hill).

We can liken Mars to a trumpet for another example. The same trumpet will sound qualitatively different in separate auditoriums. A stone room will give quite a different effect from a room made with wooden walls. Thus, Mars in its home sign of Aries can really blast away, whereas in Cancer, its sign of fall, it must play underwater. Cancer also turns energy inward, unlike the extroverted nature of Mars.

Provisos for Interpreting Planet and Sign Combinations

When interpreting planets in signs, remember this essential rule: *Planets are stronger than signs.* There are exceptions to this rule, but learn to give planets the edge. A novice astrologer can save years of bungled interpretations by remembering to give the emphasis to the planet as it is working out *through* the sign. This rule comes into play when solving problems of weighting.

For instance, what if Jupiter is in Capricorn at the Midheaven? Does Jupiter or Capricorn govern the career? This is a puzzle because of the fact that Jupiter is in its fall in Capricorn, a serious sign quite the reverse of jolly Jupiter. What should we say then? Should the vocation of this individual be Capricornian or Jupiterian?

To solve this typically encountered dilemma, always give Jupiter the emphasis. Select a Jupiterian career and see Jupiter as working through a Capricornian style or environment. Capricorn is authoritative. Therefore, we still have a Jupiterian career, but an authoritative one. (An educational administrator or the president of a publishing firm or a media director would be typical of this combination. *Never read it the other* way *around by giving the Capricorn (the sign) an interpretive dominance over Jupiter (the planet).*

Remember, planets are stronger than signs. Planets adjust or alter their energies when in contact with the vibrational environment of signs.

More Rulership Tips

Rulerships can overlap and be shared by two or more planets, or by signs and planets. This is quite natural because the universe is a very complex place. Many careers suggest a *mixture* of planets and therefore must be given multiple listings. For instance, according to Gauquelin's vocational research, Mars and Saturn are mutually prominent in the birth charts of scientists and doctors, Jupiter and Mars for generals, and Jupiter and the Moon are strong for actors and politicians. To serve the reader in understanding planetary combinations, I've included a list of planetary families and their themes in this chapter. The reader is cautioned not to skip over this list. Planetary families and combinations enter into all vocational chart interpretations.

Another important point is that sometimes a planet will not rule careers associated with the products listed for that planet. For instance, Neptune rules alcohol but not wine merchants. How could this be so? Although Neptune rules all sedatives, it does not produce the aggressive, alert temperament required of salespeople who are typically strong on Mercury and Mars. However wine merchants still require a prominent Neptune in their charts because it is, after all, the focus of their work.

It is very important for the student to impress upon his/her memory the full spectrum of rulerships by reading through these "boring" lists. The old astrologer did his/her memory work and so can others. Note: Augment this list with Rex E. Bill's *The Rulership Book* and Charles Luntz's *Vocational Guidance by Astrology*.

Sun (Rules Leo)

Universal principles: center, authority, selfhood

Vocations: stockbrokers, actors, theater owners, casino and restaurant owners, entrepreneurs, managers, foremen, presidents, coaches, people central to any activity, stars, bosses, solar power workers

Products and people: rubies, fathers, middle-aged men, bosses, kings, producers, husbands, gold, sunflowers, honey, almonds, ovens, gin, walnuts

Moon (Rules Cancer)

Universal principles: change, reception, nurturing, feeling, individual sensitivity

Vocations: tavern keepers, brewers, cooks, sailors, singers, actors, nurses, child care workers, waitresses (with Mercury, Mars), photographers, launderers, politicians, novelists, washer women, grocers, sailors, butlers, maids, fishermen, cheese makers, cottage industries, small animal farming, midwives, herbalists, shepherds, psychics (the Moon rules the public and women)

Products and people: women, mothers, wives, babies, the public, adoring fans, the masses, silver, pearls, milk, breasts, maids, food service workers, the stomach, the left eye in a man and the right eye in a woman, seafood, melon, ponds, mushrooms, ice cream (with Venus), baby food, shells

Mercury (Rules Gemini and Virgo)

Universal principles: connectivity, communication, relatedness, data *Vocations:* typists, clerks, taxi drivers, messengers, mail carriers, acrobats, journalists, writers, communication, transcribers, translators, fax machines, beekeepers, radio announcers, orators, weavers, tailors, secretaries, copy machine workers, printers, communicators, instrumentalists (who use their fingers), accountants, nutritionists, mathematicians, jugglers, pool and card players, comedians, computer programmers, editors, delivery drivers, gymnasts, small business merchants, grocery clerks, limousine drivers, reporters, telephone operators, dispatchers, butlers, waitresses/waiters, maids, tour guides

Products and people: thieves and tricksters, letters, bracelets, gloves, articles and books, editors, secretaries, books, pens, pairs of things, cars, insects, birds, small animals, phones, tickets, handymen and women, traveling salespeople, typewriters, lithe youths, Peter Pan, keys, bridges, staircases, mercury, emeralds, loose change, bicycles, motorbikes, skateboards, shoes, toys, puzzles, wind instruments, delivery persons, paper, light office supplies, letters (Mercury and Venus equal Valentines), the color green, small and agile people

Venus (Rules Taurus and Libra)

Universal principles: harmony, beauty, affinity (attraction)

Vocations: cosmeticians, artisans, singers, chefs, jewelers, orchard keepers, jewelers, confectioners, hairstylists, designers, courtesans, fashion consultants, decorators, luxurious products, sensual products, diamonds, dancers, consultants, leisure oriented careers, matchmakers, florists, toiletries

Products and people: jewelry, lingerie, pleasant art, china, lace, fine clothes, fruit, fine rugs, pretty women, unmarried women, girlfriends, cats, candy, gourmet food, copper, princesses, cakes, pies, wine, perfume, berries, flowers, singers, female genitalia, wigs, lotions, rings, the colors white and pink

Mars (Rules Aries and Co-rules Scorpio)

Universal principles: fight, defense, energy, survival of self, courage

Vocations: soldiers, mechanics, lawyers, surgeons, doctors, barbers, butchers, welders, athletes, acupuncturists, firefighters, police officers, real estate investors and developers, contractors, salesmen, packers, movers, physical laborers, tool and die makers, optometrists, loggers, garbage men, trumpet and saxophone players, locksmiths, painters, mixers, cooks, chemists, lifeguards, inspectors, investigators, hunters, soldiers, martial artists, launderers (with the Moon), sculptors, drummers, metallurgists, police officers, rock musicians, energetic dancers, boxers, engineers, janitors

Products and people: young men, muscles, iron, sharp tools, guns, dogs, cars, thorns, needles, garlic, cayenne pepper, red colors, athletic equipment, fences, alarms, soldiers, athletes, lawyers, brass instruments, red meat, blood, needles, garnets, male genitalia

Jupiter (Rules Sagittarius and Co-rules Pisces)

Universal principles: expansion, benevolence, ennoblement

Vocations: politicians, publishers, actors, ministers, preachers, teachers, generals, benefactors, promoters, producers, protectors, politicians, heads of charities and environmental organizations, department store and whole sale industries, kings, exporters-importers, clowns, financiers, pilots, loan agents

Products and people: large people, patrons, older benevolent men, elephants and whales, horses, large ships, circuses, benevolent presidents, schools, deans, universities, churches, tin, Santa Claus, yellow stones, yellow colors, turquoise, politicians, clowns, ministers, pastors, popes

Saturn (Rules Capricorn and Aquarius)

Universal principles: order, contraction, form building and maintenance, law

Vocations: priests, architects, gardeners, farmers, plumbers, graphic designers, builders, curators, scholars, researchers, archivists, solitary scholars, stone masons, bureaucrats, scientists, inspectors, physicians (allopathic), judges, accountants, engineers, physicians, scientists, mathematicians, assembly workers, printers, typesetters, typographers, statisticians, horticulturists, morticians, editors, guards, waste managers, mold makers, cement workers, funeral workers

Products and people: old men, churches, nuns and monks, donkeys, roots, grains, meat, leather, lead, pork, timber, coal, ice, building supplies, rock, black, brown, dark blue, uniforms, tests, blue sapphires, lapis lazuli, garbage, bones, concrete, fossils, clocks and watches, graveyards, large buildings, heavy equipment, solid furniture, bureaucrats, tiles, pipes

Uranus (Co-rules Aquarius with Saturn)

Universal principles: chaos, the unexpected, enlightenment, release, liberation, extremes

Vocations: astrologers, inventors, astronomers, astronauts, computer specialists, electrical work of any kind, scientists, idea people, cartoonists, revolutionaries, civil rights workers, engineers

Products and people: radicals, eccentrics, extremists, geniuses, electricity, balloons, computers, high tech equipment, science fiction producers, naturopathic doctors, aviators, astronomers, inventors, computer experts, homosexuals, transgendered individuals, androgynous people, geniuses, schizophrenics, electricity, uranium, high tech industry, space industry, cartoons, zany and shocking objects, shiny and multicolored objects, mind toys, computer games, astronomical supplies, astrology books, feminists, revolutionaries, radicals, liberals, humanists, modern artists, dadaists

Neptune (Co-rules Pisces with Jupiter)

Universal principles: entropy, dissolution, breakdown of form, escape from the material plane, sensitivity

Vocations: musicians, poets, children's book illustrators, photographers, drug dealers, fashion and glamour industry workers, water colorists, antique dealers, used book and record dealers, cooks, homeopaths, magnetic healers and subtle energy workers, psychics, social workers, sailors, shamans, dowsers, hypnotherapists

Products and people: music, fantasy, ocean, sailboats, lingerie, perfume, romance novels, film, videos, movies, fish, marijuana, sedatives, opium, fairy tales, toys, secrets, gossip, stars, viruses, bacteria, leaks, gas, oil, chemicals, psychics, dowsers, smugglers, mentally ill persons, magnets, persons close to death, diffuse New Age music, chanting

Pluto (Co-rules Scorpio with Mars)

Universal principles: exposure, purification, eradication

Vocations: exterminators, nuclear medicine, nuclear industry workers, physicists, inspectors, criminologists, detectives, refrigeration, excavators, prison guards, waste managers, recyclers, demolition workers, loggers, plumbers, breeders, underground workers, drillers and miners, Earth destroyers, bankers, chemists, genealogists, genetic scientists morticians: archaeologists, volcanologists, seismologists, cryptologists'. Egyptologists, mafioso, physicists, epidemiologists, exorcisers, waste transformation, sewer workers, exterminators, police officers, media

Products and people: evil tyrants, dictators, polluters, Earth destroyers, moguls, extremely wealthy people, plutonium, venom, poisons

North Node

The aggressive influence of this Node supports other testimonies suggesting any strongly capitalistic or athletic professions. The North Node rising suggests great energy, compulsion and sometimes an acquisitive nature with a taste for power.

Suggestions: competitive athletes, capitalists, land developers, business people, leaders, police officers, miners/loggers

South Node

The influence of this Node encourages spiritually oriented, psychic, inward-looking, reflective and compassionate careers. The South Node has a special affinity with the past. Persons born with this Node near the Ascendant may be retiring, non-materialistic and sweet. They also have great difficulty getting noticed because this Node brings the invisibility factor to their undertakings.

Suggestions: astrologers, naturopathic physicians, psychologists, psychics, monks, nuns, musicians, social workers, volunteer workers, welfare recipients, reincarnation regressionists, medievalists, scholars, historians, antique dealers, researchers

Planetary Families and Their Themes

An astrologer should find out if the majority of vocational indicators in the client's chart suggest a theme. To assist ourselves, we can make use of the planetary families chart. Each of these select planetary groupings suggests a theme. Planetary combinations can enhance the natural qualities of one or both planets and/or produce something altogether new, such as how pairing the letters "t" and "h" produces a new sound: "th".

A conjunction of two or more planets is the simplest and most obvious way of achieving a planetary family. However there are many other ways. For instance, the strongest two or three planets in the birth chart naturally combine their energies within one's character without necessarily being in major aspect. Consider also the planets flanking the Midheaven on either side.

Planetary Families

Jupiter, Sun, Mars: outgoing, impulsive, generous, loud, masculine, confident, egotistic, suggests leadership ability, successful; with Pluto, wealth

Jupiter, Sun, Saturn: authority, government, respected position, fatherly

Jupiter, Moon: convivial, sociable, influential, political, acting, producing, a chefs combination; with Neptune, ministry

Jupiter, Venus, Mars: theatrical, ceremonial, very jovial, high living, great popularity, playboys, philandering politicians, victors, heroes, crown wearers, triumphant displays, beloved and noble leaders Jupiter, Neptune: ministry, charity, religion, oceanic, benevolent, lucky Jupiter, Mars, *North Node, Pluto*: immense wealth, the heir's combination

Mercury, Saturn: intellectual, patient, critical, scholarly, technical, careful, thorough, detailed, skilled. With Venus, intelligent, refined, artistic, wise

Mercury, Uranus: mental, inventive, humorous, creative, brilliant, genius

Mercury, Mars: mechanical, sharp tools, quick tongue, alert, hand-eye coordination, exacting, cutting, intelligent, sarcastic wit, clever, cunning, savvy

Mercury, Jupiter: widely read, broad, witty, tolerant, oratorical, talkative

Mercury, Venus: pleasant expressions, diplomacy, refinement, music Saturn, Mars: medical, scientific, technical, courageous, nerves of steel, determined, tough, building, construction-destruction, industrial, intensely pragmatic, realistic, unsympathetic, the good soldier

Saturn, Pluto, North Node: dictatorial, sadistic, authority, selfish, greedy, survives famines, gives research ability, toughness and stamina

Mars, Pluto: investigative, destroying, eradicating, revealing, intense, dangerous, ruthless; with North Node, immense wealth and power

Mars, Uranus: technical and inventive, an engineer's combination, explosive

Venus, Moon: social, feminine, receptive, smooth, nurturing, supportive, provides domestic comforts, motherly, patient, kind, good cook Venus, Moon, Neptune: psychic, poetic, musical, magnetic, soothing, soft, slippery, silvery, shimmering, seductive, subtle

Venus, Saturn: beauty in form, the architectural and graphic sense, taste, elegance, etiquette, formality, traditional values, conservative, aesthetic, sincere, wisdom combines with beauty; in Libra, an excellent judge

Venus, Mars: creative, physical, passionate, sexual, artistic, motion plus beauty (the dance), the body beautiful, a massage therapist's combination

Venus, Moon, Mars: similar to Venus-Mars, the tastes, satisfaction of desires, sensual, emotional, charismatic, emotional energy, physical, creative, public magnetism

Moon, Saturn: parental, controlling, organizational, family, tribal, obeying, respect for authority and tradition, bureaucracy, hierarchical, conservative

Chapter 5

Vocational Supplements of the Birth Chart

North Node

The North Node functions in part as a great celestial portal for the entry of various cosmic energies into the Earth plane. We will strongly receive the vibratory energy of any planet closely conjunct this Node and possess a great deal of whatever this planet might symbolize in the birth chart. In most cases we can materially profit by the activities or products ruled by any planet conjunct the North Node.

Some astrologers regard the North Node (also called Caput, Rahu and The Dragon's Head) as the dharma point, or work that is right and good for us to do. In practice it does bear out that most of us will work at some time in our lives at a job suggested by the house and sign position of the North Node. General success is suggested should this point conjoin the Midheaven, its ruler, any other career significator or a planet governing the affairs of the indicated profession. For instance a successful writer might have been born when Mercury was conjunct the North Node, whereas a hairstylist might be quite popular if lucky enough to be born with Venus conjunct this point.

From the vocational perspective, connections, worldliness, power, confidence, intense activity, bringing into form, greed and materialism are associated with this point. Specific vocations associated with Rahu are listed in Chapter 4.

South Node

The vocational interpretation of this point must be handled with kid gloves. This is due to the sometimes tendency of this point to reverse the traditionally negative interpretation, instead producing quite positive results. Typically, the South Node (also called Cauda, Ketu, the Dragon's Tail) acts as a celestial portal for the exit and release of material energies and forms out of material manifestation on our plane. We can give out our energies and compassion in the area suggested by our Ketu, but seldom receive payment. Sometimes we must pay off old karmic debts represented by the house and sign position of the South Node and/or conjoining planets. Quite simply, this is the Dragon's Tail, more akin to spiritual insight than material success. Therefore, in the majority of cases, the activities and products of any planets conjoining this point will be duds. The house and sign tenanted by the South Node may experience losses or indicate an outlet for charitable giving, but will not allow for our material gain.

However, there are special conditions that will neutralize or even reverse the materially unsuccessful tendency of the South Node. If at least two of the astrological conditions in the list below exist, it is nearly certain that the grief normally associated with this point is nullified. Should three of the below conditions exist for the South Node, suspect a possible reversed interpretation, i.e. an area of remarkable success and not the failure normally expected. Sometimes an individual's work involves helping others and gainful employment in places suggested by the house place and sign of the South Node in his/her birth chart. For instance, I have witnessed several cases of those who work with the mentally challenged, deaf or educationally disabled who have Mercury conjunct the South Node. The South Node is an intensely internal point in the chart, directing our thoughts inward.

The South Node is vocationally associated with psychics, astrologers, monks, psychologists, mental health workers, naturopathic medicine, homeopathy, charity, the disabled, the terminally ill, hospices and unemployment. See page 35 for additional occupations associated with Ketu.

Neutralization of Negative Indications of the South Node

1. South Node closely conjunct Pars Fortuna. A very reliable neutralizer.

2. South Node conjunct its dispositor, i.e. the planetary ruler of the zodiacal sign the South Node tenants (see Chapter 6). Example: South Node in Taurus is disposited by Venus. Should Venus also be located in Taurus, then the South Node is conjunct its dispositor.

3. South Node closely sextile or trine its dispositor; for example, the South Node in Gemini trine Mercury in Aquarius.

4. South Node sextile, trine or opposition Jupiter; for example, Jupiter at the North Node.

5. South Node closely trine or sextile the Moon.

6. South Node closely tine or sextile Saturn.

7. South Node closely trine the Sun (less strong than the lunar aspect).

8. South Node in the ninth, tenth or eleventh houses or signs from the Ascendant (unreliable).

9. South Node in mutable signs-Gemini, Virgo, Sagittarius, Pisces (unreliable rule).

10. South Node conjunct Jupiter. The South Node is assisted by Jupiter's proximity, however this is often pretty lousy for Jupiter.

Part of Fortune

A lone survivor of scores of Arabic Parts once commonly used, the Part of Fortune has solitarily remained a mainstay of Western astrological practice. Perhaps there exists a reason for its popularity. As an exact projection of the soli-lunar phase relationship from the Ascendant degree, it was called the place of happiness and will function as such. There is no phase relationship more important than that of the Sun and Moon. Most people delight in the activities symbolized by the house and sign position of the Part of Fortune.

Also known as Pars Fortuna, this point is said by some to show how and where individuals make their money. (Or, if not, the planetary dispositor of the point. And if not that, the second or tenth houses from the point. So we see that using this part for financial meaning can be cumbersome and more or less open to interpretation.) A further difficulty confronts us with the fact that the ancient Greek astrologers reversed the calculation for night births, projecting the soli-lunar phase relationship backwards from its actual birth phase from the Ascendant.

In other words, if a person is born at night during the first quarter Moon, the Greek style Part of Fortune would be projected, as would a last quarter Moon, from the Ascendant. However, if the birth occurred during the day, the projection would be correct, i.e. first quarter, or ninety degrees forward from the rising point.

I have found the true daytime projection works quite well for nearly everyone, which may be one reason the older night reversal was apparently abandoned. Each astrologer must conduct his/her own studies to discover a preference.

The individual will enjoy and profit from the activities symbolized by the house and sign of this Part and can be fond of many things associated with any planets it conjoins or that disposit the Part. True wealth, however, depends on additional testimonies. A very strong wealth and success combination would be for one of the vocational significators to be closely conjunct both the Part of Fortune and the North Node. For more detail on Pars, see *The Part of Fortune in Astrology* (see Bibliography).

Most computer programs include the Part of Fortune. However, it can be easily calculated. Add the zodiacal sign number (Aries is sign 1, Taurus is 2, Gemini is 3, etc.), degrees and minutes for the Ascendant plus that for the Moon. Subtract from this sum the zodiacal sign number, degrees and minutes of the Sun. The result is the old style day birth *Pars Fortuna* and should mimic the precise arc between the Sun and Moon as projected from the degree of the Ascendant. Reverse the Sun and Moon for the night birth calculation, but do try both and see which one works best.

Zodiacal Degrees

Over the ages a great deal of interpretive material has been collected and recorded about the 360 zodiacal degrees. These are the degrees of ecliptic longitude that together encompass the twelve zodiacal signs (each sign represents a thirty degree sector of this 360 degree wheel).

I always take the time to go over the degree meanings of the planets in my client's chart from at least two good sources. A lot of these degree meanings regard applications and are therefore useful from the career perspective.

Note: The famous Sabian symbols are not recommended for vocational use because they are symbolic in the extreme and quite open to creative interpretation and therefore better suited to psychological astrology. The more useful degree interpretations for vocations can be found in *Practical Astrology, How to Make It Work for You* by Jerry L. Keans, Ph.D, 1967, Parker Publishing Company, Inc., West Nyack, New York, and less so in *The Encyclopedia of Astrology* by Nicholas Devore, The Philosophical Library, New York.

The most outstanding source of vocationally-oriented degree meanings is Franz Barden's *The Practice of Magickal Evocation*. This book was written for magicians rather than for astrologers. However, the accuracy of these correspondences is truly amazing and covers everything from fish tinning to botanical genetics.

Fixed Stars

Vocational meaning has been traditionally allotted to several of the fixed stars. When using fixed stars, it is important to know their true bodily position for the latitude of birth in question. This can be obtained from *Mundane Tables of Fixed Stars in Astrology* by Percival and Fox, Quick Specs, Blackwood Terrace New Jersey, 1975. If this rare book is unavailable, investigate several of the better astrology computer programs.

Getting carried away with fixed stars will prove quite useless to vocational interpretation. Never decide on careers based solely on any placement of a fixed star. Vocational aptitude must first and foremost be established by the planet-house-sign combinations and not by an exclusive assessment of stars or degrees. The stars and degrees must support and enhance testimonies already existing in the horoscope.

Pay attention primarily only to those stars conjoining the Midheaven within one degree (culminating) or conjunct the Ascendant, Sun, Moon, Midheaven ruler or Ascendant ruler, again by one degree. These fixed star conjunctions must be within one degree. The potency of any star increases if it is located within one degree of any of the four angles of the birth chart. Below is an incomplete list of vocational associations of the more prominent fixed stars.

I have not included their associated degrees of ecliptic longitude because I do not wish to encourage the bad habit of using the associated degree instead of the true position of the fixed star. Ancient astrologer-priests observed the sky and noted the actual physical position of the star, not its associated degree. For associated degree positions, use Vivian Robson's *The Fixed Stars and Constellations in Astrology* or any good computer program that includes the current fixed star positions in ecliptic longitude.

Note: The below list is from Robson's book and is given only as an incentive to obtain a copy of his book. Vivian Robson did an excellent job of listing the traditional meanings of the more important stars when found in conjunction, many with the lights and various planets and often with useful vocational application.

Achernar: public office, religion

Acrux: witches, ceremonialists, astrologers, occultists

Acubens: criminals, poison (drug, alcohol sales?)

Aculeus: eyes

Adhafera: explosives, fires, theft, military preferment (firefighters, police officers?)

Aldebaran: responsible positions and public honors, eloquence, intelligence, favors of women if at the Midheaven

Algenib: beggars, scavengers (garbage collectors, scavengers, used goods, recylcers?)

Algenubi: power of expression, destructive

Algol: mob violence, decapitation, hanging (suggested: neck and throat surgeons, butchers, mafioso)

Althena: art

Al Jabha: represent a violent nature that earns the mutiny of employees

Almach: honor, artistic ability

Alnilam: fleeting public honors

Alphard: association with drowning, poison and asphyxiation (SPCA workers?)

Alphecca: poets, artists

Alpheratz: keen intellect

Altair: positions of command, danger from reptiles

Antares: affects the nature more than choice of career; very rash, intense and headstrong character (outlaws, fugitives, assassins, runaways and sharpshooters have this star prominent in their charts)

Arcturus: voyages, navigation, art (when conjunct the Sun, a lawyer?)

Aselli: caring, responsible, charitable, fostering, donkeys, beasts of burden, burden carrying (social workers, servants, wilderness packers?)

Bellatrix: civil and military honor

Betelgeuze: marital honor

Bos: clever and piercing intellect

Bungula: beneficence

Canopus: voyages, education, wide knowledge

Capella: public positions of trust, fond of knowledge and novelties

Caphir: prophecy, courtesy

Capulus: defective eyesight (optometrist?)

Castor: success in law and publishing, horses, keen mind

Cingula Orionis: industry, memory, organizational ability

Copula: defective eyesight

Deneb: con man/woman, fraud

Deneb Adige: ingenious, clever, good at learning

Deneb Algedi: if at Midheaven, fame, receives assistance from old clergymen or similar

Difda: self-destruction through impulse, love of dance, vivid action without words (mimes?—Charlie Chaplin and Marcel

Marceau were born with the Sun near this star's degree)

El Nath: neutrality (diplomacy?)

Fomalhaut: meanings too varied and complex to list. This is the star in the fishes mouth (Pisces) and may be associated with inherited wealth and prophecy

Graffias: crime

Hamal: crime

Khambalia: argumentative (law, advocacy?)

Labrum: psychic, ecclesiastical (if near Ascendant)

Lesath: acid, poisons

Manubrium: fire, flaring, heat, courage, explosions (firefighters, blacksmiths, welders, smelters)

Markeb: educational work, religion, voyages

Mirach: brilliant mind, kindness, beauty

Nashira: struggle with evil, danger of beasts (suggested: priests, animal tamers)

Oculus: piercing mind

Pelagus: honesty, philosophical mind; science, philosophy, agriculture or education writer if conjunct Midheaven

Pleaides: many journeys, agricultural success; military commanders and kings if conjunct a luminary at Midheaven

Polaris: more of character than career given by the sources

Polis: horsemanship, martial inclinations, ambition

Pollux: boxing, poisons; occult and philosophical interests if conjunct the Sun

Princeps: research

Procyon: more character than career, association with dog bites

Rasalhaugue: athletic temperament if conjunct Sun

Vocational Astrology

Rastaban: criminals

Regulus: kings, managers military command, high government offices

Rigel: mechanical ability, sharp tools, knives, inventive abilities

Sabik: scientific, philosophical, heretical if conjunct Sun

Sadalmelik: occult studies, companies bring gain to native if conjunct Sun or Moon

Sadalsuud: psychic or occult studies if conjunct Sun or Moon

Scale, North: beneficence, high position

Scale, South: malevolence, crime

Scheat: misfortune through water and engines

Sharatan: some association with destruction by fire, war or earthquake (seismologists, nuclear industry workers?)

Sirius: dogs, protectors, guardians, custodians, curators, feeders, shepherds, groundskeepers, guards

Skat: psychics and mediums if conjunct Sun

Spica: if conjunct Sun, Ascendant or Midheaven, ecclesiastical success, great fortune and joy, good for government office

Unakalhi: anger of poison and betrayals, intrigue, plots, banishment (especially conjunct Moon); politics?

Vindemiatrix: widows, grapes, gives falsity; bad credit, business failure if conjunct Sun

Wasat: chemicals, gas, poisons, destructiveness (pharmaceutical and chemical manufacturers, anesthesiologists, oil and gas workers?)

Zaniah: lovable nature, educators if conjunct Sun

Zavijava: combat

Zosma: more on character than career

Vedic Nakshatras

Valuable career suggestions can be found from the sidereal positions of the Sun, Ascendant and particularly the Moon in the Vedic, or Indian style chart.

Caveat: To obtain the sidereal zodiac, one must first subtract the *ayanamsha* or correct amount of motion from the tropical zodiac. However, at least five respected *ayanamshas* exist, each having a suggested number of degrees to subtract from the tropical zodiac to obtain the sidereal zodiac. Vedic astrologers of India vary greatly as to their preferences, and no one really knows which *ayanamsha* is correct. These preferred methods differ as much as six degrees.

Once the dubiously correct ayanamsha is obtained and subtracted, each planet and the Ascendant is afforded a true degree in the sidereal zodiac and also a *nakshatra* (sign), or lunar mansion of 12.51.25 degrees. Due to the above problem of unresolved ayanamsha, the correct *nakshatra* (and also zodiacal sign positions) for all planets is undetermined, especially if their position is sidereally located near a cusp, or border between two *nakshatras*.

Although brief, the best vocational listing by Vedic nakshatra can be found in *The Light of Life* , an excellent book by Hart Defoux and Robert Svoboda.

Sun and Moon as Vocational Indicators

Chapter 2 presents a detailed discussion on the special role of the Sun, Moon and Ascendant as temperamental indicators. These three factors should ideally be satisfied in some way for a happy career. However, it has also been shown that careers are most often described by the best career planets, regardless of the birth chart's temperamental preferences. This incompatibility between career and temperament is the basis for most visits to the vocational counselor. Indecision is the second.

However, there are many cases where the blend of Sun and Moon will aptly describe the career. This is the method: *Envision the Sun as the center of interest. Then see the Moon as carrying out the will of the Sun into daily life expression. The Moon also represents likes and needs* as described in Chapter 2. Rely on this method to pinpoint careers for those charts that otherwise might be baffling.

Example: A client had a horoscope that indicated she was extremely talented. There were so many strong career planets that I was left somewhat confused as to which to choose. At the same time, the Sun and Moon positions were radically different. Her Sun (center of interest) was in the fourth house (properties) in strategic, manipulative Scorpio, whereas her Moon (likes, needs and carrying out the will of the Sun) was in the ninth house of education and travel in feisty, outspoken Aries.

Solution: The client's center of interest (the Sun's natal position by sign and house) will be related to the strategy and resource management (Scorpio) of homes, lands or properties (fourth house). The favored area of expression (the Moon's natal position by sign and house) of this center of interest (Sun) would be education or travel (ninth house) carried out in an assertive, inspiring manner (Aries). She is a traveling educator/promoter for the real estate and banking industries.

As an aside, Mars, a planet that simultaneously disposits her Aries Moon and Scorpio Sun (because it rules both those signs) is located in Capricorn in the sixth house. This double earth placement for an already practical, property-oriented planet provided additional testimony toward the business end of professional choices.

Chapter 6

Planetary Strength and Weakness

How to Use Planetary Dignity/Debility

To correctly use the ancient doctrine of planetary dignity, we must first understand what dignity is and how it impacts the nature of the planet. There is an unfortunate tendency to regard planets in their signs of dignity as good, and in their debility as bad. The foolishness of this immediately reveals itself when we see that a condition of dignity affects only the purity of the planetary character, while not necessarily creating either negative or positive *application* of its energies. In viewing the purity of a planet's natural functioning, we can also see that sometimes a dignified planet can indicate an *excessive* trait.

Let us take Mars for our first example. The sign of Aries allows Mars to act in a purely Martian way-aggressive, impulsive, straightforward. Although useful for some activities, this is also the mark of the proverbial hothead. We can now see that the dignity of Mars in Aries means only that Mars is very much itself. The goodness or badness of this placement depends on how it is applied by the native.

Conversely, Mars is debilitated in Libra, the opposite sign. Mars cannot act independently in Libra because it must act through others, in partnership. Is this bad or good? Again, this depends on how it is applied. Pure action on behalf of self may be more difficult for Mars in Libra than for Mars in Aries. However, a debilitated Mars in Libra gives far greater diplomatic power than the dignified Mars in Aries.

Ancient doctrine holds that dignified planets indicate strong developments related to the traditional activities of the dignified planet in former lives. In reverse, a debilitated planet might indicate a past life area of neglect or misuse. This is one reason behind the greater worldly success allotted to vocations ruled by dignified planets over their debilitated brothers. However, this never precludes a useful vocational application of a debilitated planet. A debilitated Mars in Taurus makes a superb builder, and Mercury in Sagittarius makes a gifted story teller, although debilitated. Nothing is wasted in vocational astrology. All planetary positions can be useful if put to a good use.

A debilitated planet will never be weak if it is in sect). In fact, in such a condition it can become exceptionally strong quantitatively, although its qualitative energy differs with each sign.

Planetary Dignity and Debility

Planet	Rulership (Dignity)	Exalted (Dignity)	Detriment (Debility)	Fall (Debility)
Sun	Leo	Aries	Aquarius	Libra
Moon	Cancer	Taurus	Capricorn	Scorpio
Mercury	Gem/Virgo	Aquarius	Sagittarius	Leo
Venus	Taurus/Libra	Pisces	Scorp/Aries	Virgo
Mars	Aries/Scorpio	Capricorn	Libra	Cancer
Jupiter	Sagit/Pisces	Cancer	Gem/Virgo	Capricorn
Saturn	Cap/Aquarius	Libra	Cancer/Leo	Aries
Uranus*	Aquarius	Scorpio	Leo	Taurus
Neptune*	Pisces	Cancer	Virgo	Capricorn
Pluto*	Scorpio	Aries	Taurus	Libra

*Due to their relatively recent discovery, the traditional rulerships for the trans-Saturnian planets are speculative.

Sect, the Doctrine of Day/Night Birth

Ancient Greek astrologers paid a great deal of attention to the sect of a horoscope, i.e. whether it represented a day or night birth. Project Hindsight did much to clarify this important doctrine. Unfortunately, space isn't available here to go into all the subtleties of this tradition. For our purposes it is enough to understand that a planet in sect can be very strong regardless of its condition of dignity or debility.

Night Sect

Mars, the Moon and Venus are in sect and thus very strong for night births when located above the horizon and in feminine (earth and water) signs. This is even more effective should these planets also be located between the Descendant and Midheaven.

For Mars, this seems to cool it down and make its energy at once more useful and less destructive. Overall, night births incline to less ambition than day births and prefer a life away from the limelight. I have witnessed many night birth clients pass up promotions because they didn't feel right.

Day Sect

Jupiter, the Sun and Saturn are in sect and thus very strong for day births when located above the horizon and in masculine signs. The effectiveness of this condition is increased should these planets also be located between the Ascendant and Midheaven.

In my experience, these planets so placed will prove very powerful and fortunate for the native's career. Leadership is often indicated if supported by additional testimonies. This condition seems to warm up Saturn, enhancing this planet's wisdom quality and decreasing its power to limit the native.

Neutral Sect

Mercury is neutral in that it can be in sect for either a day or night birth, depending on special conditions.

Mercury is in sect for a day birth if it rises ahead of the Sun and is located between the Ascendant and Midheaven or the Descendant and Nadir.

Mercury is in sect for night births if rising after the Sun and located between the Ascendant and Nadir or the Descendant and Midheaven.

Vocational Strength for Planets

Potential vocational strength is enhanced by the following conditions: Any planet enjoying two or more of the below conditions of placement becomes a strong candidate for vocational consideration. Strengthening conditions are as follows:

1. Planet is dignified (in the sign of rulership or exaltation).

2. Planet is located within thirty degrees of the Midheaven (the closer the better).

3. Planet is within thirty degrees of the Ascendant (the closer the better).

4. Planet is conjunct the North Node.

5. Planet rules the Midheaven.

6. Planet is located in the sixth or second house.

7. Planet rules the tenth, sixth or second house (in that order of preference).

8. Planet trines or sextiles the Midheaven within one degree of orb.

9. Planet rules the sign of the Sun, Moon or Ascendant and simultaneously rules or tenants any of the three vocational houses (second, sixth, tenth).

10. Planet is conjunct the Sun or Moon and simultaneously rules or tenants any of the three vocational house (second, sixth, tenth).

11. Planet is the doryphory, an old term meaning "spear bear-

er" to the Sun. This means that the planet is the last planet to rise preceding the rise of the Sun. Therefore, it rises directly before the Sun in the same or contiguous sign. A strongly placed, dignified doryphory must never be neglected in vocational interpretation.

12. A planet is in sect (see the section above on sect).

13. A planet is stationary direct. This condition greatly intensifies the planet's energy and also slows down to a crawl its influence in time. Select only the slow, enduring fields of any careers associated with a stationary planet.

Vocational Weakness for Planets: The Avoids

The vocational unsuitability of a planet is furthered by the following conditions. Any planet enjoying two or more of these weakening conditions of placement may prove to be an unfortunate career significator.

1. The planet is debilitated through location in a sign of its detriment and fall.

Note: Planets are potentially debilitated in the signs of their fall and detriment. This condition does not necessarily detract from a useful vocational application of the planet's energy. However, detriment and fall can affect the success of activities associated with the planet, being rarely as lucky as planets in rulership and exaltation positions.

Should the planet in fall or detriment be well placed and aspected, expect a moderate success and talent described by the planet and its position. For instance, the "horrifying" double debility of Mars in Cancer in the fourth house is ideal for home demolition, neighborhood protection and fence building. The equally "negative" Mars in Cancer in the tenth house quite frequently produces a good cook, mechanic, cleaning person or nurse.

A debilitated planet's difficulties are to some degree neutralized should it be disposited, conjunct, square or opposite a planet in rulership or exaltation; a planet ruling its own exaltation sign; conjunct the North Node; or receiving a trine or sextile aspect from Jupiter.

2. Any planet closely conjoined the South Node (see Chapter 5 for factors that nullify or reverse this rule). A conjunction of no greater than three degrees will be powerful. However, there will be some South Node effect for proximity of up to fifteen degrees regardless of sign boundaries, provided no other planet stands between them.

3. Planet neither rules nor tenants any of the three career houses (second, sixth, tenth or Midheaven). Be sure to use the old style Ptolemaic rulers for this rule (not Uranus, Neptune and Pluto).

4. Planet is not within a thirty degree proximity of the Midheaven or Ascendant. This lack of proximity to the primary vocational angles will not disqualify the planet as a vocational indicator, nor necessarily reduce its strength. However, the planet is disqualified preferentially should another planet be strong by sign and well aspected in either of the above locations.

5. Planet receives a quincunx from any other planet and is simultaneously squared or opposed by other planets.

6. Planet is out of sect (see section on sect). A planet out of sect is only mildly weakened if it is strong in another way. However if it is in sect its strength is greatly enhanced.

7. Planet squares, opposes or quincunxes the Moon.

8. Planet opposes or quincunxes Saturn. For best results Saturn must agree with the enterprise and therefore cannot be in disharmony with the planetary ruler of that enterprise. These aspects and, to a lesser extent the square of Saturn, indicate a harder row to hoe. However, success can still be achieved with patience, hard work and a helpful aspect from Jupiter.

9. Planet square or quincunx the Midheaven exactly within one degree of orb.

10. Any planet in the last three degrees of a sign. This weakening condition is strongest for the air and fire signs and will cause a lack of steam and motivation for this planet's activities. Should the planet also be void of course (completing no major aspect to slower planets than itself or faster planets retrograding before exiting its current sign), the "fading out" quality of the planet is certain. However, a void-of-course planet is useful for philanthropic and charitable forms of employment and for spiritual expression.

11. A retrograde planet. This is tricky because if it is near stationary it sometimes will be exceptionally strong and successful. More typically, however, the retrograde condition gives the planet a slow start or indicates the flowering of this planet's affair later in life after a period of latency, delay or frustration.

The activities and occupations ruled by any planet that is stationary retrograde will back up and stop. This resembles a super retrogradation. Stationary retrograde occur whenever a planet slows to a stop, or stations, and then turns retrograde.

Locate the day of the station in an ephemeris and see if that date is accompanied by the letter "R" under the planet column. If so, check how many days preceding the station this planet makes no apparent motion (remains on the same degree and minute as on its stationing date). This motionless period functions inclusively as the period of stationary retrograde. Be careful in making judgments because a stationary direct planet looks similar (it has a "D" instead of an "R") and will sometimes prove very strong rather than weak for career matters.

12. The planetary ruler of the tenth house, Midheaven or sixth house is located in the twelfth house (limitations) and poorly placed by sign with few supportive aspects. However, do keep alert to a very important point: The traditionally "evil" houses-

six, eight, twelve-have no natural power to injure the career success of any planet. More typically they simply indicate the sphere of the career action. For example, the ruler of the Midheaven, well placed by aspect and sign and located in the twelfth house, usually shows work in labs, hospitals, remote places or ashrams.

The planetary ruler of the tenth house, or Midheaven, located in the eighth house is an excellent placement for surgeons and psychologists. And of course the sixth house is itself one of the three employment houses and cannot be evil in that context. Instead, it is useful. (See Chapter 7.)

Chapter 7

House Rulerships in Vocational Astrology

The twelve divisions of the celestial sphere constitute the traditional twelve astrological houses. There are several alternate methods of dividing the celestial sphere. The existence of so many house systems creates a valid confusion, i.e. which house system to use. Every astrologer must solve this age-old riddle to his/her own satisfaction. Whatever house system is used, be sure to include the two methods described below in the vocational interpretation.

1. The Midheaven, identical for all house systems, is the traditionally preeminent angle for career analysis. Therefore, the Midheaven, its sign and its planetary ruler's condition and house plus sign placement, plus all planets nearest to this point (within an orb of thirty degrees, the closer the better) must always be foremost and central to the career analysis.

2. Use the house system that works best for you. Placidus, Koch and, to a lesser degree, Campanus appear to be the Western favorites. However, keep the ancient whole sign houses in mind and include them in the analysis. What is a whole sign house?

Whole Sign Houses

Whole sign houses are probably the oldest and certainly the simplest method of house division, still widely in use among the Jyotish (Vedic astrologers). In this system the entire ascending sign (not the Ascendant degree) constitutes the beginning of the first house. The second sign from the Ascendant becomes the second house, the third sign from the Ascendant will have a third house influence, and so on through the remaining houses. Try it and see if it works. So far I haven't met one astrologer who isn't well satisfied with the results. Once this cyclic-based system of house division is incorporated, a curiosity will be noted:

The Midheaven can occur in the eighth, ninth, tenth or eleventh signs as counted counterclockwise from the Ascendant (in mid-northern latitudes).

This floating Midheaven phenomenon leads me to speculate that the earliest astrologers (as do many modem Jyotish) always set out the chart into twelve equal divisions beginning either with the ascending sign or the Ascendant degree. Ancient astrologers knew the tenth sign from the Ascendant was the house of career matters. Over time, the Midheaven was also discovered to powerfully impact vocational matters, professional choice and the timing of events. Ptolemy clearly knew of the Midheaven and wrote of its vocational importance as early as 140 A.D.

Therefore (and here was the faulty leap of logic), the Midheaven must now become the cusp of the tenth house, superseding the traditional vocational function of the tenth sign. The superimposition of a floating tenth house cusp over an equally sectioned wheel created a real problem in house division mechanics because the Midheaven will only be exactly ten signs from the Ascendant (and therefore within the boundaries of the natural tenth house) in some charts, depending on the latitude and time of birth. The Midheaven is equally likely to fall within the boundaries of the natural eighth, ninth or eleventh houses. It would seem thus more naturally cyclical to spin out a cycle of twelve equal houses from the Midheaven and to use this as a secondary chart for vocational purposes. But Western astrologers insisted on attempting to force a new tenth house—the Midheaven—over a chart that already contained a tenth sign from the Ascendant, the whole sign house divisional chart.

The result is seen today in a variety of methods called house systems, some ingenious and others awkward, because of dividing up the chart so as to accommodate both an Ascendant as starting the first house and the Midheaven as beginning the tenth house. And what of the traditional tenth sign from the Ascendant? Sadly, it is ignored in its career implications unless the individual is lucky enough to have the Midheaven fall within its boundaries.

We must ask this question: Why can't the tenth sign from the Ascendant rule career implications and have the Midheaven simultaneously be a strong vocational indicator? Well, why not? In practice this question answers itself. Both the tenth sign and the Midheaven contain information valid to the vocation. There is no real need to insist on the Midheaven starting the tenth house just because the tenth is the traditional vocational area. Treat the tenth sign and the Midheaven angle as separate career indicators, including both in the career analysis.

House Rulerships in Vocational Astrology

First House: Visibility, face, "the person is the career," initiators, leaders. Exerts energy and start the ball rolling. The role one plays in most situations.

Second House: Food, eating, money, finances, the body, ear-nose-throat, vocal cords, teeth, physical objects, appetites, precious metals and stones, form. One of several artistic house (emphasis on beauty, form, senses). A mathematical house.

Third House: Writing, talking, communication, fine arts, literature, short trips, taxis, messenger work, neighborhoods, siblings, commuting, trade, intellectual development, languages, play, mind games, data, newspaper columns, bits of information, arms, fingers, nervous system, lungs, breath, oratory, singing, juggling, instrumentalists, dexterity, a mathematical house, telephones, typewriters, computers, books, bookstores, numbers, penmanship, stationery.

Fourth House: Real estate, property, cemeteries, beds, baths, kitchens, domesticity, mothers, home businesses, gardens, ports, enclosures, reservoirs, centering principle, night work, privacy, hidden things, emotional life and feeling, home gardening, canning, cottage industries, Earth energies, mining, buried wealth, below, darkness, private gardens, vaults, mines, reservoirs, safes.

Fifth House: Theaters, casinos, vacations, recreation, parks, management, youth, sports, dance, painting, creativity, speculation, pleasure, money from real estate, exposition of self, children, games, fun, attention attractors. An artistic house (emphasizes color).

Sixth House: Real estate processes (inspecting, appraising), nursing, food preparation, medicine, preparation, social services, armed forces, data, facts, filing, employment as a topic, employees, work teams, utilities, clothing, building supply, subordinates, coworkers, proletariat, health as a topic, support, jobs, common work, work methodology and processes, business development, conveyor belt, useful animals, farmed animals and farm animals, useful skills, farming, sorting objects, weaving, manufacturing, blue collar trades.

Seventh House: Negotiations, contacts, diplomacy, cooperation, competitors, law as a profession, balance, social graces, war, partners of any kind, associates, alliances, conflict resolution, one of several artistic houses (emphasizes balance, harmony and portraiture), observations, wisdom, judgment, interviewing, listening, chairpersons, mediators, representatives. A strong house for psychologists (with the eighth and twelfth).

Eighth House: Surgery, death and dying, chemistry, physics, analysis and research, criminology, detection, others' money, recycling, resource management, money management, banking, investing, insurance, inheritance, benefits packages, crisis control, epidemiology, bacteriology, sex, genetics, transformational work, psychology, investigations, crisis management, waste management, economic analysis.

Ninth House: Publishing, newspapers, media, radio, academia, international affairs, connections of any kind, import-export, immigration, migration, long journeys, flying, collegiate education, philosophy, religion, thought packages, group-think, libraries, conferences, conducting, coordinating, Internet.

Tenth House: Reputation, personal mission, highest achievements, vocation in general, material and life goals, presidents, bosses, corporate heads and builders, land development, capitalism, initiation, "name," status.

Eleventh House: volunteer work, adoptions, humor, science, inventive ability, creative thinking, large groups, senate, board meeting, legislation, overview, visualization, humanitarianism, philanthropy, humanity, the public, brotherhoods, sisterhoods, idealized projects, lectures, conferences, New Age expose, planetariums, aquariums, visioning, anthropology, other people's children, the world's children, leisure time, large social movements, equality, idealism, utopia, sweeping social fads, electricity, high tech inventions, socially enlightening organizations, other people's creativity, elderly people, quality of life enhancement, prayer, miracles, hope, mentors, benefactors, coaching. A mathematical, scientific and inventive house.

Twelfth House: Retreats, ashrams, sleep, spiritual work, psychological processing, fear, psychic tendency, hidden things, subconscious, inhibitions, prisons, backwaters, garages, forgotten lots, remote places, unkempt parts of the house or land, wilderness, wild animals, sea creatures, untamed, oceans, monasteries, monks and nuns, selfless service, charity, hospitals, institutions (the red tape that runs itself), faith, prayer, night environments, dark rooms, illegal activities, swamps, diving, research, ancient things, the past, used items, music, antiques, psychic residue, ghosts, paranormal, insanity, addictions, recovery, the poor, poverty, escapes, unemployment. A musical, mystical house.

Chapter 8

The Three Vocational Houses

Three of the twelve astrological houses are associated with vocation. This trilogy is comprised of the second, sixth and tenth astrological houses.

Although all twelve houses have useful vocational associations, it is this vocationally oriented triad that predicts what we will do for a living.

These three vocational houses are hierarchical in that the tenth house is supreme over both the sixth and the second, whereas the sixth house is vocationally stronger than the second in most cases. Exceptions to this rule are described below.

Hierarchically above these three houses stands the Midheaven, that preeminent vocational point located often, but not always, in the tenth house (applying whole sign houses, the tenth house is identical to the tenth sign as counted counterclockwise from the Ascendant). Many astrologers prefer to call the Midheaven the beginning point or cusp of the tenth house. If this is your method, continue but do not neglect a study of the tenth sign should the Midheaven not fall within its borders. For more information on whole sign houses, refer to Chapter 7.

The Three Vocational Houses and the Midheaven

The Midheaven (MC)

This angle reflects the individual's life calling, the profession, status, rank, authority and greatest achievements. The Midheaven is the career point par excellence. Think of it as kind of a mission statement for life. One's material accomplishments and professional aspirations are represented here. It also can indicate outer events that seem to control the life externally, from above as it were.

This essential career point can fall within the boundaries of either the eighth, ninth, tenth or eleventh signs from the Ascendant (as counted counterclockwise).

Always carefully observe the sign located at the Midheaven, those planets nearest the Midheaven (within thirty degrees; planetary strength increases with increased proximity to the Midheaven) and especially the planetary ruler of the Midheaven-its sign and house placement, strength and ties by aspect to the rulers of the second, sixth and tenth houses as counted from the Ascendant.

Notice the tenth sign from the Ascendant is not necessarily identical with the Midheaven of the Western tenth house cusp unless the Midheaven is within the boundaries of the tenth sign from the Ascendent.

A strongly placed or dignified planet near the Midheaven (either side) and not void of course or square, opposite or quincunx to either the Moon or Saturn will manifest as a career at some point in life.

The zodiacal sign of the Midheaven also can be important. The Midheaven and its planetary ruler will dominate over the signs and rulers of the remaining two career oriented houses, the sixth and the second. Always give the planets near the Midheaven and the ruler of the Midheaven precedence in vocational selection unless unfortunate or weakened in the ways described in Chapter 6. Only a dignified planet near the Ascendant can vie for vocational power with a strong and well-aspected planet near or ruling the Midheaven.

The Tenth Sign from the Ascendant

Use this sign and its planetary ruler identically as described for the Midheaven and its ruler. Remember, the Midheaven and tenth sign will only be identical should the Midheaven fall in the tenth sign from the Ascendant. Should the two not be identical, be sure to allow the Midheaven sign and its planetary ruler precedence over the tenth sign and its planetary ruler unless the former is conspicuously weaker than the latter. In reverse, the tenth sign house holds precedence over the sixth and second vocational houses for career choice.

The Sixth House or Sixth Sign from the Ascendant

This vocational house rules gainful employment, coworkers, work relations, subordinates and all jobs done just for the money. Never confuse the labor of the sixth house with professional callings as shown by the tenth whole sign house and the Midheaven unless the Midheaven ruler is located in the sixth house or vice versa.

This area governs jobs as distinct from life work or greatest life achievement. The position of the planetary ruler of this house or any planets within its boundaries may suggest positions of employment held by the native at some point in his/her life. Should the Midheaven rulers be weak while the sixth house rulers are strong, consider the sixth house ruler to be a dominant vocational significator. Vocationally, this house governs many activities, including coworkers, employees, health, work environment, work equipment and improvements, skill development, real estate development, useful animals, product development, conveyer belt, utilities, support systems, teamwork, efficiency.

The Second House or Second Sign from the Ascendant

The second house testifies to earning power, money and business sense, and hints at the kinds of businesses and products from which one may profit. This last and traditionally weakest of the three vocational houses governs food, money and earning power. Planets strongly placed by sign in this house may bring wealth to the native according to either the products they govern or their specific activities. For instance, Venus in Libra in the second house might bring money through the sale of fine china or any products ruled by Venus. Or it can mean that it is the native's diplomatic graces (a trait associated with Venus in Libra) that assist him/her in business.

The planets tenanting this house area, or the planetary ruler of the second house, become vocational significators in the event that 1) a dignified planet (one in its sign of exaltation or rulership) tenants the second house, 2) the rulers of the tenth house and the Midheaven are weak, poorly placed or out of the running, 3) the rulers of the sixth house are weak or debilitated, and 4) the strongest vocational significators, such as the Midheaven ruler, are found in the second house and are simultaneously strong by sign and aspect.

One observation is that persons with very strong second houses and weaker tenth and sixth house will strongly incline toward business activities or prominently product-oriented and/or money-related careers.

Analyzing the Vocational Houses and Their Rulers

Those planets nearest the Midheaven by thirty degrees are always studied first for strength and for the quality of aspects made with other planets. These culminating planets signify definite careers in life. If not, then they will show the planetary forces most influential to the career. For instance, Uranus conjunct the Midheaven at birth can mean the individual is an electrician or that the career is prone to unexpected "electrical" changes or reversals. It can even mean that one's reputation is peculiar or one is renowned for his/her brilliance. A variance of interpretation depending on the overall quality of the chart must therefore be allowed.

Occasionally, several planets cluster near the Midheaven and/or tenth house. This can indicate a checkered career or separate careers, each of several years duration. Generally speaking, a Midheaven planet equals a career.

A planet in its sign of rulership or exaltation, tolerably aspected and especially in sect, will absolutely indicate a strong career for that person as described by the planet and sign. An example would be the occurrence of Jupiter in Pisces near the Midheaven further supported by a pleasant trine aspect to the Moon in the second house of money matters. This person would engage in a lucrative Jupiterian occupation as working out through Pisces. Perhaps he/she would be a successful minister, chef or naval officer. Sections on how to interpret planet-house and planet-sign combinations are given in this chapter and Chapter 4.

The planet not necessarily near but ruling the sign of the Midheaven is next in line for specifying the nature of the career. Observe its position by house and sign.

Note: Should the Midheaven not coincide with the tenth house sign, locate the tenth sign from the Ascendant, counting counterclockwise. This tenth whole sign house stands second in vocational importance to the Midheaven. Take note of any planets in this region, their signs and their aspects. What sign governs the tenth sign and what planet rules this sign? Locate the house and sign position of the tenth house ruler.

Midheaven or Tenth House Ruler in the First House: The individual is his/her career. One's "face," energy or personality will be the stage where career activities will manifest, and he/she will be noticed.

Midheaven or Tenth House Ruler in the Second House: An emphasized area of vocational activity will be money, objects, the body, Earth or food (one or more).

Midheaven or Tenth House Ruler in the Third House: An emphasized area of vocational activity will be communication, language, writing, neighborhood affairs, speaking, the fine arts (one or more).

Midheaven or Tenth House Ruler in the Fourth House: An emphasized area of vocational activity will be property, home, family, Earth (one or more).

Midheaven or Tenth House Ruler in the Fifth House: An emphasized area of vocational activity will be pleasure, theater, youth, art, recreation, management (one or more).

Midheaven or Tenth House Ruler in the Sixth House: An emphasized area of vocational activity will be employment, data or food processing, health, services (one or more).

Midheaven or Tenth House Ruler in the Seventh House: The partner may be the career. An emphasized are of vocational activity will be marriage, negotiations, diplomacy, contracts, law (one or more).

Midheaven or Tenth House Ruler in the Eighth House: An emphasized area of vocational activity will be death, surgery, healing, crises, analysis, other people's money (one or more).

Midheaven or Tenth House Ruler in the Ninth House: An emphasized area of vocational activity will be teaching, traveling, religion, law, publishing or media (one or more).

Midheaven or Tenth House Ruler in the Tenth House: A very strong career placement. Powerful reputation and life work. Excellent power to attain one's highest ambitions. Gives recognition and leadership in one's field. The native will pursue an occupation that is ruled by this planet, especially if it is dignified.

Midheaven or Tenth House Ruler in the Eleventh House: An emphasized area of vocational activity will be groups, social contribution, philanthropy, altruism, creative thinking, board meetings, science, companies, humanity, idealistic projects (one or more).

Midheaven or Tenth House Ruler in the Twelfth House: An emphasized area of vocational activity will be hospitals, clinics, ashrams, the spiritual life, psychology, remote places, research, prison, charitable works (one or more).

Ruler of the Sixth House Through the Twelve Houses

To reiterate, the planets nearest the Midheaven are observed first, followed by those located in the tenth sign from the Ascendant (see Chapter 7). We also look to both of the rulers of the Midheaven and the tenth sign and judge their vocational viability from their strength and aspects (Chapter 6).

Although the sixth house is subordinate to the Midheaven, the tenth house and their rulers, we must consult it for information about employment and work environment. Most individuals spend years in various jobs before arriving at their chosen work, as shown more decisively by the Midheaven, planets nearest the Midheaven and the Midheaven ruler. Planets located in the sixth house and the sign and house position of the planetary ruler of the sixth house will show where it is we work. Additionally, much information about the work environment, job issues and useful skills can be found in the sixth house.

Ruler of the Sixth House in the First House: The individual is seen as a worker, and is his/her work, possibly working alone. There may be healing abilities or work as a healer, and he/she may be a master of a trade or outstanding in the chosen field.

Ruler of the Sixth House in the Second House: The work environment involves money, food, objects, form, beauty, the body (one or more).

Ruler of the Sixth House in the Third House: The work environment involves communications, phones, computers, typing, commuting, neighborhoods, siblings, fine arts, connections (one or more).

Ruler of the Sixth House in the Fourth House: The work environment involves the home, family, parents, property, real estate, land, night, privacy, restaurants or pubs (one or more).

Ruler of the Sixth House in the Fifth House: The work environment involves children, sports, art, dancing, theater, painting, dancing, recreation, pleasure, romance, fun, gambling (one or more).

Ruler of the Sixth House in the Sixth House: The work environment involves employment, employees, teams, technical detail, industry, details, utilities, services, medical occupations, animals, teams, nursing, subordinate positions, health, food processing, manufacturing (one or more). This position gives excellent job opportunities and work reputation.

Ruler of the Sixth House in the Seventh House: The work environment involves partners, consulting, counseling, law, competition, sales, others, marriage, alliances, diplomacy (one or more).

Ruler of the Sixth House in the Eighth House: The work environment involves other people's money, surgery, crises, transformation, medicine, analysis, chemistry, physics, psychology, investigation, death (one or more).

Ruler of the Sixth House in the Ninth House: The work environment involves teaching, traveling, colleges, religion, knowledge, media, publishing, radio (one or more).

Ruler of the Sixth House in the Tenth House: The work environment involves authority, ownership, having employees, manufacturing, power. This position gives rank and reputation in relation to one's work, skills and coworkers. A strong indication for medical work. May have employees or work with labor teams.

Ruler of the Sixth House in the Eleventh House: The work environment involves groups, social awareness, creative thinking, idealized projects, friendships, good will, leisure, mentoring, coaching, visioning, abstract thinking, science, humor, composition, genius, contribution, philanthropy, humanity (one or more).

Ruler of the Sixth House in the Twelfth House: The work environment involves ashrams, retreats, hospitals, psychology, rest homes, clinics, animal shelters, bars, the night, the hidden, research, fantasy, sleep, the poor, charities, unemployment (one or more).

Ruler of the Second Vocational House Through the Twelve Houses

The Second house becomes vocationally important in three ways:

1. There are no planets in the tenth or sixth houses and their planetary rulers are weak or indisposed by the various "avoids" listed in Table 3 (Chapter 6). In this case we must study the second house, the planets therein and the placement by house and sign of the planetary ruler of the second house.

2. The best vocational planets, that is the Midheaven or sixth house rulers, are located in this house, dignified and well aspected.

3. A planet in its own sign is located in the second house. Such a planet will profit the native through the activities or products it rules.

Ruler of the Second House in the First House: Earning power is very strong. The individual will be profit oriented and sensual.

Ruler of the Second House in the Second House: Money is obtained from the activities or products associated with this planet. If well aspected, this is an excellent indication of good earning power and financial success.

Ruler of the Second House in the Third House: Earning power and money sources are connected with writing, communication, intellect, computers, commuting, siblings, speaking, the hands, fine arts (one or more).

Ruler of the Second House in the Fourth House: Earning power and money sources are connected with real estate, homes, parents, family, land, restaurants, Earth (one or more).

Ruler of the Second House in the Fifth House: Earning power and money sources are connected with youth, pleasure, sports, art, creativity, drama, speculation, recreation management, entrepreneurial activities (one or more).

Ruler of the Second House in the Sixth House: Earning power and money sources are connected with health, nursing, secretarial work, employment, service, the trades, technical work, real estate transactions, animals (one or more).

Ruler of the Second House in the Seventh House: Earning power and money sources are connected with marriage, business partnership, consulting, counseling others, diplomacy, law, alliances, competition, war (one or more).

Ruler of the Second House in the Eighth House: Earning power and money sources are connected with inheritance, estates, other's money, benefits, insurance, alimony, divorce, banking, investment, death, medicine, psychology, physics, engineering, chemistry, analysis (one or more).

Ruler of the Second House in the Ninth House: Earning power and money sources are connected with knowledge, publishing, religion, spirituality, teaching, education, traveling and travelers, foreign countries, media (one or more).

Ruler of the Second House in the Tenth House: Earning power and money sources are connected with the profession, authority, power, rank, reputation, father, boss (one or more). This is one testimony of financial success. One may pursue a career in finance, business, economics or any money-related profession (especially if the planet is in an earth sign).

Ruler of the Second House in the Eleventh House: Earning power and money sources are connected with friends, groups, volunteer work, collectives, outside income, ideas, special projects, coaching, humanitarianism, creative thinking, science, humor, abstract thought, brain children, conferences, inventions, favors, luck (one or more). This is a fairly lucky position for the finances.

Ruler of the Second House in the Twelfth House: Earning power and money sources are connected with retreats, hospitals, inheritances, windfalls, unemployment compensation, charitable work, prisons, psychology psychic work, research, solitude, past karma (one or more). This position is either very good or very poor in regards to wealth. The earning power can be seriously harmed if the planet ruling the second house is weak and badly aspected. However, a strong and well-aspected second house ruler in the twelfth house will protect the native, bringing miraculous help, inheritances and similar events.

How to Interpret the House-Sign Combination of the Midheaven Ruler and Other Important Vocational Planets

The twelve houses have countless items under their rulership. My house rulership listings (Chapter 7) are incomplete because they include only the vocational implications of each house. These become important should the Sun, Moon, Midheaven ruler or tenth house ruler be placed in any particular house. In this case the affairs of the house *(en toto* or select), gain prominence of vocational activity. Still we cannot neglect to blend the planet-house interpretation with the sign the planet is in. Below is a step-by-step example demonstrating how to proceed.

First, find the Midheaven ruler. In what house is it? Now check the house position. Think of the activities listed as the area of vocational activity. (Use the above lists to get the feel of planet-house combinations.) Naturally only some of the house meanings will fit the individual case. (All house meanings are related, but it is still impossible to always include the full gamut.)

So we see that the house tells us the "where" of vocational activity. Now assess the sign the planetary ruler of the Midheaven inhabits. (Reread Chapters 1 and 3 for a review of sign qualities.) Now locate the sign placement of the Midheaven ruler. This sign tells us *how* the planet will work out. In summary, the planet must be viewed as "what," the main energy, whereas its house position shows "where" this energy will work out and the zodiac sign it tenants describes "how."

Example Synthesis of Planet with Sign and House

Below is a hypothetical example designed to assist the reader in the interpretation of the house-sign placement of the Midheaven ruler.

Let us say that the Midheaven sign is Taurus, which is ruled by Venus. Therefore, Venus is the main career energy. Where is Venus? In what house and in what sign is this planet?

Let's again pretend that Venus is located in the fourth house and is in the sign Scorpio. Therefore, the fourth house is the stage where the vocational activity must work out. The Venus-type activity, that is!

What items are suggested by the fourth house? Property, homes, gardens, beds, kitchens, etc. We can say that at least some of these listed items will constitute an important stage for professional activity. But how? To answer this, we must look to the zodiac sign that Venus is located in at birth.

Next observe the sign Scorpio because Venus is in this sign. (Venus may rule Taurus, but it is not in Taurus all the time.) Our hypothetical chart locates Venus in Scorpio, which has many fine qualities but not all of which exactly fit Venus. Only the sexy, alluring and sensually pleasurable qualities of Scorpio meld well with the naturally sweet and soothing energy of Venus. What aptitudes might this energy suggest?

Put it together: planet, house and sign. At first, just concentrate on the one indicator of Venus in Scorpio. (This takes intuition and practice at first, but you will catch on.)

Venus in Scorpio in the fourth house would be ideal for a bath supplies shop or sauna business, a women' shelter or a dealer in exotic rugs and bedroom accessories. We could speculate further, but will stop here. Use this method also for interpreting the rulers of the additional vocational houses (second, sixth, tenth, first).

Once some skill in interpreting simple planet-house-sign combinations is acquired, you will graduate to synthesizing all vocational factors in the chart.

Chapter 9

Reading the Vocational Horoscope

What It Takes

What special skills enable an astrologer to interpret vocational horoscopes? First, it is important to realize that vocational astrology is not easy and cannot be accomplished through "cookbook" or computer program astrology. The vocational astrologer must bring to the craft a certain amount of previous accomplishment in chart reading. He/she should already be proficient and experienced in the interpretation of natal charts as well as progressions and transits.

Vocational astrology is the art of astrological applications. In other words, how can Mars in Aries best be used? What skills does a sixth house Saturn in Taurus best describe? If you are one of those people who looks at horoscopes and immediately sees applications, then you are a natural for vocational chart interpretation.

However it is also important that the psychological nature of each planet and house is well understood. A little background in medical astrology also will come in handy, especially for selecting branches of medicine for medical students. Do learn the body rulerships by sign. For instance, Pisces governs the feet, so an emphasis of benefic planets in Pisces might be a clue to a potentially lucrative career in shoe sales.

Above all, the vocational astrologer needs a good memory. I make no attempt to jest when I insist that the contents of Rex E. Bills' *The Rulership Book* should be committed to memory. Careers, types of people, things and activities should be understood according to their sign, planet or house connections.

Next, a vocational astrologer must be adept at what is known in astrology as synthesis. To synthesize means to bring many factors together in an understandable whole. The chart reader must be able to observe and absorb the entire pattern of the birth chart and then intuit the vocations that best satisfy at least several of the native's many sides.

A great deal of intuition is part and parcel to vocational reading. The lists provided in this book are therefore essential only from the technical standpoint. The art of vocational chart reading must come from within and will be individual to each practitioner. This does not mean that memorizing these lists should be neglected. Only when the technical material is stored through memorization in the subconscious can the ability to synthesize be operative and the intuitive art well applied. (Natural psychics of the caliber of Edgar Cayce may be excused from their studies.)

Sometimes a picture or word will appear in your mind regarding an individual's work and many times this image will be accurate. Is this your psychic ability at work? Maybe. But more likely it is the synthesizing function of your own subconscious mind quietly working away on problems while your conscious mind is elsewhere preoccupied. Hand the subconscious a problem, such as remembering someone's name you have forgotten, and at some unexpected moment the name will pop into your conscious mind, located at your request by the subconscious. It is much the same with vocational chart synthesis, albeit more complicated. Your subconscious is able to sort through the scores of vocational indicators and suddenly flash ideas forward to your conscious mind. With practice, this can become a reliable process in vocational chart interpretation. But first your memory bank must include the full contents of the rulership lists included in this book and exercised through practice in interpreting charts. Let's start now.

Weighting

Most charts are full of strange contradictions and opposite planetary testimonies. This brings up the important concept of weighting the vocational testimonies. In weighting, look for a strength of tendencies in any one direction given by the majority of career indicators. Each chart will have a minimum of three vocational rulers-the planetary rulers of the three vocational houses. Most horoscopes have at least five important indicators plus the temperamental indicators of Sun, Moon and Ascendant. In weighting, look for either 1) a majority of planetary indicators in either the feminine signs (earth and water) or the masculine signs (air and fire) because planets in same-gendered signs harmonize with one another or, 2) whether a majority of vocational indicators in the chart suggest any one direction or theme. To assist in doing this, use the Planetary Families chart in Chapter 4.

The Best Planets

There may be several strong and well-aspected planets in the chart, but do any of them rule or tenant a vocational house? If they do, then these planets are automatic vocational candidates, and the individual should excel at some of the talents in their association.

Hopefully you have read the previous section and thoroughly understand planetary strength, or dignity, and planetary weakness, or debility. To interpret vocational charts, you must be able to judge the strength or weakness of any planet in the birth chart. This ability is needed in order to select the best or strongest vocational planet(s), and also to ferret out the worst.

Below is a step-by-step hierarchical guide to finding the best planet(s) for vocational purposes. Begin always with the planets nearest and/or ruling the Midheaven.

1. Planets Nearest the Midheaven. Are any of these planets also in their rulership or exaltation signs or in sect or receiving a trine or sextile aspect from the Moon or the ruler of any vocational house or strong in any of the other ways listed in Chapter 6? If no "avoids" are functional, the planet is an automatic career contender.

2. The Midheaven Ruler: Note the precise position by sign and house (and number of signs from the Ascendant) of the Midheaven ruler. Be sure to use the old style Ptolemaic rulers given in Chapter 6. Is this ruler well placed by sign and aspect? Are no "avoids" functional? If the Midheaven ruler is strong by sign (exalted or in rulership) and has good aspects, it is a prime career candidate. Again, the Midheaven ruler takes preference over any other planetary ruler of a career-related house (first, second, sixth).

3. The Nadir Planet(s): Should the Midheaven and tenth sign from the Ascendant be empty of planets, check three degrees on either side of the Nadir. This angle is exactly opposite the Midheaven and, as such, any planet here can influence the vocation. Any planet found in its rulership or exaltation sign near the Nadir may describe the person's career provided there are no dominant planets near the Midheaven. This rule is extremely reliable should the planet so described closely aspect by conjunction trine or sextile a planetary ruler of any career house (the Midheaven, tenth, sixth or second) or is itself a ruler of a career house.

4. Tenth Sign: If the Midheaven does not fall within the boundaries of the tenth sign, focus attention on any planets located in the tenth sign from the Ascendant. The best of these planets are those strongest by sign position—not in detriment or fall and hopefully in their signs of rulership and exaltation. They also can be very strong if they are in sect, a condition dependent on day/night birth.

5. Rising Planet(s): Is there a planet conjunct the Ascendant within seven degrees (preferably within three degrees)? This region functions as a place of honor for planetary qualities obvious in the personality. Should no "avoids" be functional, the process is nearly complete. If the rising planet is well aspected, especially to any rulers of vocational houses or the Midheaven angle, then its associated careers qualify as prime vocational choices. Note: In my experience, it doesn't seem to matter if this planet is in fall or detriment.

6. Sixth House Planets: Proceed now to the sixth house (sixth sign from the Ascendant). Are there any planets in this house? Are they strong and well aspected? Is the sixth house without "avoids"? If so, then some of the careers associated with this planet(s) qualify for career consideration.

7. Sixth House Ruler: Locate the planetary ruler of the sixth sign and judge its condition. Is it conjunct, sextile or trine the rulers of the second or tenth house or, most especially, the Midheaven ruler?

8. Second House Planets: The last vocational house to observe is the second. Locate the second sign from the Ascendant. Are there any planets therein? Are they strongly placed by sign and without "avoids"? Are any of these planets conjunct, sextile or trine any of the rulers of the Midheaven, tenth house or sixth house? If so, the careers associated with these planets qualify for potentially lucrative vocational consideration.

9. Second House Ruler: Locate the ruler of the second house. Is it strong by sign and well aspected? Are there any "avoids" functioning? Is the second house ruler conjunct, trine or sextile a ruler of the sixth house, tenth house or Midheaven? If so, the careers associated with this planet qualify for potentially lucrative vocational consideration.

10. No Best Planet: Occasionally a chart has no vocational ruler in an acceptable condition. In this case, the strongest planet in the chart must be selected, regardless of its vocational association by house or rulership.

Beginning Synthesis: Comparing the Best Vocational Planets with the Sun, Moon and Ascendant

Now that the best vocational planets have been identified, it is imperative to learn if they agree with the temperamental rulers: the Sun, Moon and ascending signs. If they don't, the individual may not be happy in a career in which he/she excels. Proceed by comparing the best vocational planets with the Sun, Moon and Ascendant through the following steps (see Chapter 2).

1. *Comparison of the Best Career Planets with Sign and House Positions of the Native's Sun*: Does this planet conjunct, sextile or trine the Sun in a harmonious pattern? Or does it square, quincunx or oppose the Sun? How does the best planet relate to the central life purpose or main value as indicated by the Sun's position? In other words, if the career rulers are all saying "banking" and the main value is spiritual (Sun in the ninth house, perhaps in Pisces), would employment as a banker be fulfilling?

2. *Compare the Best Career Planet with Emotional Likes and Needs as Described by the Moon's Sign and House Placement*: Will he/she be happy with the careers ruled by the selected planet? Does this planet conjunct, sextile or trine the Moon in a harmonious pattern? Or does it square, quincunx or oppose the Moon? For example, suppose Saturn is the best career planet, located in the tenth house and its own sign, Capricorn. This indicates an administrative position, but the native's third house Gemini Moon is quincunx Saturn in Capricorn. This person would be too jumpy, fun-loving and inconstant for a predictable desk job.

What should be advised? In this case, it's important to remember some of Saturn's other careers that might harmonize better with the Gemini Moon, or forego a Saturnian career altogether.

One solution: Saturn in Capricorn provides an excellent graphic sense, and a Gemini Moon loves to draw. This combination could indicate a good cartoonist or architect.

3. *Compare the Best Planet with the Ascending Sign*: What kind of outlook on life does this Ascendant suggest? How does the specific outlook of this ascending sign support the occupations suggested by the best career planets? Use the Ascendant to gain insight into the specific role or specialty within a chosen profession. (For example, a Libra Ascendant should always be in the counseling and diplomatic side of any profession, whereas a Virgo Ascendant should go for the technical and service roles.)

Example Vocational Analysis

Here is a very good, very classic chart of a bartender (chart shown on the next page). A walk through the outlined steps explains why this is so.

Remember the three vocational houses—second, sixth and tenth and the all-important Midheaven? Begin the vocational analysis with the Midheaven and proceed from there in order through the tenth, sixth and second vocational houses and the house and sign placements of their planetary rulers.

First, study the Midheaven, its sign and the closest planet to this point. The Midheaven is in gregarious Aquarius. Since that sign also governs ministers and coaches, why a bartender? The Moon (public, people, environments, change) in Aquarius is the nearest planet. Look up the vocational meanings for the Moon in Chapter 4 and also likes and needs in Chapter 2.

An Aquarius Moon likes people. Next, notice that Jupiter is near the Moon in neighboring Capricorn. This Jupiterian trait influences the mood of the Aquarius Moon further, toward the convivial side of the sign. (Note: Should Saturn have been near the Moon instead of Jupiter, the convivial spirit of Aquarius would have been dampened and the more scientific and intellectual sides of the sign would have been enhanced.)

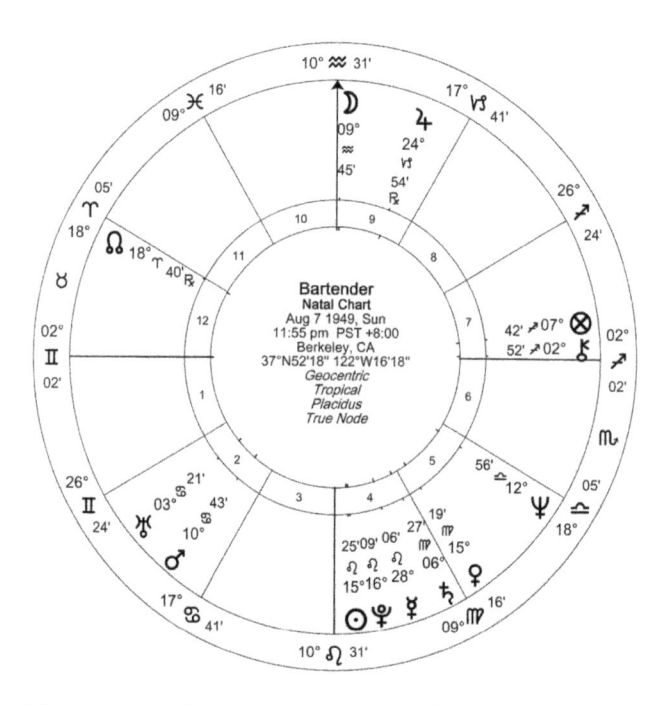

What planet rules the sign on the Midheaven? First, find the sign on the Midheaven, which is Aquarius. The rulerships list, Table 1 (page 50) says that Aquarius, the sign on this Midheaven, is ruled by Saturn and co-ruled by Uranus. Now locate Saturn (and later Uranus) by sign and house placement within the horoscope.

Saturn is in the practical sign Virgo in the fourth house of properties. Virgo is admittedly pretty dry and does not suggest bartenders. Here it is important to consider weight. Which is stronger-Saturn in Virgo or the majority of the other vocational testimonies as shown by the other vocational house rulers, the planet(s) nearest the Midheaven and also the Sun, Moon and Ascendant (temperamental indicators). An overwhelming number of vocational testimonies are in social "bartender" placements.

So what does this Midheaven ruling Saturn in Virgo in the

96   Reading the Vocational Horoscope

fourth house mean? Easy. As a side career, the bartender invests in real estate (Saturn, fourth house, Virgo) and looks forward to owning a restaurant (places, fourth house). Note: Saturn in Virgo gives the care with detail necessary in food a drink preparation. As a trait, Saturn in Virgo or the sixth house is typical for chefs.

What sign rules the tenth sign from the Ascendant? Counting counterclockwise from the Gemini Ascendant, the tenth sign is Pisces. Pisces rules many things, including alcohol. Pisces has two rulers, Jupiter and Neptune. Jupiter is retrograde, void of course and in detriment. As a career planet, Jupiter is somewhat handicapped, although it lends its convivial quality to the personality by being so near the Moon in Aquarius.

Neptune is in the fifth house (pleasure) in Libra (others, relationships) and close to the South Node, a point associated with escape from reality. Neptune trines the Moon at the Midheaven, harmoniously supporting it. Additionally, Neptune rules alcohol. Neptune forms a partile (exact) aspect by trine to the Midheaven. This combination seems fairly perfect for a bartender, and the Moon-Neptune combination is strong enough to describe a primary career. The next step, finding the sixth house ruler, will be secondary unless it can outperform the Midheaven conjunct Moon trine Neptune combination.

Where is the ruler of the sixth house and/or the sixth sign from the Ascendant? (I always prefer the sixth sign from the Ascendant, as it is more accurate.) In this chart, the sign is Scorpio and its two planetary rulers are Mars and Pluto. Mars is in the second house (food, mouth, money) in the water sign Cancer. Furthermore, Mars in Cancer is closely associated with painters, chemists, cooks and those who mix things together. The bartender also is a gourmet cook.

Mars is well aspected by sextile to Saturn, the Midheaven ruler, and also quincunx the Moon. As Mars and Saturn both rule properties, this makes for a strong real estate combination.

However, Mars cannot be selected for an exclusive career ruler because of a prominent "avoid": the quincunx to the Moon (see Chapter 6). His emotional preference for friendly socializing as shown by his Aquarian Moon would not be satisfied by more purely financial careers (as shown in his chart by the sixth house ruler Mars placed in the second house and sextile Saturn).

The new style ruler of the sixth house sign is Pluto, which is in fun-loving Leo near the Nadir (places), an ideal combination for work in a recreational environment.

Continue to the second vocational house (or the second sign from the Ascendant, as is my preference), where the sign Cancer is placed. Note: Gemini risings always have Cancer as their second sign.

As previously observed, the sixth house ruler Mars is here. So where is the ruler of the second house? The Moon conjunct the Midheaven, which kicks the Moon up a notch as a vocational indicator by ruling a vocational house and also culminating.

What is this individual's center of interest? Look first to his Sun's position by sign and house.

The Sun in Leo is at the Nadir and is interpreted as being at the center (Sun) of attention (Leo) in a place (Nadir). Leo is also the third sign from the Ascendant, so he likes to be the center of attention in communication (third house). What describes bartending more than this? This Leo Sun seems to augment rather than oppose the Moon-Neptune vocational favorites. Notice how the Sun exactly sextiles Neptune. Furthermore, a Full Moon in the Leo-Aquarius polarity is occurring across the vocationally inclined Midheaven-Nadir axis. This combination alone would immediately say "bartender" or something similar to a seasoned vocational astrologer. This man would find a sense of fulfillment as the center of a party, as a host or as a bartender.

Are his emotional needs and likes going to be satisfied in a bartending career? Look to the Moon for a resounding "yes"! The

Moon rules tavern keepers and brewers (Chapter 4). Located in Aquarius and near Jupiter, and also closely trining the fifth house Neptune, the planetary ruler of alcohol, and in its full phase, this Aquarius Moon strongly testifies to the high degree of comfort this person finds in highly social environments. The Leo-Aquarius Full Moon always accents the social and pleasure sides of life. (When working with a Full Moon chart, be sure to give plenty of weight in vocational interpretation to the houses and signs of the Full Moon polarity. These houses will be dominant.)

How about his ascending sign? What is his approach to life? What branch of a social Moon-Jupiter-Aquarius career would best suit this person? A Gemini Ascendant always means that a communication role within any occupation would be most suitable. Gemini Ascendants love to gad about. This person is best suited in verbal, constantly changing, stimulating environments that offer ample opportunity to chat and pick up information about a wide range of life experiences. Bartending! (Caveat: This does not mean that working with alcohol in a night club environment is spiritually good for this individual. In fact, it is likely to be highly destructive to him, a separate inquiry that should considerably interest the vocational consultant.)

This chart was easy. The majority of vocational and temperamental significators described in the previous chapter are compatible with the bartending life. Of course, bartending is a very specific occupation. Although this man is well suited for it, there are many other possible and healthier applications for the astrological symbology of his friendly birth chart—club or restaurant owner, theater owner, chef, coach, host, youth worker, minister, adoptive parent.

Chapter 10

Vocational Time Clocks

"We cannot come to terms with the present until we learn to think of it 1) as a part of the distant future (as it will someday be), and 2) as part of the distant past (as it once was). "—Robert Grudin

Astrologers largely concern themselves with three types of time cycles. The planetary time clock is formed as outer cycles (transits) work in unison with internal cycles (progressions) in ticking off major life passages.

Internal Cycles: These are peculiar to the individual, constituting an internal time clock, or program, much as the seed is already programmed with the seasons of its future unfoldment into a tree. These cycles occur regardless of the current outside planetary stimulus, although many rely on such for triggering of external events or internal states. Western internal cycles are known as progressions, directions and solar arc. There are many kinds of Western-style progressions and directions. Vedic astrology utilizes a system of internal timing known as one's *dasas* and *buktis,* or planetary periods in life. Internal time clocks are important vocational barometers. Those interested in the why and how of progressions should consult my article, "Octaves of Time, How Progressions Work" (see Bibliography).

Outer Cycles: The current planetary positions are called transits and describe a sort of planetary weather shown to correlate with and stimulate activity and events both personally and nationally.

The Cycle of Ages: These are not useful to vocational practice except in the historical availability of career occupational trends. (The female presence in the workplace or the proliferation of the computer might relate, in part, to the very gradual change of the Ages from Pisces to Aquarius.) Eastern and Western astrologers have documented several larger planetary and star cycles believed to signal the great historical eras and to guide the gradual evolution of humanity and the solar system.

Saturn's Vital Role in Vocational Timing

Saturn is the chief significator of career matters in general and of time in particular. Ancient astronomers named this slowest moving of the seven visible planets as a *chronocrat*, or timekeeper, an appellation most appropriate to the subject. (Jupiter was also a *chronocrat*, but is somewhat less associated with one's vocation.) One of Saturn's Vedic aliases is *shanishcharacharya*, or "teacher who moves slowly."

As the planetary significator of time and discipline, Saturn's transits (current motion in a birth chart) flag the specific areas of life requiring focus, planning and serous attention. For example, should Saturn transit through the second house of finances, its message is to buckle down on finances. Or else. That's right; as Father Time, Saturn tells when one can expect to reap what has been sown in a particular life area. This is one reason why Saturn is allegorically depicted as an old man carrying a sickle, and Saturn as karmic reaper also marks out the chapter of one's life story. At birth, life stretches before people like a highway. On this highway, each has varying degrees of room for diversion and adventure. However, it is impossible to avoid meeting the milestone of physical age, as well as other important road signs designating entry and exit of various states and other events. The highway will have some built-in limitations such as width, length, scenery and speed at which one can legally travel. Each person travels a unique highway with its own milestones and set limitations.

It is to this life structuring process and its work to which Saturn's hand on the celestial clock points. A graduation, a first baby and the death of a parent are all typical Saturnian experiences. Saturn brings that which one must inevitably meet and tells when to expect it. Its motion establishes the lessons and limitations people must endure. Its movement signals life's harvest times; reward greets those who, upon Saturn's arrival, have accomplished their given work.

Length of Saturn's Effects

Due to its period of retrograde motion each year, Saturn will typically make two or even three passes over each angle, planet or Node described below. The strongest effects of each transit therefore are felt for roughly one year. However, the lingering effects of Saturn's transit might continue as long as Saturn remains in the same sign as the point listed, and sometimes much longer.

Saturn's Transit of the Four Angles

Note: Saturn's arrival, once in each cycle of 29.48 years, at any one of the planetary birth chart's four angles has powerful vocational significance.

Saturn Conjunct the Ascendant: A new beginning. This is a point signaling the maximum output of hard work toward structuring an external life. Sometimes this period brings an entirely new direction in life, more recognition or a coming into one's own after a long period of waiting. Here is where the vocational cycle is sown, and it is a point of independence.

Saturn Conjunct the Nadir: Saturn's swing to the lowest angle of the wheel corresponds to an obscure period for outer works. This is the time to pay attention to the home. It is the high point for one's personal, property and family concerns. Because this is the house of foundations, many people establish an office or begin a new career when Saturn transits this point. However, if Saturn on the Nadir is a career low, this is because it is not the time for outer works, but for inner ones. A low point in the outer life can equal a peak in the inner life. As an example, one woman was ordained as a rabbi at the time of Saturn's exact conjunction to this point in her chart.

For older folks, retirement is often signaled by Saturn's passage over the Nadir. Responsibilities concerning parents and families will preoccupy some, and it is an appropriate time for a sabbatical.

Note: For Libra Ascendants and charts with emphasis on the lower hemisphere, Saturn's swing to the Nadir could be a career high point, reversing its normal meaning. This only holds true in some cases.

Saturn Conjunct the Descendant: This is one of those transits that coincides with seeking vocational guidance. Many experience this transit as the great standstill of life, where a pause (a concept absent from Western culture) is needed after much has been accomplished. Mostly, people feel frustrated and blocked when Saturn transits the Descendant. That is because they are supposed to be! This is not the time for action, but for contemplation, which requires a form of nonaction.

It is the time to look, weigh and finally decide what to do next. Stay in the present career or start anew? Marry or divorce? Move or stay? This is the seventh house angle, the midpoint of the chart, the symbolic scales where all must be weighed. Saturn at this cusp acts to encourage objectivity and wisdom, of observing and getting to know oneself. A critical point or turn in the career life often accompanies this transit. For some it is a time of reaping what has been sown.

Saturn Conjunct the Midheaven: As Saturn culminates, it signifies a career peak. If positive, people acquire position and achieve their greatest external power and maximum responsibility. Life works are accomplished and one's name is recognized. For older people, this transit might signify retirement. If negative, Saturn's transit coincides with downfalls, scandals and humiliations in the career.

Saturn's Most Important Vocational Transits

Saturn Conjunct Saturn: The Saturn return. The past is wiped away and a new life begins. A new career. The first Saturn return marks a completion of the physical growth cycle. By now, most people are physically, mentally and emotionally formed. Patience and discipline are ingrained through experience. At the first return, we are finished products, physically. A separation from the parents might occur. Individualization.

Saturn Square Saturn (waxing): Life is busy under this transit as people work hard to build their careers. They often must rebuild or rework a past career. It is a time to build something new based on what has already been achieved. A profound disenchantment with one's work might be experienced.

Saturn Square Saturn (waning): This coincides with a psychological or philosophical crisis in the career. The person must often rebuild or rework the career. A time to build something new based on what you have achieved. A profound disenchantment may be experienced with one's work.

Saturn Conjunct Sun: The sense of life purpose is defined, and for some it is a career peak, a time of hard work and dedication. Many experience a greater sense of their own destiny and fulfillment; others collapse in depression.

Saturn Opposition Sun: The career is blocked or at a low ebb. It is a period of questioning life's purpose and meaning, and is similar to Saturn's transit of the Descendant.

Saturn Conjunct the North Node: A time when material obligations and opportunities enter people's lives. An excellent time to assume responsibility and build or buy property. One's *dharma,* or life work, is clarified. An important position might be offered.

Saturn Conjunct the South Node: Not always a vocational death knell, this transit does signal a time for letting go of much of what Saturn rules—foundations, property and, sometimes, careers. The transient nature of striving is pointed out, and for many this time is best enjoyed as a sabbatical to be used for deep spiritual seeking and time out. This is not a time for fame and fortune unless several other transits disagree. It is an excellent time to pay off debt, something which might be forced or unavoidable (the planet of *karma* comes to the *karmic* payment point).

Saturn's South Node transit is not the time for beginning a new career or position. Anyone in a stable job should stay there because new employment might be difficult to find. Plenty of rest is necessary because this transit might coincide with mental states wholly inappropriate to the workaday world. It is too bad people cannot respect these more introverted times in their lives, feeling compelled instead to always keep working.

Saturn Square the Nodes: The great crossroads and an important life juncture where people must choose between two paths, this is an important transit that should not be overlooked. Sometimes this crossroads is literal, such as a choice between two nations, and often it requires that a choice be made between two sets of values. Sometimes this transit represents making a decision between two careers. If this is the case, each should be analyzed according to the strongest values they encourage in the individual. Once this is understood, people realize that their career choices are actually spiritual choices, with one career benefitting the individual's evolution.

Additional Vocational Transits and Progressions

Transiting Jupiter Conjunct the Midheaven: Career opportunities. This transit is best for water and fire Ascendants or those with a prominent natal Jupiter. A good time to seek promotion.

Transiting Jupiter Conjunct Sun: Duplicate of above. Might also meet important men. For women, marriage.

Transiting Jupiter Conjunct Midheaven Ruler: Duplicate of Midheaven transit except it also will bring opportunities related to the precise vocational rulerships, products or people as signified by the transiting planet. Best for fire and water ascending signs.

Transiting Jupiter Conjunct North Node: This brings excellent work opportunities should it occur in a career house (second, sixth, tenth) and should Jupiter be strong in the natal chart. Best for fire and water ascending signs. A time for requesting favors and raises.

Progressed or Solar Arc Saturn, Jupiter or Midheaven Ruler Moves to a New Degree: This signals a new stage in the career life and an internal readiness for something new. This is very pronounced if the planet also enters a new sign, and even more pronounced if into a solstice or equinox degree (zero degrees of cardinal signs).

Progressed or Solar Arc Midheaven Ruler or Midheaven Degree Moves into a New Sign: A new internal development of the planet is indicated along the lines of the new sign. Still, this internal development must be triggered by a transit. Once triggered, a new day in the career begins. The new urges will be described by the newly inhabited sign and remain internal unless triggered by a transit. All progressions to the Midheaven are useful only if the exact minute of birth is known.

Progressed Planet Turns Stationary: A very powerful influence for vocational affairs, products and industries associated with this planet. Stationing progressions are vocationally useful should the planet in question rule the actual career activities of the native. Allow one year on either side of the precise station. A stationing planet will turn either retrograde or direct once it completes its station. Stationary direct is much more helpful as

Vocational Astrology

it "turns on" the planet. Stationary retrograde will begin to slow down or "shelve" the affairs of the planet. However, while the planet is stationing, it is very strong regardless of direction.

Progressed Midheaven to Natal Planet: To use the progressed Midheaven, the birth time must be accurate to the minute. This information is only known for sure if someone with a stopwatch was attending the birth. Memories and birth certificates are not reliable sources of the exact minute of birth. However, if the exact minute of birth is known, the progressed Midheaven conjoining any planet will bring that planet's activities into the professional arena for one year on either side of the conjunction as long as it is triggered by transits.

Progressed Planet to Natal Midheaven: Read above.

Progressed Moon Conjunct Midheaven or Midheaven Ruler: This progression coincides with a great deal of interest in the activities signified by the Midheaven sign or the planet that rules the Midheaven and its sign and house position (depending on which the progressed Moon is conjoining). This will last for three months on either side of the exact conjunction.

Eclipses and Nodal Transits

There are four kinds of eclipses—solar eclipse at the North Node, solar eclipse at the South Node, lunar eclipse at the North Node and lunar eclipse at the South Node.

The North Node solar eclipse generally is positive, and the remaining three are generally negative. This is because only the North Node solar eclipse does not immediately involve the South Node (although it can do so at the opposite point in the chart).

The negative South Node and positive North Node interpretations are subjective. Cosmic energies enter at the North Node and exit at the South Node. This does not mean that what enters at the North Node is necessarily good or that an ending indicated by the South Node is a bad thing. The outward manifestation of eclipses depends a great deal on whether something is ready to enter or exit, as the case may be. Anything positive or negative that is ripening will tend to pop and come to a head at the time of an eclipse, especially the lunar variety.

Because the world is negative, many eclipses are the same. Also, human beings tend to cling to people and objects. When these must exit their lives, the events are interpreted as negative. But this is a subjective interpretation. Sometimes a seemingly negative South Node eclipse brings surprisingly positive results. After all, it might be a good thing for a difficult situation to exit. It is liberating! In the reverse, a positive North Node eclipse could bring in a lot of unwanted energy. One year's North Node solar eclipse in Virgo brought too much work to many and a medical worker's strike occurred the same day. Sometimes the effect of either type of eclipse is altogether unexpected and can be good just as often as bad. In practice, however, it is wise to expect exits at South Node eclipses and entries at North Node eclipses. Then, giving no value judgment as to positive or negative, wait to see what will happen.

North Node Solar Eclipse Conjunct Midheaven: A strong professional activity commences. The native's work receives energy and publicity, and he/she might come before the public eye. A major event in the career or with one's boss is to be expected within the quarter (usually within thirty days). Property ownership and landlord issues are stimulated.

South Node Solar Eclipse Conjunct Midheaven: Most frequently these signal a collapsing influence to the career, events and trials. A relocation might be indicated. Less frequently there is great excitement concerning events and activities along a positive direction. Strikes, layoffs, mergers, unexpected changes, management changes and general hubbub are typical. The reputation should be guarded and scandal avoided. This is not a time to be playing around with the boss' wife.

Lunar Eclipses Conjunct Midheaven/Nadir: Similar to above.

North Node Conjunct Midheaven or in the Tenth House: Similar to above. Energy is made available in the region of professional activities. This is a good time to pursue ambitious goals and material accomplishments. The reputation is generally good and one's professional affairs are moving ahead.

South Node Conjunct Midheaven or in the Tenth House: Energy is drained from the career, ambitions and selfish pursuits. Disappointments, disillusionment and a sense of giving out more than is received are typical manifestations. On the positive side, one can become more interested in the spiritual aspects of the career. Emotional and spiritual values supersede material values.

This transit can be excellent for those in the ministry, social work, workers with the handicapped or mentally ill. It is an excellent time to work from the heart, holding no thought for personal gain or credit. The reputation should be guarded, however, as there is some tendency to undo oneself in the professional arena. (Princess Diana was aptly born with the Moon, Jupiter and South Node in Aquarius.)

Many people experience burnout and a Joss of ambition. However, it's important to try to do a good job even if little recognition is forthcoming at this time. The South Node is a karmic payment point and provides an opportunity to pay off old debts through selflessness and charitable works.

North Node Conjunct Natal Planet: The products and careers associated with this planet receive a powerful celestial boost. The tide oflife and times seems now to be with this planet. It is a promising time to connect with people described by the planet, and excellent for gains related to the planet in combination with its sign and house indications.

Planet Conjunct North Node: The planet's energy abounds at this time, and there are favorable connections with/from the people and products ruled by the planet.

South Node Conjunct Natal Planet: Circumstances and timing might appear to go against the enterprises or products related to this planet. People described by the planet may depart or require help, and past associations symbolized by the planet may crop up again. It is a time to give selflessly of the planet's energy, expecting little credit or gain. If aspects are exceptionally good, projects related to the planet's rulerships may be released at this time. This is not the time to begin a materially gainful enterprise related to the planet (and its sign and house). Spiritual, psychological and charitable use of the planet's energy are more appropriate. The time is excellent to get rid of products and objects related to the planet (for example, junk the car when South Node crosses Mars).

Planet Conjunct South Node: This planet's rulerships go down the tubes, which in this case is the Dragon's Tail. When Mars crosses the South Node, it's a good time to sell a car. However, resumes should never be sent when Mercury transits here, and the same applies to Venus and haircuts!

Appendix A
A-Z Vocational Listings: Planet, Sign, House Emphasis

Accountant
Dominant Planets: Mercury, Saturn
Primary Sign: Virgo
Secondary Signs: Taurus, Scorpio
Primary Houses: 2, 3, 8
Secondary House: 6

Actor
Dominant Planets: Jupiter, Sun, Moon
Supportive Planets: Neptune, Uranus, Mars, Venus
Primary Sign: Leo
Secondary Signs: Scorpio, Pisces
Primary Houses: 5, 3
Secondary Houses: 1, 7

Acupuncturist
Dominant Planets: Mercury, Mars
Supportive Planets: Saturn, Uranus (electrical forces), Pluto *(chi)*
Primary Signs: Virgo, Scorpio
Secondary Signs: Pisces, Capricorn
Primary Houses: 6, 8
Secondary Houses: 12, 1, 7

Airline Attendant
Dominant Planets: Moon, Mercury
Supportive Planet: Jupiter
Primary Signs: Gemini, Virgo, Pisces (mutable quadruplicity), mutability
Primary Houses: 3, 9, 6
Secondary Houses: 7, 11

Ambulance Worker
Dominant Planet: Mars

Vocational Astrology

Supportive Planets: Uranus, Jupiter, Mercury, Pluto, Saturn, Moon (only in Aries, Scorpio, Taurus, Virgo or Capricorn)
   Primary Signs: Virgo, Scorpio
   Secondary Signs: Aries, earth emphasis
   Primary Houses: 8, 12
   Secondary Houses: 3, 6, 11
Anthropologist
   Dominant Planets: Jupiter, Moon, Mars
   Primary Sign: Aquarius
   Secondary Sign: Sagittarius
   Primary House: 11
   Secondary Houses: 3, 9
Appraiser (Real Estate)
   Dominant Planets: Mercury, Saturn, Mars
   Supportive Planet: Pluto
   Primary Sign: Scorpio
   Secondary Signs: Virgo, Libra
   Primary Houses: 4, 8
   Secondary Houses: 6, 7
Arborist
   Dominant Planets: Venus, Mars, Saturn
   Supportive Planet: Moon
   Primary Signs: Taurus, Cancer
   Secondary Signs: Virgo, Capricorn
   Primary Houses: 4, 6
   Secondary Houses: 8, 10
Architect
   Dominant Planet: Saturn
   Supportive Planets: Mars, Mercury, Venus
   Primary Signs: Capricorn, Taurus
   Secondary Signs: Gemini, Aquarius, Cancer
   Primary Houses: 2, 3, 4, 10
Artist
   See Computer Graphics, Graphic Artist, Fashion Illustrator. "Artist" in general is not included in this book because there

are so many varieties of artists. However, a few comments can be made about the planetary combinations most often seen in the charts of fine artists and modern artists. In the fine arts there is an emphasis on the third, fifth and seventh houses. A strong seventh house brings art appreciation and a sense of observation of forms and balance. The Sun or Venus in the seventh house is rather typical of career artists. The second house (form) and the eleventh house (mental images) are also often strong, as is the fifth house of art in general.

Venus (beauty) is always prominent, followed by Saturn (form). Venus is most often near the Ascendant or Midheaven or in the second, third, fifth or seventh houses. Saturn is often near the Ascendant or very strong by sign and aspect. Mercury is required for delicate and ornamental work. The imaginative planets Uranus and Neptune love to shock and are strong in modem artists. Much art today is Plutonian rather than Venusian because Pluto's disturbing and psychically violent images are seen everywhere. Frequently, Leo or Aquarius ascends with planets in both Leo and Aquarius. Artists are more typically astrologically dominant in one element—fire, earth, air or water—which typifies their artistic style. Modem artists are strong in fire signs, especially Aries. A Sun or Mars in Aries is typical. Fire signs love what is big, bold and colorful. Water signs prefer the romantic, impressionistic and water color styles. Air signs love landscapes, portraiture and thoughtful, detached art. Air is more concerned with design and balance than with artistic mood or passion. The air type is a fine artist, although fire is necessary to produce the "old master." Earth signs love sculpture, pottery and graphic arts. Taurus is the best designer, and Capricorn is the unexcelled commercial artist.

Baker
Dominant Planets: Venus, Saturn
Supportive Planets: Moon, Mars
Primary Signs: Taurus, Capricorn

Secondary Signs: Virgo, Cancer
Primary Houses: 2, 4, 6
Banker
Dominant Planets: Saturn, Jupiter, Pluto, North Node
Supportive Planets: Venus, Mars
Primary Signs: Taurus, Leo, Scorpio
Secondary Signs: Capricorn, Cancer
Primary Houses: 2, 8
Secondary Houses: 5, 10, 11
Bartender
Dominant Planets: Moon, Jupiter, Neptune
Supportive Planets: Venus, Sun
Primary Signs: Leo, Aquarius, Gemini, Taurus
Secondary Signs: Scorpio, Cancer, Pisces
Primary House: 4
Secondary Houses: 3, 7, 5, 11, 12
Beekeeper
Dominant Planets: Mercury, Mars
Supportive Planets: Venus
Primary Sign: Virgo
Supportive Signs: Capricorn, Cancer (if not a squeamish Cancerian) Primary Houses: 4, 6, 8
Secondary House: 2
Beautician
Dominant Planet: Venus
Secondary Planets: Moon, Mars, Mercury
Primary Signs: Taurus, Virgo
Secondary Signs: Cancer, Scorpio (for dyeing), Libra
Primary House: 6
Secondary Houses: 1, 7, 3, 4, 8
Belly Dancer
Dominant Planets: Venus, Neptune
Supportive Planets: Mars, Moon, Uranus (in our culture)
Primary Signs: Virgo, Scorpio
Secondary Signs: Cancer, Pisces, Gemini

Primary House: 5
Secondary Houses: 3, 6, 8
Boat Builder
Same as below. However, include Aquarius with Taurus as a dominant sign.
Builder (Homes)
Dominant Planets: Mars, Saturn
Supportive Planets: Pluto, North Node
Primary Sign: Taurus (earth emphasis)
Secondary Sign: Capricorn
Primary House: 4
Secondary Houses: 2, 10, 8 (if demolition is involved)
Calligrapher
Dominant Planets: Mercury, Venus, Saturn
Supportive Planet: Mars
Primary Signs: Virgo
Secondary Signs: Cancer, Libra, Taurus, Capricorn
Primary House: 3
Secondary Houses: 4, 5 (9, if a Torah or Bible calligrapher)
Carpet (Fine) Dealer
Dominant Planets: Venus, Saturn
Supportive Planets: Mars, Moon, Mercury, Neptune
Primary Signs: Virgo, Capricorn, Taurus
Secondary Signs: Cancer, Scorpio
Primary House: 2, 3, 4
Secondary House: 7
Chef
Dominant Planets: Moon, Venus
Supportive Planets: Mars, Jupiter
Primary Signs: Taurus, Cancer, Scorpio
Secondary Signs: Leo, Aquarius
Primary Houses: 2, 6
Secondary Houses: 4, 10
Chemist
Dominant Planets: Saturn, Pluto

Supportive Planets: Mars, Neptune
Primary Sign: Scorpio
Secondary Signs: Pisces, Virgo, Taurus, Capricorn, Aquarius
Primary Houses: 2, 8 (12 if a research chemist or lab worker)

Child Care Worker
Dominant Planet: Moon
Supportive Planets: Mercury, Neptune
Primary Signs: Cancer, Gemini, Pisces
Secondary Sign: Libra
Primary Houses: 3, 4, 5
Secondary Houses: 9, 10

Colonic Irrigationist
Dominant Planets: Mars, Pluto, South Node
Supportive Planets: Saturn, Mercury
Primary Sign: Scorpio
Secondary Signs: Virgo, Pisces
Primary Houses: 6, 7, 8
Supportive House: 12

Computer Programmer
Dominant Planets: Mercury, Uranus
Supportive Planets: Saturn
Primary Signs: Virgo, Aquarius Secondary Sign: Gemini
Primary Houses: 3, 6
Secondary House: 11

Conflict Resolution
Dominant Planet: Venus
Supportive Planets: Jupiter, Saturn
Primary Signs: Libra (Aries-Libra polarity)
Secondary Sign: Scorpio
Primary Houses: 1-7 polarity
Secondary Houses: 3, 9

Contractor/Land Developer
Dominant Planets: Saturn, Mars
Supportive Planets: Sun, Jupiter, Pluto Primary
Sign: Capricorn

Supportive Signs: Cancer, Scorpio, Taurus
Primary Houses: 4, 10
Secondary Houses: 2, 8

Dancer
Dominant Planets: Mars, Venus, Moon
Supportive Planets: Neptune, Uranus
Primary Signs: Aries, Cancer, Pisces
Supportive Signs: Leo, Sagittarius, Virgo (Gemini for tap)
Primary Houses: 5, 6 (7 for partner dancing)
Secondary Houses: 1, 3

Death Educator
Dominant Planets: Jupiter, Saturn, Neptune, Pluto, South Node
Primary Signs: Scorpio, Sagittarius
Secondary Sign: Pisces
Primary Houses: 8, 12
Secondary Houses: 7, 9

Dentist
Dominant Planets: Mars, Saturn
Supportive Planets: Mercury, Pluto
Primary Signs: Taurus, Virgo, Capricorn, Aries, Scorpio
Primary Houses: 2, 8
Secondary Houses: 3, 6

Economist
Dominant Planets: Saturn, Mars, Jupiter
Supportive Planets: Mercury, Moon
Primary Signs: Virgo, Cancer, Capricorn, Taurus
Secondary Sign: Libra
Primary Houses: 2, 8, 10
Secondary House: 7

Editor
Dominant Planets: Mercury, Saturn
Supportive Planets: Mars, Pluto
Primary Sign: Virgo
Secondary Signs: Libra, Scorpio, Gemini, Capricorn

Primary Houses: 3, 6
Secondary Houses: 7, 9
Electrician
Dominant Planets: Uranus, Mercury
Supportive Planets: Saturn (grounding)
Primary Signs: Aquarius, Gemini
Secondary Sign: Virgo
Primary Houses: 3, 4, 6
Electrical Engineer
Dominant Planets: Uranus, Mars, Saturn
Supportive Planet: Mercury
Primary Sign: air signs—Gemini, Libra, Aquarius
Secondary Signs: Aries, Sagittarius
Primary Houses: 2, 3, 6, 8
Secondary House: 12
Events Organizer
Dominant Planets: Moon, Jupiter
Supportive Planets: Uranus, Saturn, Venus, North Node
Primary Signs: air and fire signs—Gemini, Libra, Aquarius, Aries, Leo, Sagittarius
Primary Houses: 1, 5, 9, 11
Supportive Houses: 2, 3, 8
Environmentalist
Dominant Planets: Jupiter, Pluto, Mars
Supportive Planets: Uranus, Saturn
Primary Signs: Cancer, Virgo
Supportive Signs: Sagittarius, Capricorn, Aquarius
Primary Houses: 4, 6
Supportive Houses: 3, 9, 10
Fashion Illustrator
Dominant Planets: Venus, Mercury
Supportive Planets: Uranus, Neptune, Saturn (for form)
Primary Signs: Aries, Leo, Taurus
Secondary Signs: Libra, Pisces
Primary Houses: 3, 5

Secondary Houses: 1, 7, 11
Female Impersonator
Dominant Planets: Venus, Mars, Uranus
Supportive Planets: Neptune, Moon
Primary Signs: Libra, Leo, Aquarius, Scorpio, Pisces
Secondary Sign: Gemini (mimicry)
Primary Houses: 1, 5, 8
Secondary Houses: 2 (the body), 7, 12
Feng Shui Practitioner
Dominant Planets: Moon, Neptune, South Node
Supportive Planets: Jupiter, Uranus, Pluto, Venus
Primary Signs: Cancer, Pisces, Libra
Secondary Sign: Scorpio
Primary House: 4
Secondary Houses: 7, 12
Film Editor
Dominant Planets: Mercury, Neptune, Mars
Primary Signs: Virgo, Pisces
Supportive Signs: Taurus, Scorpio
Primary Houses: 3, 6, 9, 12 (the cadent houses)
Secondary Houses: 5, 8
Film maker
Dominant Planet: Jupiter
Supportive Planets: Sun, Moon, Mars
Primary Signs: Aries, Leo, Aquarius
Secondary Signs: Scorpio, Pisces (essential for fantasy, whimsical topics or children's programming)
Primary Houses: 1, 7, 5, 10, strong Aquarius—Leo and Aries—Libra polarity in "odd" houses seems typical
Secondary Houses: 3, 9, 12
Firefighter
Dominant Planet: Mars
Supportive Planets: Jupiter, Uranus, Pluto
Primary Signs: Aries, Leo
Secondary Signs: Virgo, Scorpio

Vocational Astrology

Primary Houses: 4, 8
Secondary Houses: 6
Flautist
Dominant Planets: Venus, Neptune
Supportive Planets: Mercury, Moon
Primary Signs: Gemini, Pisces
Secondary Signs: Taurus, Cancer, Libra
Primary Houses: 3, 5
Secondary House: 12
Fund raiser
Dominant Planets: Mars, Jupiter
Supportive Planets: Venus, Neptune
Primary Signs: Aries, Libra, Sagittarius
Supportive Signs: Leo, Aquarius, Scorpio
Primary Houses: 1-7 polarity, 2-8 polarity
Secondary Houses: 3, 9, 11
Gardener
Dominant Planets: Moon, Saturn
Supportive Planets: Mars, Jupiter, Venus
Primary Signs: Virgo, Capricorn
Secondary Signs: Taurus, Cancer
Primary House: 4
Secondary Houses: 2, 6
Guard
Dominant Planets: Saturn, Mars
Supportive Planets: North Node, Pluto, Mercury
Primary Signs: Aries, Taurus, Leo, Scorpio
Secondary Sign: Capricorn
Primary Houses: 1, 3, 8
Secondary House: 4
Harpist
Dominant Planets: Venus, Mercury, Neptune
Primary Signs: Gemini, Libra
Secondary Signs: Pisces
Primary Houses: 3, 5

Secondary House: 12

Healer
Dominant Planets: Mars, Pluto
Supportive Planets: Venus, Neptune, Uranus
Primary Signs: Aries, Sagittarius (fire). Energy output must be high.
Supportive Signs: Varies widely; usually a side emphasis in either earth (body) or water (subtle and emotional energy).
Primary House: 8
Supportive Houses: 1, 7, 3, 4

Health Administrator
Dominant Planets: Mercury, Saturn
Supportive Planets: Mars, Moon
Primary Sign: Virgo
Secondary Signs: Capricorn, Cancer, Libra
Primary Houses: 6, 10
Secondary Houses: 4, 8, 11

Herbalist
Dominant Planets: Moon, Mercury
Supportive Planets: Neptune, Venus, Saturn
Primary Sign: Cancer, Pisces
Secondary Signs: Taurus, Scorpio
Primary House: 6
Secondary Houses: 2, 4, 8

Homeopath
Dominant Planets: Mercury
Supportive Planets: Neptune, Pluto, Uranus, South Node, Saturn
Primary Sign: Virgo
Secondary Signs: Libra, Capricorn, Pisces
Primary Houses: 6, 12
Secondary Houses: 4, 8

Homemaker
Dominant Planets: Moon, Saturn
Supportive Planet: Mercury

Vocational Astrology

Primary Signs: earth and water signs—Taurus, Virgo, Capricorn, Cancer, Scorpio, Pisces
Primary House: 4
Secondary Houses: 2, 5, 6, 7, 8

Hospice Worker
Dominant Planets: Moon, South Node, Neptune
Supportive Planet: Jupiter
Primary Signs: Virgo, Scorpio
Secondary Signs: Cancer, Pisces (unless too sensitive)
Primary Houses: 8, 12
Secondary Houses: 6, 4, 7

Interior Decorator
Dominant Planets: Moon, Venus
Supportive Planets: Neptune, Uranus
Primary Sign: Cancer
Secondary Signs: Taurus, Libra, Capricorn
Primary House: 4
Secondary Houses: 2, 7, 12

Inventor
Dominant Planets: Uranus, Saturn
Supportive Planets: Mercury, Neptune, Pluto
Primary Sign: Aquarius
Supportive Signs: Aries, Gemini, Capricorn, Pisces
Primary Houses: 11, 8
Secondary Houses: 1, 2, 3, 12

Janitor (Sanitary Engineer)
Dominant Planets: Mars, Saturn, South Node
Supportive Planet: Mercury
Primary Sign: Virgo
Secondary Signs: Pisces, Cancer, Scorpio (water signs)
Primary Houses: 4, 6, 12
Secondary House: 8

Jeweler
Dominant Planets: Venus, Mercury
Supportive Planets: Mars, Sun (for gold), Moon (for silver)

Primary Signs: Virgo, Taurus
Secondary Sign: Cancer
Primary Houses: 2, 3
Secondary Houses: 1, 4, 6

Lawyer
Dominant Planets: Mercury, Mars
Supportive Planets: Saturn, Jupiter
Primary Signs: Libra, Scorpio
Secondary Signs: Gemini, Aries
Primary Houses: 7, 9
Secondary Houses: 1, 3, 8

Librarian
Dominant Planet: Mercury
Supportive Planets: Jupiter, Saturn (archivists), Moon (for librarians who interact with the public)
Primary Signs: Virgo, Libra, Pisces, Cancer
Secondary Signs: Gemini, Aquarius
Primary Houses: 3, 9
Secondary Houses: 6, 7, 12

Madame
Dominant Planets: Mars, Sun, Pluto
Supportive Planets: Venus, Neptune, North Node, South Node
Primary Signs: Leo, Scorpio
Secondary Signs: Virgo, Libra
Primary Houses: 8, 12
Secondary Houses: 1, 2, 4, 5, 7

Martial Artist/Teacher
Dominant Planet: Mars
Supportive Planet: Neptune
Primary Signs: Aries, Taurus, Sagittarius
Supportive Signs: Pisces (for mystical martial arts), Scorpio
Primary Houses: 1, 2, 3, 5, 6
Supportive Houses: 7 (8 and 12 for the mystical martial arts)

Vocational Astrology

Massage Therapist
   Dominant Planet: Mars
   Supportive Planets: Moon, Venus
   Primary Signs: Taurus, Scorpio
   Secondary Signs: Virgo, Capricorn, Aries
   Primary Houses: 1, 7, 8
   Secondary Houses: 3 (the hands), 6

Meat Packer
   Dominant Planets: Mars, Saturn
   Supportive Planet: North Node
   Primary Sign: Taurus
   Secondary Signs: Virgo, Capricorn, Scorpio (butchers)
   Primary Houses: 2, 6, 8

Mechanic
   Dominant Planets: Mars, Mercury
   Primary Signs: Gemini, Aries, Virgo
   Secondary Signs: Scorpio, Aquarius
   Primary Houses: 3, 6, 8
   Secondary House: 12

Merchant Seaman
   Dominant Planets: Mars, Moon, Neptune
   Supportive Planet: Mercury
   Primary Sign: Gemini, Virgo, Pisces, Sagittarius (mutable signs)
   Supportive Sign: Aquarius
   Primary Houses: 6, 3, 9
   Secondary House: 11

Metaphysical Bookseller
   Dominant Planets: Mercury, Neptune, Uranus
   Supportive Planets: Saturn, South Node
   Primary Signs: Gemini, Virgo, Pisces, Sagittarius (mutable signs)
   Primary Houses: cadent houses (3, 6, 9, 12)

Microbiologist
   Dominant Planets: Mercury, Saturn

Supportive Planets: Pluto, Mars
Primary Signs: Cancer, Virgo
Supportive Signs: Scorpio, Pisces
Primary Houses: 6, 8, 12
Secondary House: 11

Military Command
Dominant Planets: Mars, Jupiter
Supportive Planets: Sun, Saturn, North Node
Primary Signs: Aries, Cancer, Libra, Capricorn (cardinal signs), Scorpio (Libra and Scorpio are the favored combination for generals)
Primary Houses: 1, 7, 8, 10
Secondary House: 5, 9

Minister
Dominant Planets: Jupiter, Moon, Neptune
Supportive Planets: Saturn, South Node
Primary Signs: Aquarius, Scorpio
Secondary Signs: Pisces, Libra
Primary Houses: 7, 8, 9 (third quarter), 10, 11, 12 (fourth quarter)
Supportive House: 4
Note: A strong 4-10 axis is typical, similar to day care center operators and health administrators.

Music Educator
Dominant Planets: Jupiter, Neptune
Supportive Planets: Venus, Moon, Mars
Primary Signs: Cancer, Libra, Pisces
Supportive Signs: Aries, Sagittarius
Primary Houses: 5, 11, 9
Secondary Houses: 3, 1, 7

Novelist
Dominant Planets: Moon, Mercury
Supportive Planets: Neptune, Uranus
Primary Sign: This seems to depend on the genre. The water signs (Cancer, Scorpio, Pisces) love romance and mystery,

Vocational Astrology

and adventures are more akin to Sagittarius (as in story telling). Aquarius is ideal for science fiction, and Gemini rules writers in general.
Primary Houses: 3 (writing), 9, 11, 12
Nun/Monk
Dominant Planets: Saturn, South Node
Supportive Planets: Jupiter, Moon, Neptune
Note: The Moon is usually in aspect to Saturn. A life of austerity is indicated if the Moon separates from Saturn and makes no further major Ptolemaic aspects.
Primary Signs: Cancer, Scorpio, Pisces (water signs)
Secondary Signs: Virgo, Capricorn
Primary Houses: 9, 12
Secondary Houses: 4, 6, 8
Nurse
Dominant Planet: Moon
Supportive Planets: Mercury, Mars, Saturn, Neptune, Pluto
Primary Sign: Virgo
Supportive Signs: Cancer, Capricorn, Scorpio
Primary Houses: 6, 8
Secondary Houses: 4, 12, 7
Optical Engineer
Dominant Planets: Saturn, Mars, Uranus
Supportive Planet: Mercury
Primary Sign: Aries, Aquarius, Virgo
Secondary Signs: Scorpio, Capricorn
Primary Houses: 8, 11
Secondary Houses: 3
Paralegal (Legal Secretary)
Dominant Planets: Mercury, Saturn, Mars
Supportive Planets: Jupiter, Pluto
Primary Sign: Scorpio
Secondary Signs: Virgo, Libra, Capricorn
Primary Houses 3, 6, 7, 8
Secondary House: 9

Photographer
  Dominant Planet: Neptune
  Supportive Planets: Moon, Mars
  Primary Sign: Pisces
  Secondary Signs: Aries, Cancer, Aquarius
  Primary House: 7
  Secondary Houses: 1, 3, 4, 5, 12

Pilot
  Dominant Planets: Mercury, Mars, Jupiter
  Supportive Planet: Uranus
  Primary Signs: Gemini, Libra, Aquarius (air signs), Taurus, Virgo, Capricorn (earth signs)
  Primary Houses: 3, 4, 9, 10
  Secondary House: 11
  Note: The charts of many professional airline pilots are curiously strong in earth signs. A common feature is an earth sign Sun in the fourth house. Why? Pilots need to be absolutely reliable, dependable, grounded, unflappable and practical. A pilot functions as the "rock" of the flight crew and also as a parental security figure for the passengers. The air element describes only the element of travel and gives an interest in flying, providing of itself little of the temperament necessary for a professional pilot.

Plumber
  Dominant Planets: Saturn, Mars
  Supportive Planets: Mercury, Pluto
  Primary Sign: Scorpio
  Supportive Signs: Taurus, Pisces, Capricorn
  Primary Houses: 4, 8
  Secondary Houses: 3, 12

Police Officer
  Dominant Planets: Mars, Sun, Saturn
  Supportive Planets: Pluto, North Node
  Primary Sign: Leo, Scorpio, Capricorn
  Supportive Signs: Cancer (for defense, must hold strong

Vocational Astrology

planets), Aries
Primary Houses: 1, 8, 12
Secondary Houses: 3, 6, 7

Priest
Dominant Planets: Saturn, Jupiter
Supportive Planets: Moon, South Node
Primary Signs: Virgo, Pisces, Capricorn
Supportive Signs: Cancer, Scorpio
Primary Houses: 9, 10, 12
Secondary Houses: 4, 7, 11

Printer
Dominant Planets: Mercury, Mars, Saturn (Mars in Virgo or Capricorn in the sixth house seems typical of printers, binders, book construction)
Primary Signs: Capricorn, Virgo
Supportive Sign: Gemini
Primary Houses: 3, 6
Secondary House: 9

Producer (Film, Advertising, TV, Film Maker)
Dominant Planet: Jupiter
Supportive Planets: Sun, Moon, Mars
Primary Signs: Aries, Leo, Aquarius
Secondary Signs: Scorpio, Pisces (essential for fantasy, whimsical topics or children's programming)
Primary Houses: 1, 7, 5, 10, strong Aquarius-Leo and Aries-Libra polarity in "odd" houses seems typical
Secondary Houses: 3, 9, 12

Prostitute
Dominant Planets: Venus, Mars
Supportive Planets: South Node, Neptune, Pluto
Primary Signs: Scorpio, Virgo (absolutely!)
Secondary Sign: Taurus
Primary Houses: 2, 7, 8
Secondary Houses: 12, 5 (environments)

Psychiatric Nurse
Dominant Planets: Mercury, Neptune, Moon
Supportive Planets: South Node, Mars, Saturn
Primary Signs: Pisces, Virgo, Scorpio
Secondary Sign: Gemini
Primary Houses: 3, 6, 12

Psychic
Dominant Planets: Neptune, Moon
Supportive Planets: Pluto, South Node, Jupiter
Primary Signs: Pisces, Cancer, Scorpio
Secondary Signs: Taurus (for the Moon only as this steadies the mind and give the ability to listen inwardly), Sagittarius lends the ability to see into the future
Primary House: 12
Secondary Houses: 7, 8, 9

Psychologist
Dominant Planet: Mercury
Supportive Planets: Neptune, Pluto, South Node, Mars, Venus
Primary Signs: Virgo, Libra, Scorpio
Primary Houses: 7, 12, 8
Secondary Houses: 1, 3, 7

Publisher
Dominant Planet: Jupiter
Supportive Planets: Mercury, Saturn
Primary Sign: Sagittarius
Secondary Signs: Pisces, Virgo, Gemini
Primary House: 9
Secondary Houses: 3, 7, 10

Radio Host
Dominant Planet: Mercury
Supportive Planets: Venus, Moon, Jupiter, Uranus, Neptune
Primary Sign: Gemini
Secondary Signs: Aquarius, Libra, Taurus
Primary Houses: 3, 9, 11

Secondary Houses: 1, 7, 5
Real Estate Agent
Dominant Planets: Mars, Saturn, Moon, Mercury
Supportive Planets: Jupiter, Venus
Primary Signs: Cancer, Capricorn, Libra
Secondary Signs: Scorpio, Taurus
Primary Houses: 4, 7
Secondary Houses: 2, 3, 8, 10
Sailing Instructor
Dominant Planets: Moon, Neptune, Mars
Supportive Planet: Jupiter
Primary Signs: Cancer, Pisces, Aries
Primary Houses: 3, 9, 12
Secondary Houses: 1, 4 (The fourth house rules the boat. It also partially governs the capacity for receptive feeling and responsiveness, two qualities necessary to sailing.)
Social Worker
Dominant Planets: Jupiter, Neptune, Moon, Mars
Supportive Planets: Venus, Saturn
Primary Signs: Virgo, Libra, Aquarius
Secondary Signs: Cancer, Pisces
Primary Houses: 11, 12
Secondary Houses: 7, 5 (work with youth)
Songwriter
Dominant Planets: Moon, Neptune, Venus, Mercury
Supportive Planets: Uranus
Primary Signs: Gemini, Pisces
Secondary Signs: Aries, Cancer
Primary Houses: 3, 12
Secondary Houses: 9, 5
Stockbroker
Dominant Planets: Mercury, Jupiter, Mars
Supportive Planets: Neptune, Venus
Primary Signs: Gemini, Libra, Scorpio
Secondary Signs: Aquarius, Leo, Virgo

Primary Houses: 2, 3, 5, 8
Secondary Houses: 7, 11
Stuntman/woman
Dominant Planets: Mars, Mercury, Jupiter
Supportive Planet: Pluto
Primary Signs: Aries, Gemini, Sagittarius
Supportive Sign: Pisces (especially for clowns)
Primary Houses: 3, 8
Surgeon
Dominant Planets: Mars
Supportive Planets: Mercury, Saturn, Pluto
Primary Signs: Scorpio, Aries
Supportive Sign: Virgo
Primary House: 8 (a common combination for surgeons is Sun, Mercury or Mars in Aries in the eighth house, and a Scorpio Ascendant)
Secondary Houses: 2, 3, 6, 7, 12
Teacher (High School, College)
Dominant Planet: Jupiter
Supportive Planets: Mars, Mercury, Moon, Saturn, Uranus
Primary Signs: Aries, Sagittarius
Secondary Signs: Capricorn, Aquarius
Primary House: 9
Secondary Houses: 1, 3, 5, 10, 11
Note: A strong third house is necessary for individual tutoring work and also for grade school educators.
Technical Writer
Dominant Planets: Mercury, Saturn
Supportive Planets: Mars, Pluto
Primary Signs: Virgo, Gemini
Secondary Signs: Taurus, Capricorn
Primary Houses: 3, 6
Secondary Houses: 8, 9
Telephone Operator
Dominant Planet: Mercury

Supportive Planets: Venus, Moon
Primary Sign: Gemini
Secondary Signs: Libra, Virgo (less)
Primary Houses: 3, 7
Secondary Houses: 4, 9

Travel Agent
Dominant Planet: Mercury
Supportive Planets: Jupiter, Moon, Venus
Primary Sign: Virgo
Secondary Sign: Gemini
Note: Sagittarius rules long distance travel and thus may be expected to be prominent in the birth charts of travel agents, but does not describe their temperament. Because Sagittarius is an extremely restless sign, it is too impatient to perform the tedious detail required of travel agents.
Primary Houses: 3, 6, 9
Secondary House: 7

Typist
Dominant Planet: Mercury
Supportive Planets: Mars, Saturn
Primary Signs: Gemini, Virgo
Primary Houses: 3, 6
Secondary House: 9

Veterinarian
Dominant Planets: Mars, Saturn, Mercury
Supportive Planet: Moon
Primary Sign: Virgo
Secondary Signs: Taurus, Scorpio, Capricorn
Primary Houses: 6, 8, 12 (primarily for zookeepers and those who work with wild animals or sea creatures)

Waste Manager
Dominant Planets: Saturn, Pluto, Mars
Supportive Planet: South Node
Primary Sign: Scorpio
Secondary Signs: Capricorn, Leo (for management in general)

Primary Houses: 4, 8, 12
Supportive House: 2
Weaver
Dominant Planet: Mercury
Supportive Planets: Mars, Venus, Moon
Primary Sign: Virgo
Secondary Signs: Sagittarius (not for patience, but for its coordinating ability; this sign rules the sciatic nerve and produces weavers when connected with Virgo), Cancer, Gemini
Primary Houses: 3, 6
Secondary Houses: 4, 5
Welder
Dominant Planets: Mars, Pluto
Supportive Planet: Mercury
Primary Signs: Gemini, Virgo, Scorpio
Secondary Signs: Aries, Leo (fire signs)
Primary Houses: 1, 3, 6
Secondary House: 8
Writer
See Novelist, Technical Writer

Appendix B
Glossary of Vocational Terms

Ascendant: The eastern point where the ecliptic crosses the horizon at the time and exact latitude and longitude of birth. Planets near this degree often are vocationally strong.

Artha: The Vedic name for the three vocational houses-second, sixth and tenth.

Aspect: A geometric relationship between the planets.

Benefic: The traditional good guys, Jupiter and Venus. Vedic astrologers also consider the Full Moon, and occasionally Mercury, as benefic in effect. Western astrologers often describe the North Node as possessing a benefic influence (a view not shared by Vedic practitioners.)

Besieged: When a planet is flanked by two malefic (traditionally Mars and Saturn) planets and they are in the same or adjacent signs with no other planets between themselves and the besieged planet.

Culmination: The arrival of a planet at the Midheaven.

Conjunction: An aspect of zero degrees. Harmony or disharmony depends entirely on the two or more planets involved.

Cusp: The division point between two signs or houses.

Debility: Any condition that weakens a planet. There are many kinds of debilities, both essential and accidental. Refer to any standard encyclopedia of astrology. Chapter 6 includes vocational debilities.

Descendant: The angle of the birth chart opposite the Ascendant. Here the ecliptic intersects the western horizon. Also called the setting point.

Degree: There are 360 degrees of ecliptic longitude that make up the twelve zodiacal signs. Each degree has its own influence and interpretation.

Detriment: A condition of debility based on sign. See Chapter 6.

Dignity: Any condition that strengthens a planet. There are many kinds of dignities, both essential and accidental. Refer to any standard encyclopedia of astrology.

Dispositor: The planet ruling the sign that another planet tenants. The former planet disposits the latter. Example-Mercury would disposit any planet located in the signs it rules, Gemini and Virgo. (See Chapter 6.)

Doryphory: See explanation in Introduction and Chapter 6.

Element: There are four elements in Western astrology-fire, earth, air and water. See Chapter 3.

Exaltation: A condition of dignity based on sign. See Chapter 6.

Fall: A condition of debility based on sign. See Chapter 6.

Fortified: A planet enjoying dignity in any number of ways is considered fortified.

House: A division of the celestial sphere, either spatially or by time. There are several alternate methods of dividing the celestial sphere and, therefore, diverse system of house division. See Chapter 7. Houses rule various activities of life and are extremely important in vocational astrology.

Malefic: The traditional bad guys, Saturn and Mars. However, any planet can have a malefic influence under certain astrological conditions. Vedic astrologers consider the Sun, the waning (and especially) the balsamic Moon and the North and South Nodes as potential malefics. Western astrologers include the South Node, Pluto, Neptune and Uranus as conditional malefics.

Midheaven: Also referred to as the MC, *medium coeli*. The conjunction of two great circles, the ecliptic and the meridian, i.e. the great circle passing north-south. This is the south point of the birth horoscope.

Mode: There are three traditional modes in Western astrology-cardinal, fixed and mutable. Modes describe the rate of matter in motion. See Chapter 3.

Nadir: The angle in the birth chart directly opposite the Midheaven. The north point. Here the ecliptic intersects the great meridian in the north.

Native: The owner of the birth chart.

Opposition: An aspect of 180 degrees. Disharmonious, but not always. Sometimes it indicates a balance rather than a war.

Orb: Any distance of ecliptic longitude form one point to another, orbs are spoken of in degrees. This term usually applies to an allowable amount of orb given to various aspects between two planets.

Partile aspect: An exact aspect.

Platic aspect: An inexact aspect.

Quincunx: An aspect of 150 degrees. It indicates a disconnection is occurring between the two planets so placed. Many astrologers insist on a one degree orb for this aspect, although it can work well with a larger orb. Disharmonious.

Rising/Rising Sign: A common term for the Ascendant. Also called the rising point. An intersection of the local horizon with the ecliptic plane.

Rulership/Ruler: Every planet rules a sign (sometimes two). A planet also is said to rule a house if its sign is on the cusp of that house.

Sect: Refers to various strengthening planetary conditions based on day or night birth. (See Chapter 6.)

Sextile: An aspect of sixty degrees. Harmonious.

Sign: A season of thirty days. In Western astrology there are twelve "tropical" seasons or signs, and the wheel begins on the spring equinox, or zero degrees Aries. The spring equinox presents a yearly constant for Earth-Sun relationship, as do all four quarters. This definition of sign does not hold for the various star-based "sidereal" zodiacs. Sidereal zodiacs divide the ecliptic plane into sectors of thirty degrees, starting with the slowly retrograding longitude of a star, Aswini. These sectors are called "signs." There are at least four sidereal zodiacs currently popular with Vedic astrologers.

Significator: A generic ruler over an object or topic, e.g. Jupiter is the significator of children in general, regardless of what planets may personally indicate offspring in the birth chart.

Square: An aspect of ninety degrees. Inharmonious, although not invariably so. An energetic and problem solving aspect.

Trine: An aspect of 120 degrees. Harmonious.

Vedic astrology: The term commonly used for the astrology of India.

Zenith: The Midheaven.

Appendix C
Collection of Vocational Horoscopes

The planetary birth charts in this collection were selected according to the following criteria:

• Birth times are preferably from the birth certificate. If that could not be obtained, they are from the mother's memory.

• The individuals whose birth charts are displayed here represent successful careers in full capacity.

• The individuals whose birth charts are represented here enjoy their work.

In order to protect the anonymity of the birth chart owners, their names are not included. However, I am prepared to demonstrate the authenticity of individual birth charts to the seriously inquiring, provided I can obtain permission from the owner of the birth moment.

Because the vast majority of professionals reflect their horoscopes beautifully, there was no picking and choosing to find charts that look like the occupations they represent. No charts were discarded because they did not turn out as expected. What I saw is what you get. However, particular birth charts were deliberately included for topical interest. This collection represents a selection from my astrological practice from 1969 to 1997.

There are many house systems, each with its own merits. For convenience, all charts here are constructed in Placidus. It is important to always include a whole sign house approach in vocational readings. Why? Because it works. This is an ancient method that was used by the earliest Greek astrologers and is still popular with many Vedic practitioners.

Whole sign houses work like this: The sign on the Ascendant, regardless of degree, functions as the first house. (The Ascendant and Midheaven remain absolutely essential points for natal conjunctions, natal interpretation, planetary transits and progressions.) The second sign as counted forward in the order of the signs from the Ascendant constitutes the second house, and so on through the twelve houses. Notice how within the borders of the North American/Western European latitudes, the all-important Midheaven can occur in the ninth, tenth or eleventh sign from the Ascendant. Although the Midheaven and its ruler will target professional concerns, never neglect to also observe the tenth sign from the Ascendant and its ruler. This house methodology is thoroughly explained in Chapter 7.

Whole sign houses have an excellent cyclic basis supported by the work of the late scientist Arthur M. Young in his book *The Geometry of Meaning*. However, if whole sign houses do not suit you, use your preferred house system exclusively.

Seasoned and lay astrologers will enjoy perusing the following birth chart collection "as is." However, the serious student is guided to compare the charts with the vocational listings in Appendix A. Here I have described the represented careers using planetary combinations followed by the astrological signs of prominence and houses in emphasis. My selections are based on traditions, i.e. the conclusions of previous authors regarding planetary, house and sign rulerships for most careers in combination with my thirty years of observation based on more than 5,000 personal readings. This especially holds true in the special case of "new" occupations.

Keep in mind that no single birth chart represents an absolute fixed picture of what the horoscope of someone in that profession must necessarily look like. Vocational aptitude arises through a combination of planets, signs and houses, and these combinations are nearly infinite. However, it is true that persons engaged in identical work will share many of these astrological combinations, e.g. two nurses will share more astrological themes with each other than with two construction workers. If this were not true, then this book and its vocational chart collection would be of no use to anyone.

The preceding chapters contain all vocational lists, tables and methodologies necessary to acquire the useful skill of accurately interpreting horoscopes from the vocational perspective.

Chart collections have seen publication before, but never from an absolutely vocational perspective. This fascinating collection of more than I 00 vocational horoscopes represents a diverse collection of professional occupations. Deliberately included are those careers emphasizing the four elements and three modes, as well as various planetary energies, houses and signs. A thorough study of these charts should be of great assistance in gaining a solid working knowledge of vocational astrology.

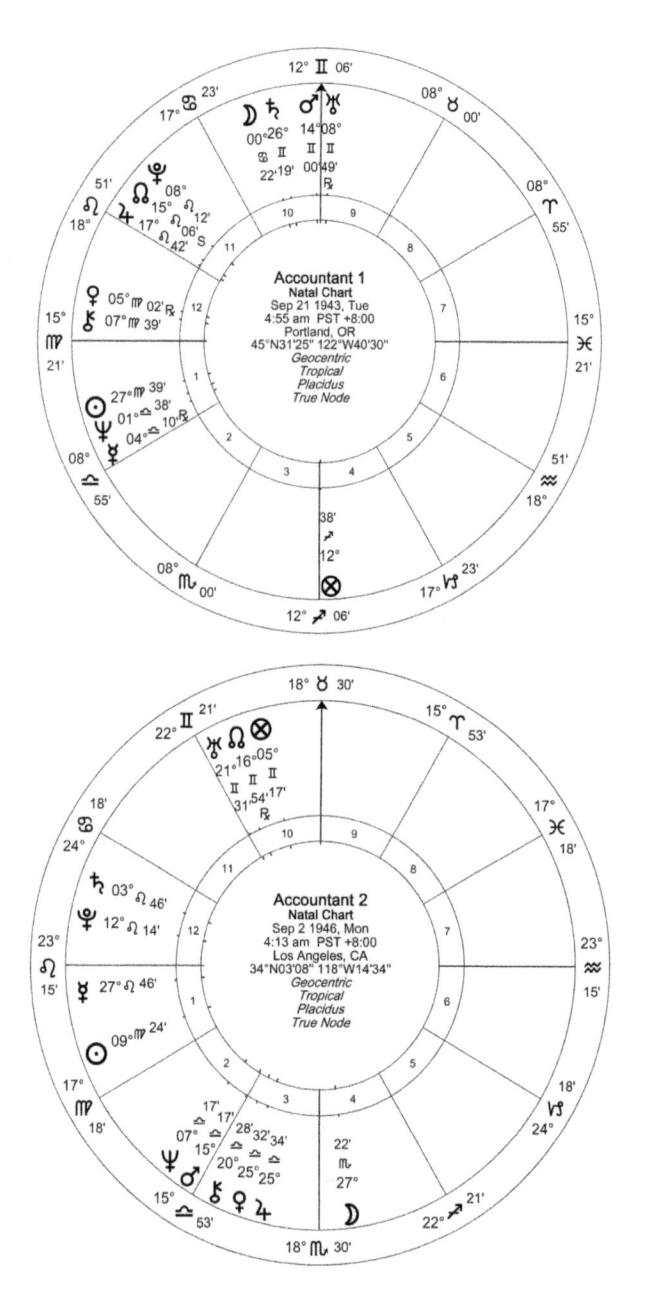

Appendix C: Vocational Horoscopes

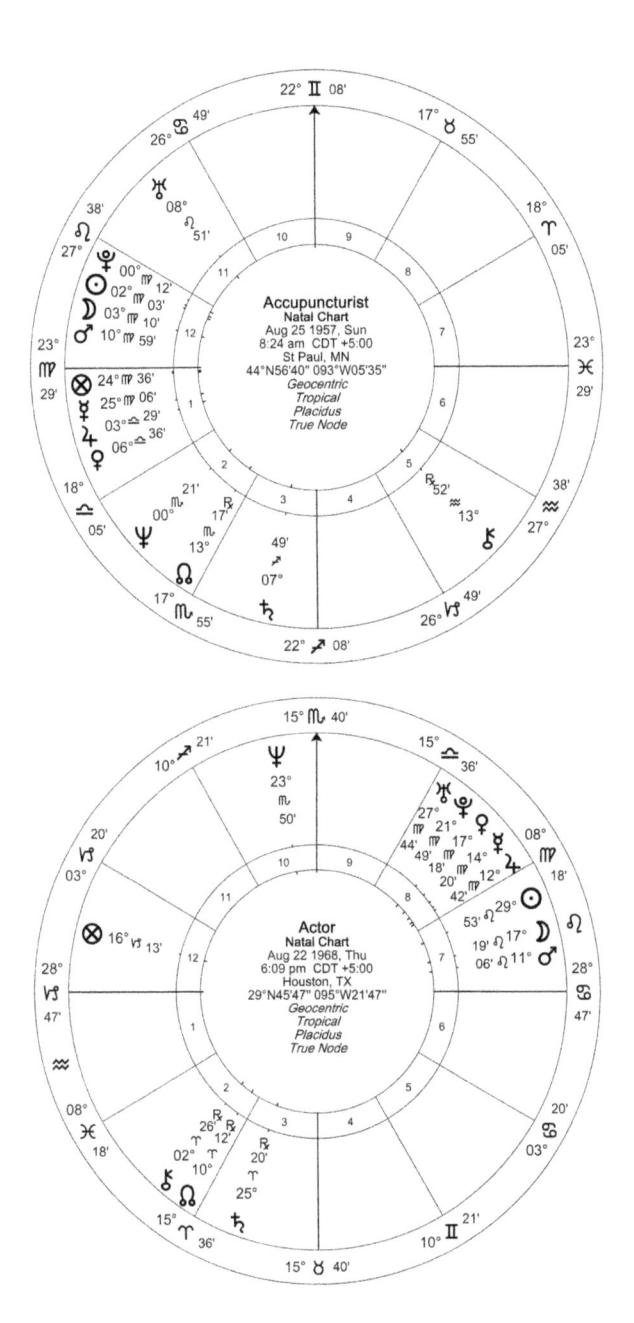

Vocational Astrology

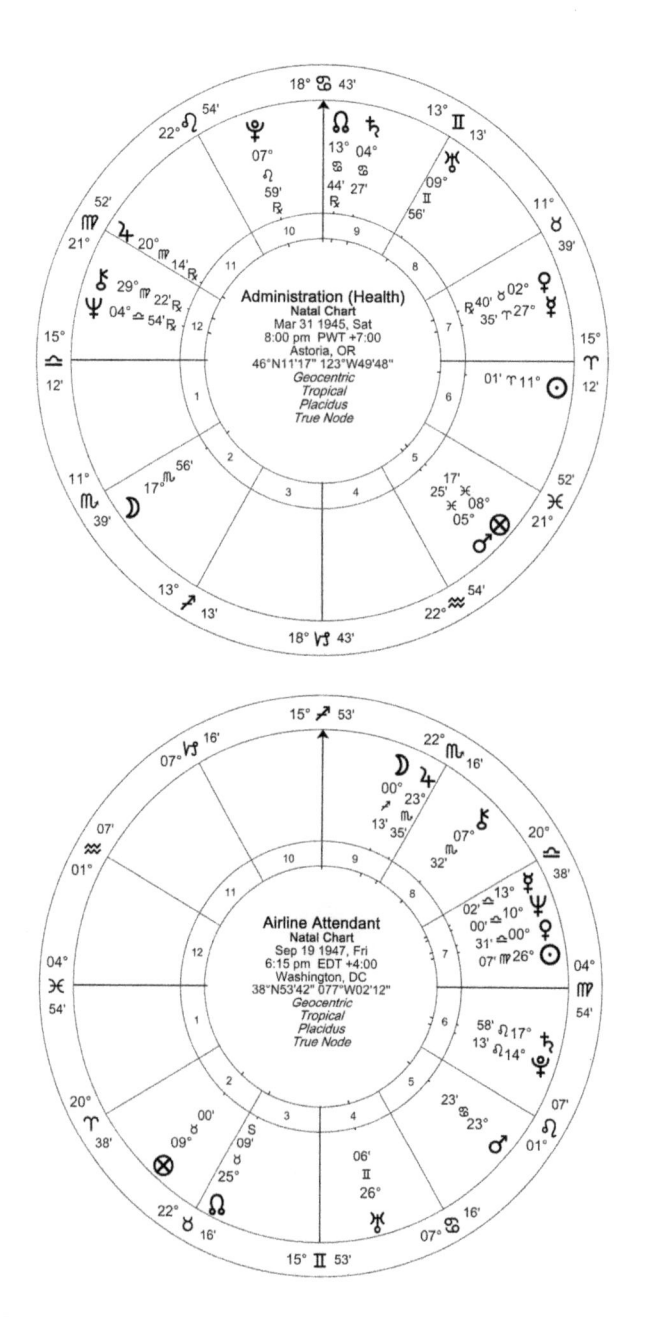

Administration (Health)
Natal Chart
Mar 31 1945, Sat
8:00 pm PWT +7:00
Astoria, OR
46°N11'17" 123°W49'48"
Geocentric
Tropical
Placidus
True Node

Airline Attendant
Natal Chart
Sep 19 1947, Fri
6:15 pm EDT +4:00
Washington, DC
38°N53'42" 077°W02'12"
Geocentric
Tropical
Placidus
True Node

Appendix C: Vocational Horoscopes

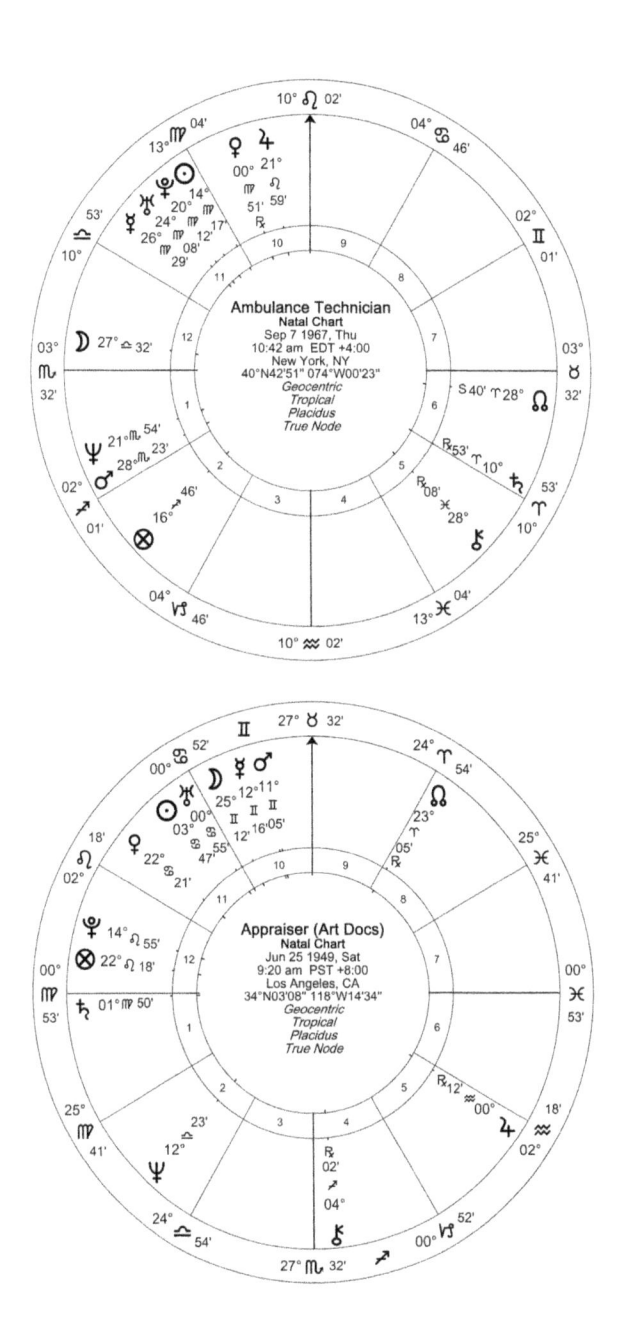

Vocational Astrology

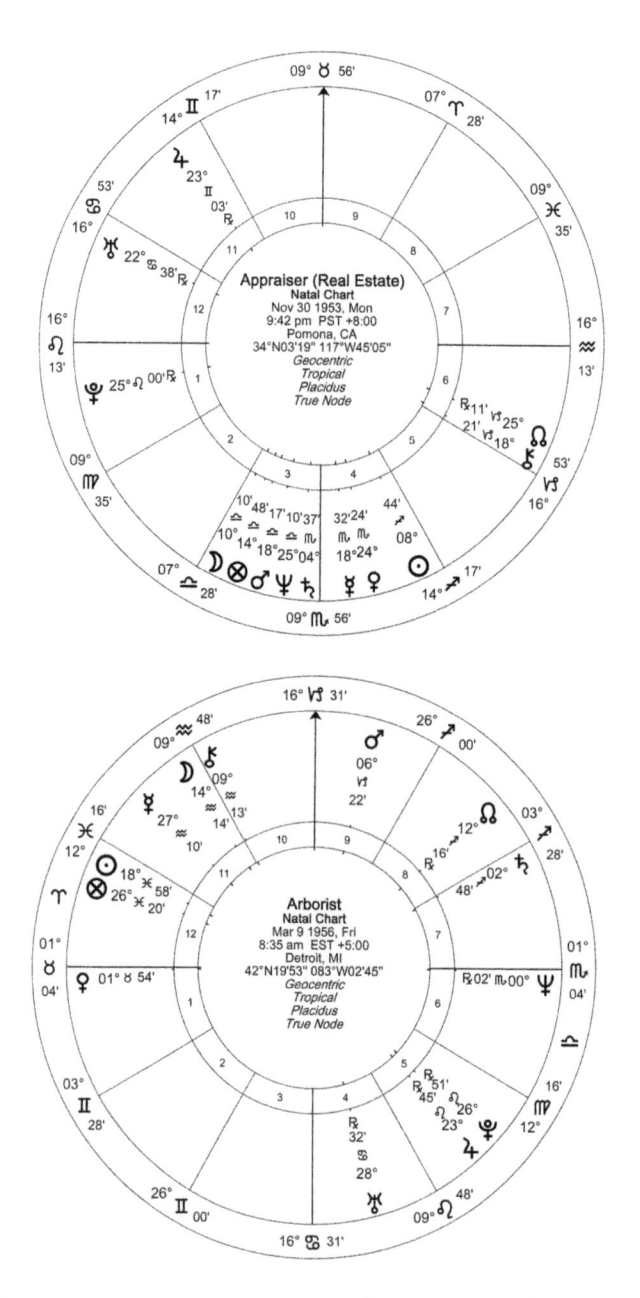

Appendix C: Vocational Horoscopes

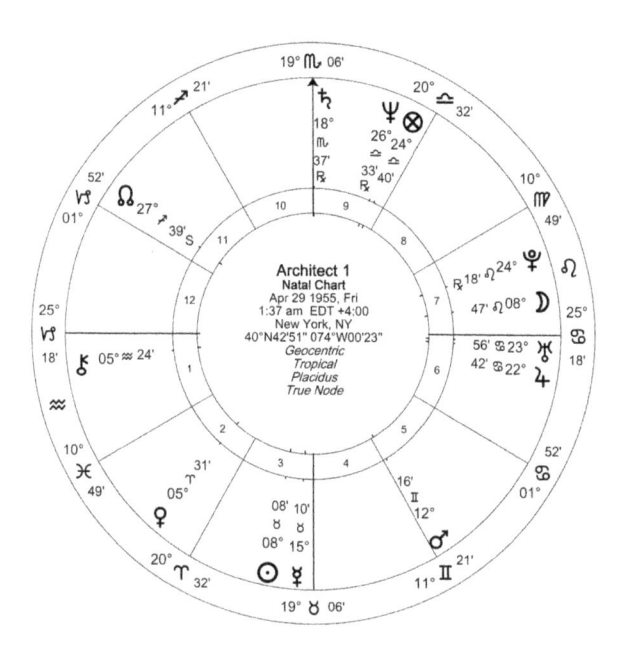

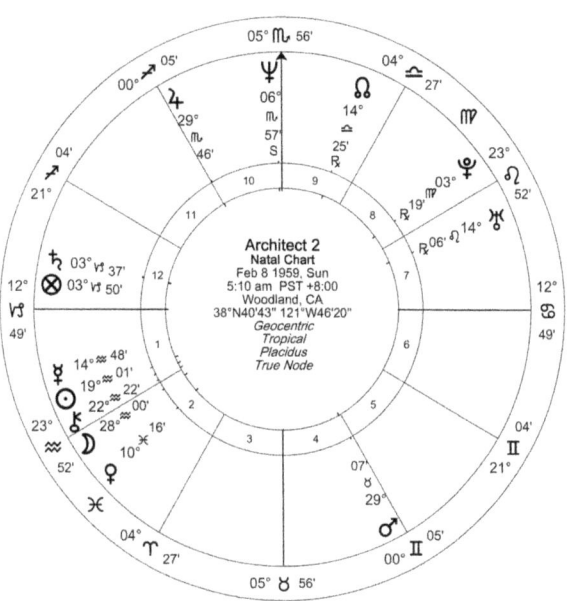

Vocational Astrology

Appendix C: Vocational Horoscopes

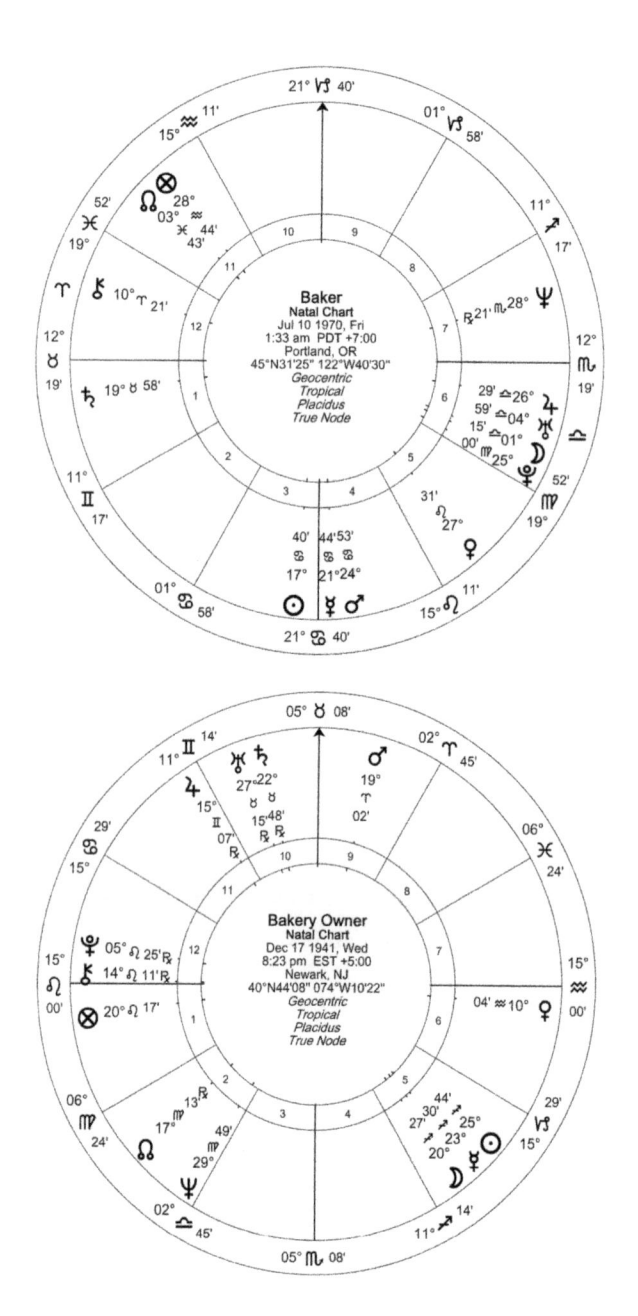

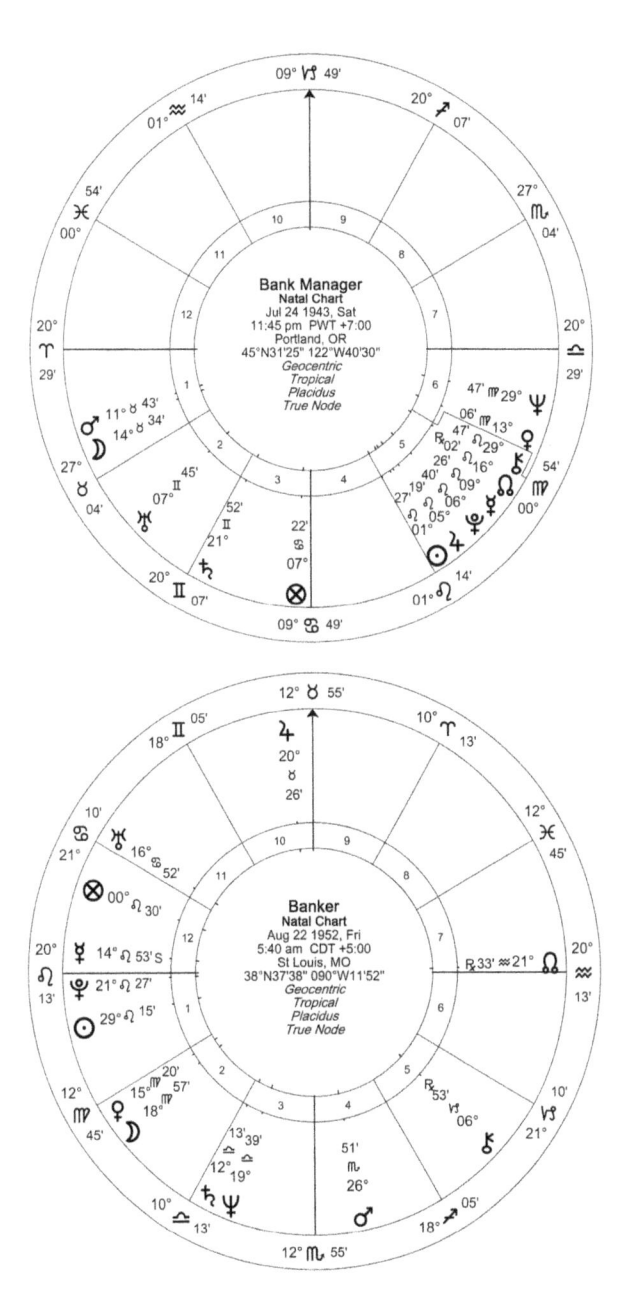

Vocational Astrology

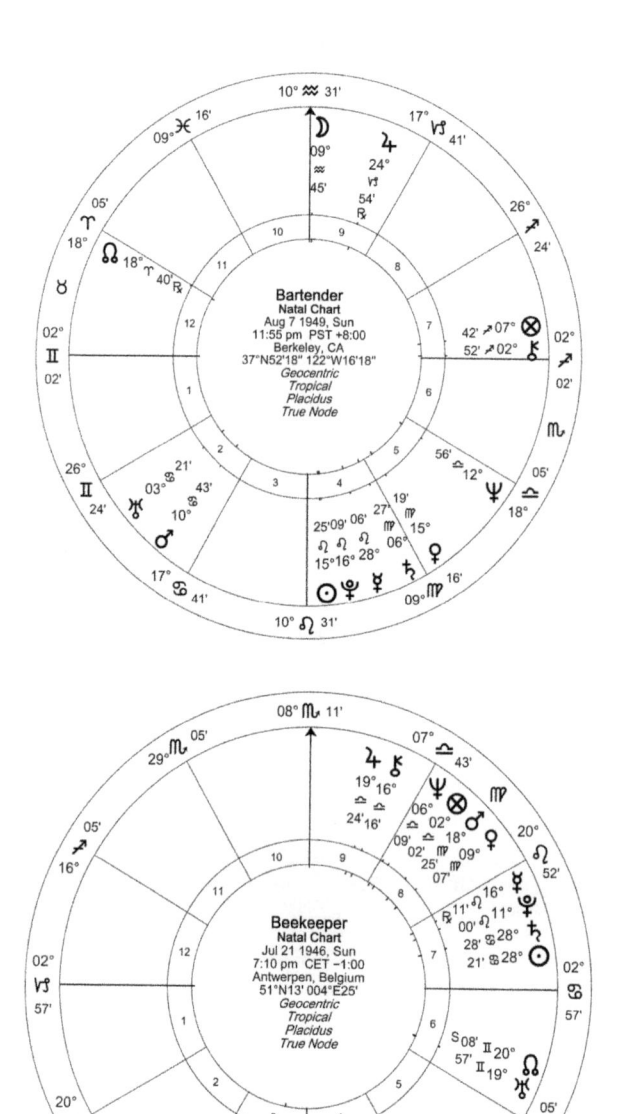

Appendix C: Vocational Horoscopes

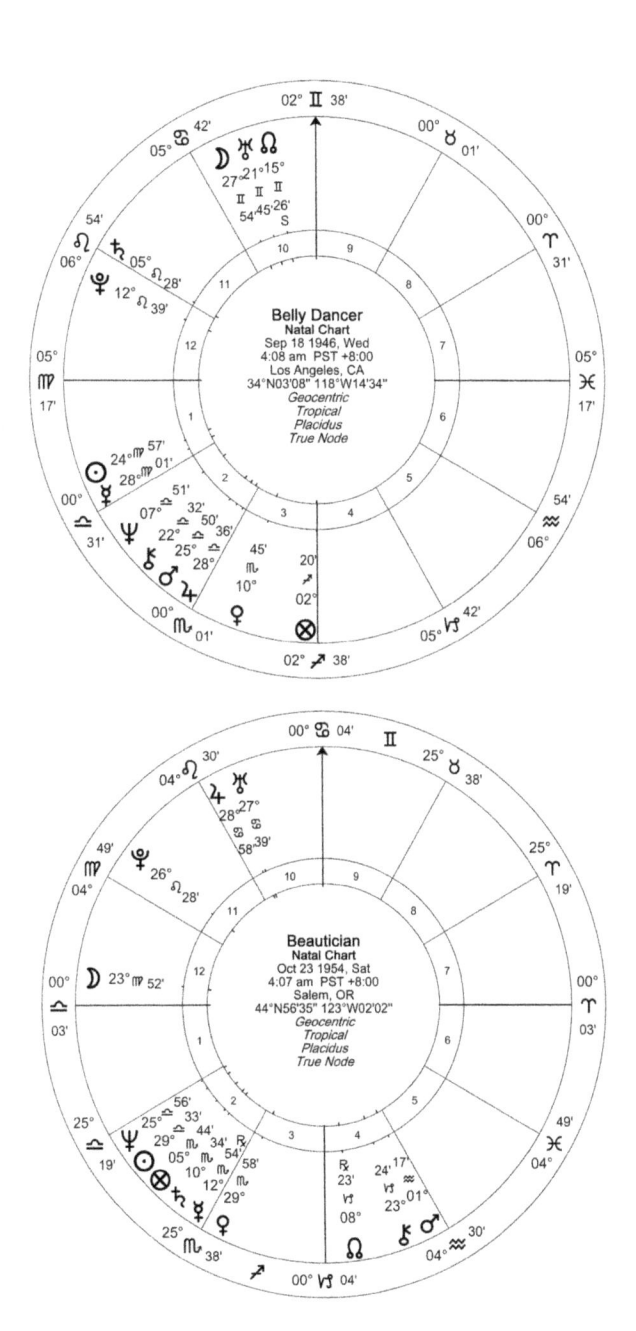

Belly Dancer
Natal Chart
Sep 18 1946, Wed
4:08 am PST +8:00
Los Angeles, CA
34°N03'08" 118°W14'34"
Geocentric
Tropical
Placidus
True Node

Beautician
Natal Chart
Oct 23 1954, Sat
4:07 am PST +8:00
Salem, OR
44°N56'35" 123°W02'02"
Geocentric
Tropical
Placidus
True Node

Vocational Astrology

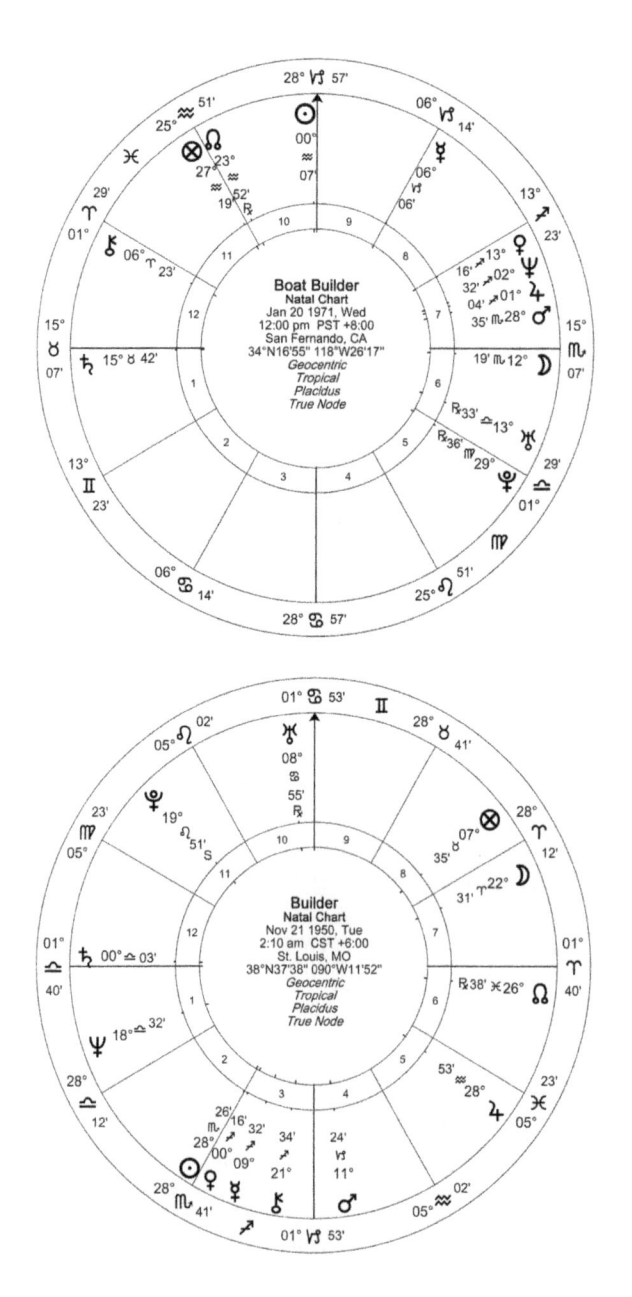

Appendix C: Vocational Horoscopes

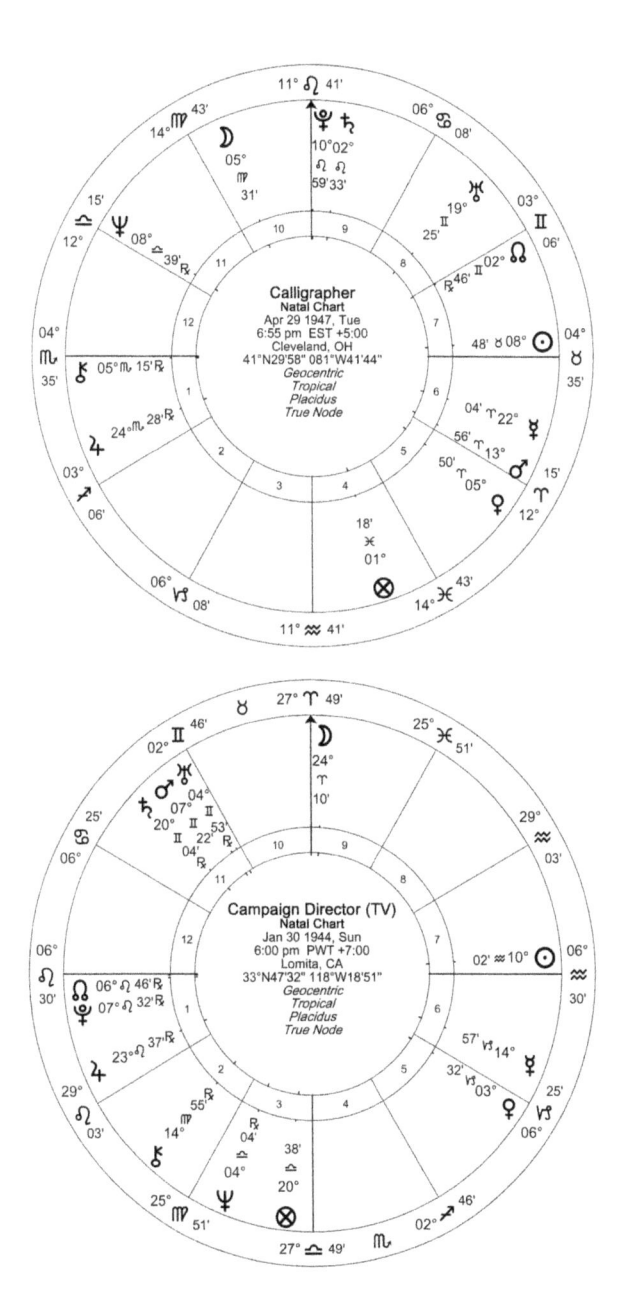

Vocational Astrology

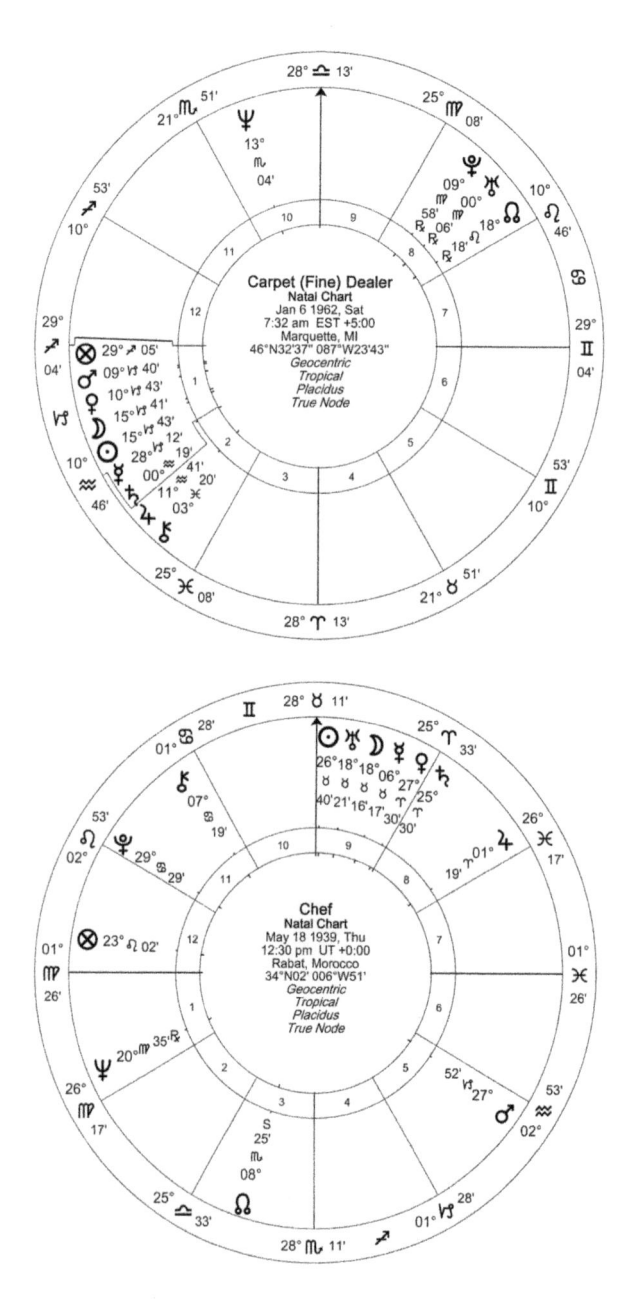

Carpet (Fine) Dealer
Natal Chart
Jan 6 1962, Sat
7:32 am EST +5:00
Marquette, MI
46°N32'37" 087°W23'43"
Geocentric
Tropical
Placidus
True Node

Chef
Natal Chart
May 18 1939, Thu
12:30 pm UT +0:00
Rabat, Morocco
34°N02' 006°W51'
Geocentric
Tropical
Placidus
True Node

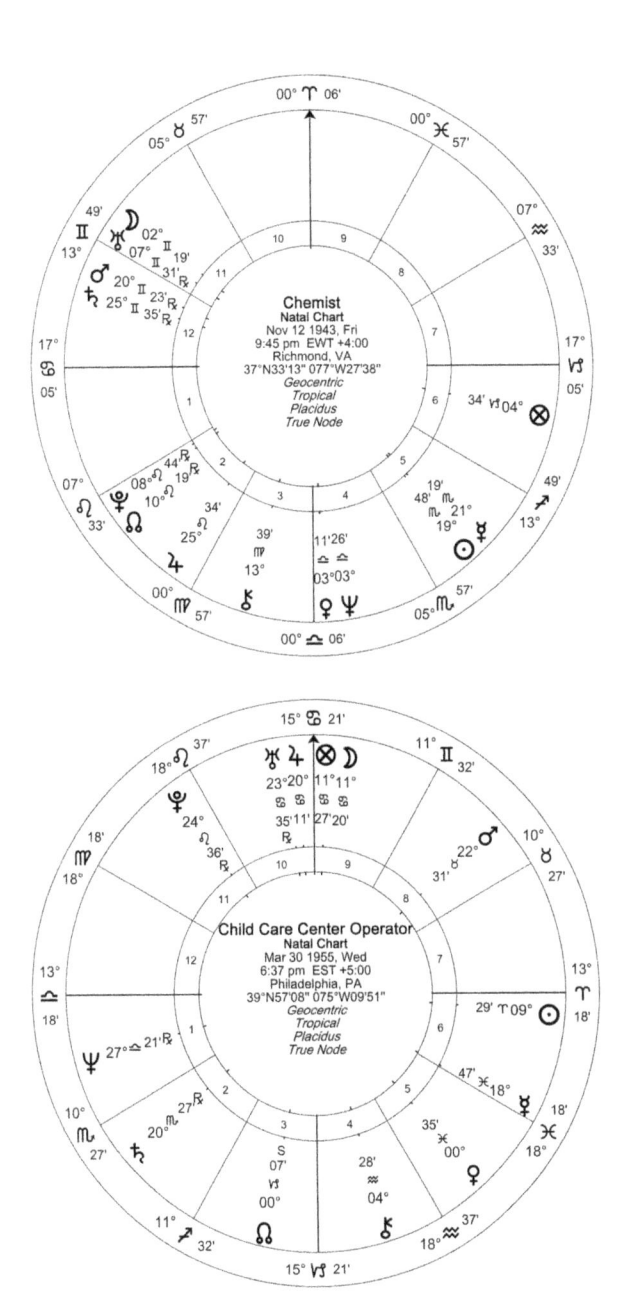

Vocational Astrology

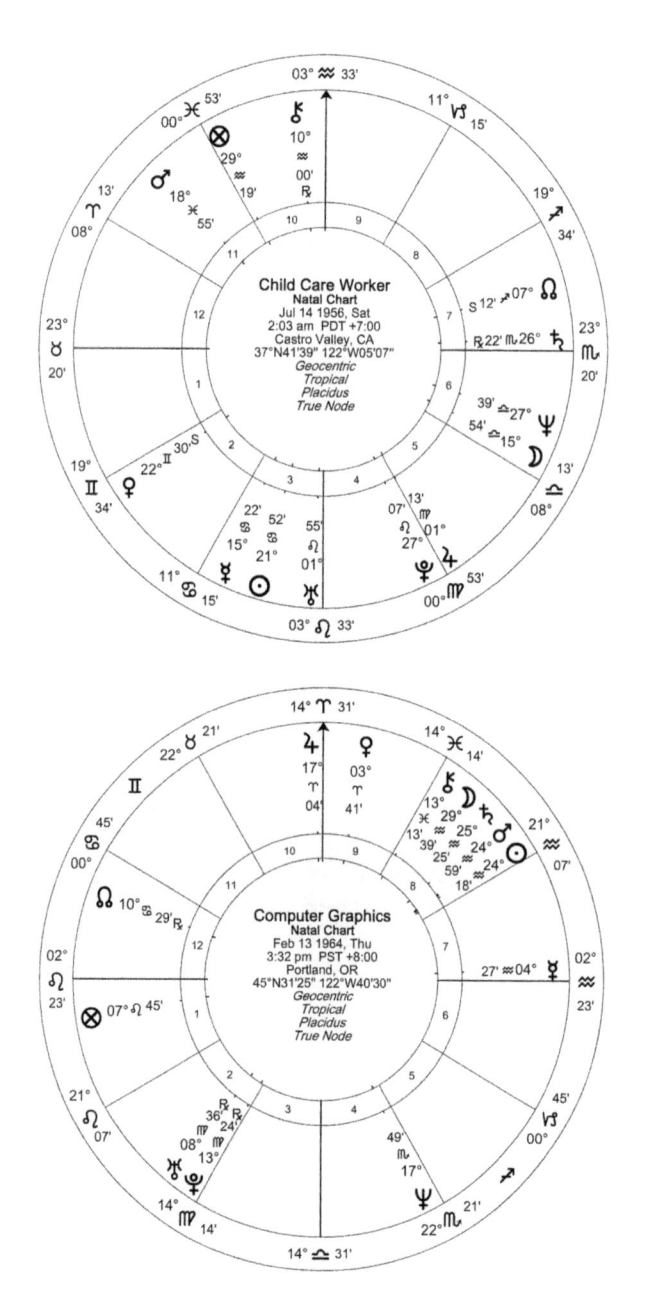

Appendix C: Vocational Horoscopes

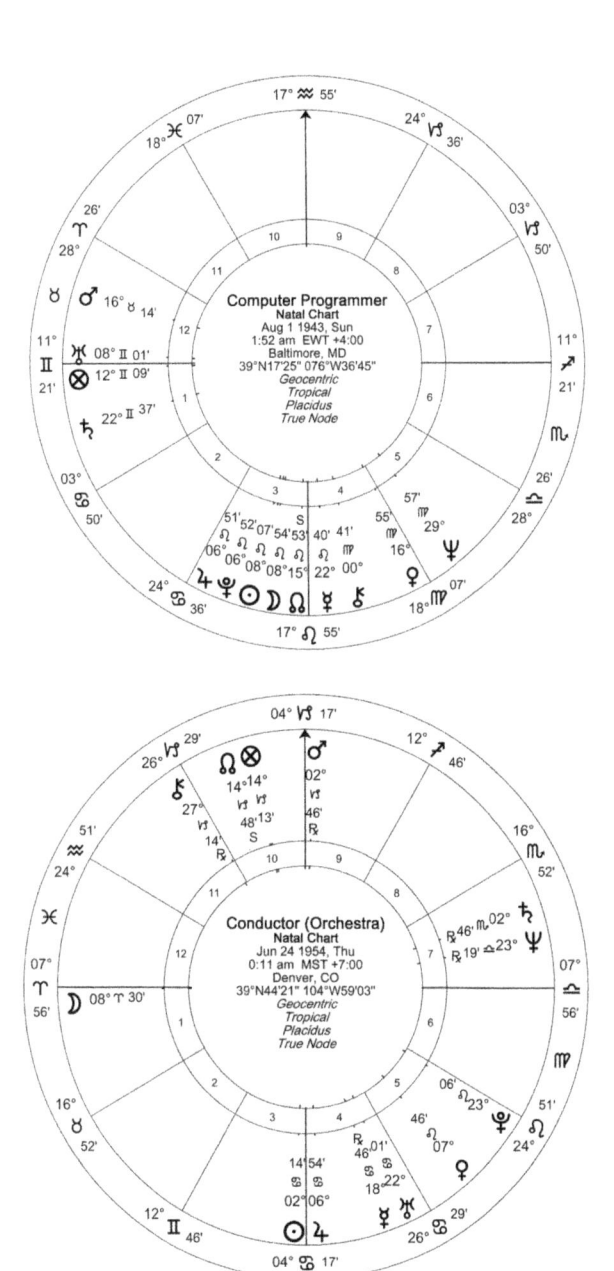

Vocational Astrology

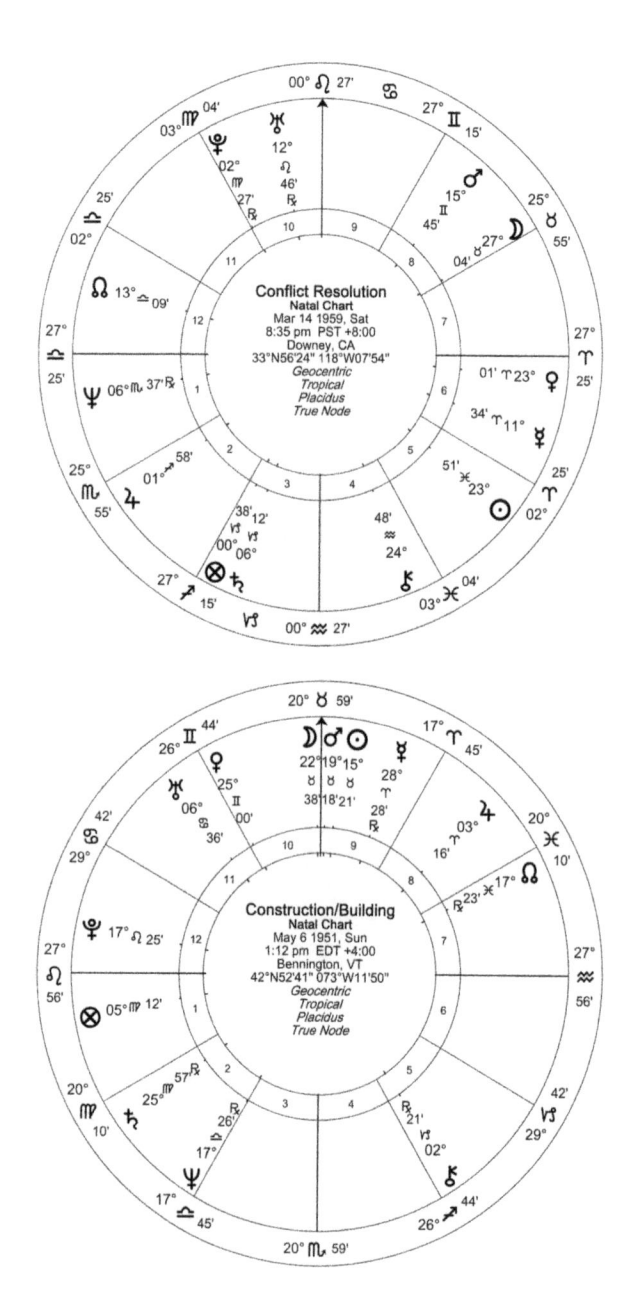

Appendix C: Vocational Horoscopes

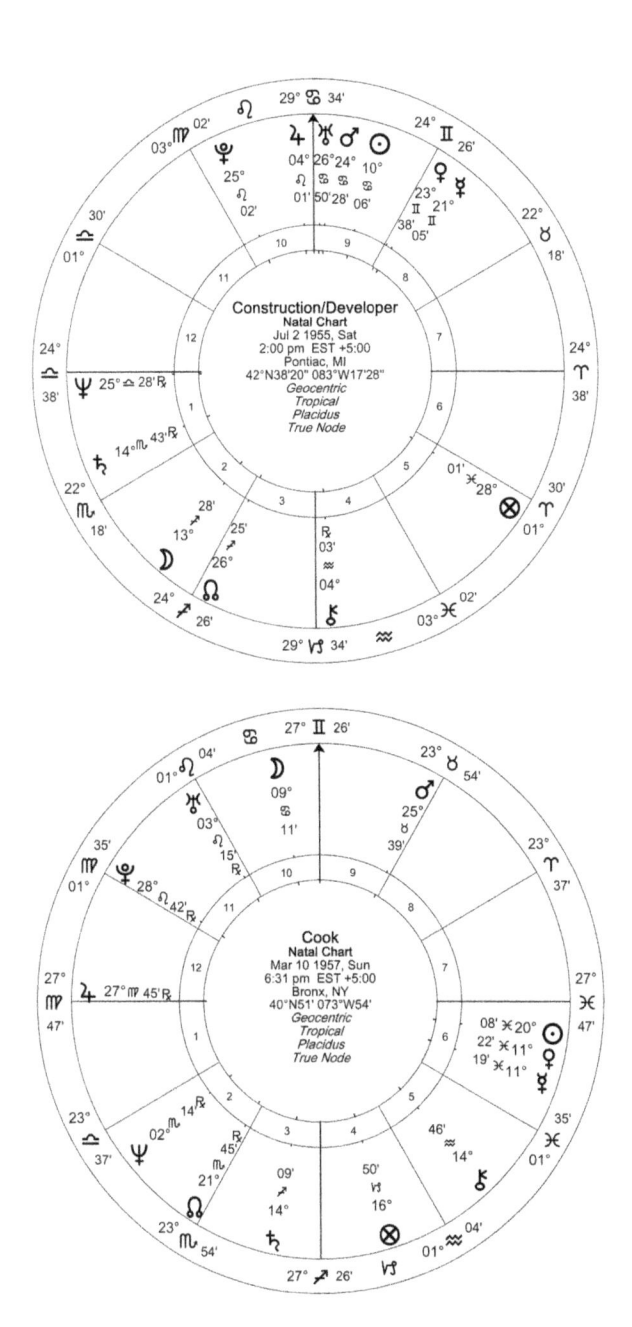

Vocational Astrology

Appendix C: Vocational Horoscopes

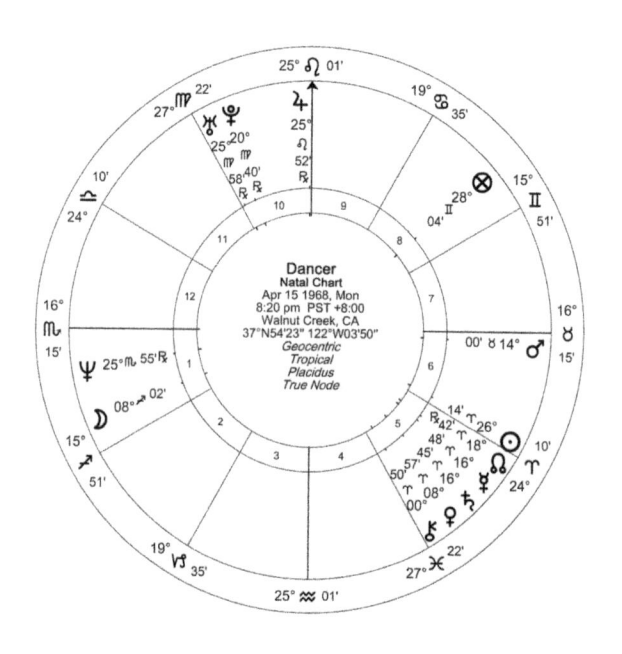

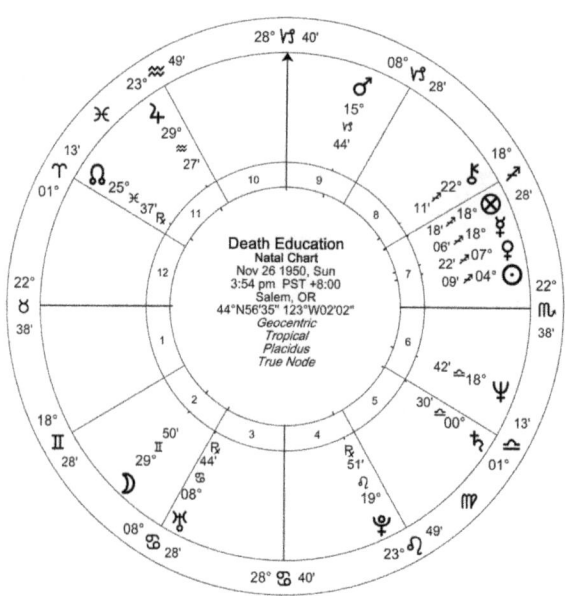

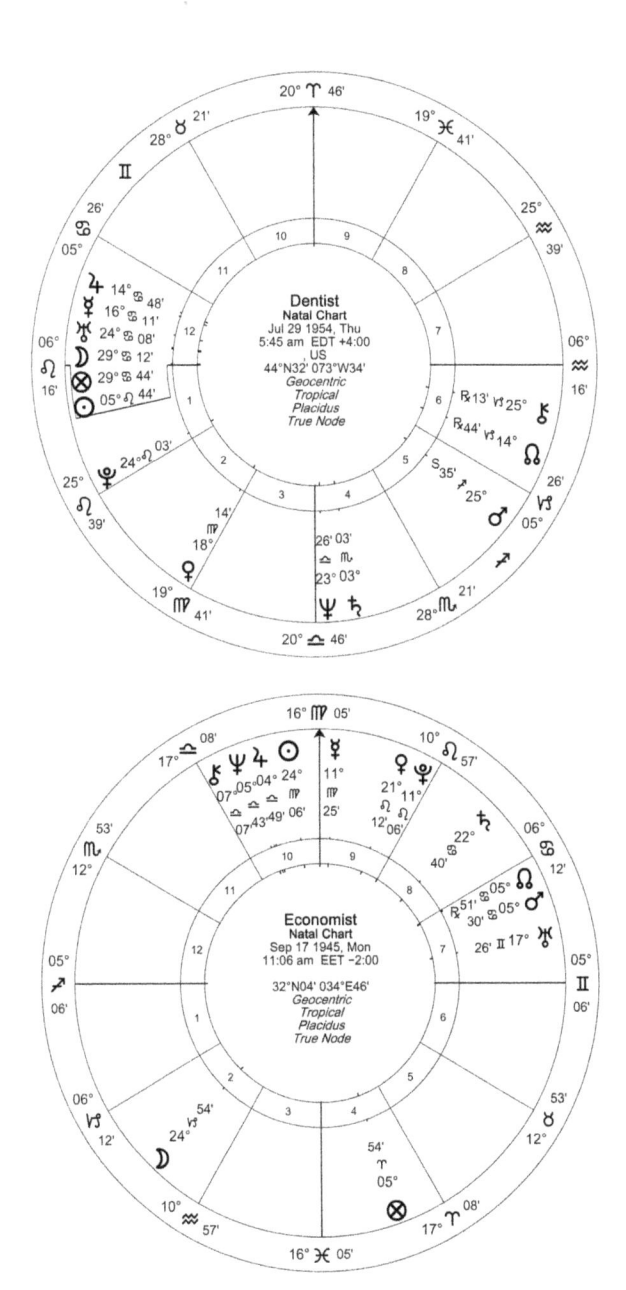

Vocational Astrology

Appendix C: Vocational Horoscopes

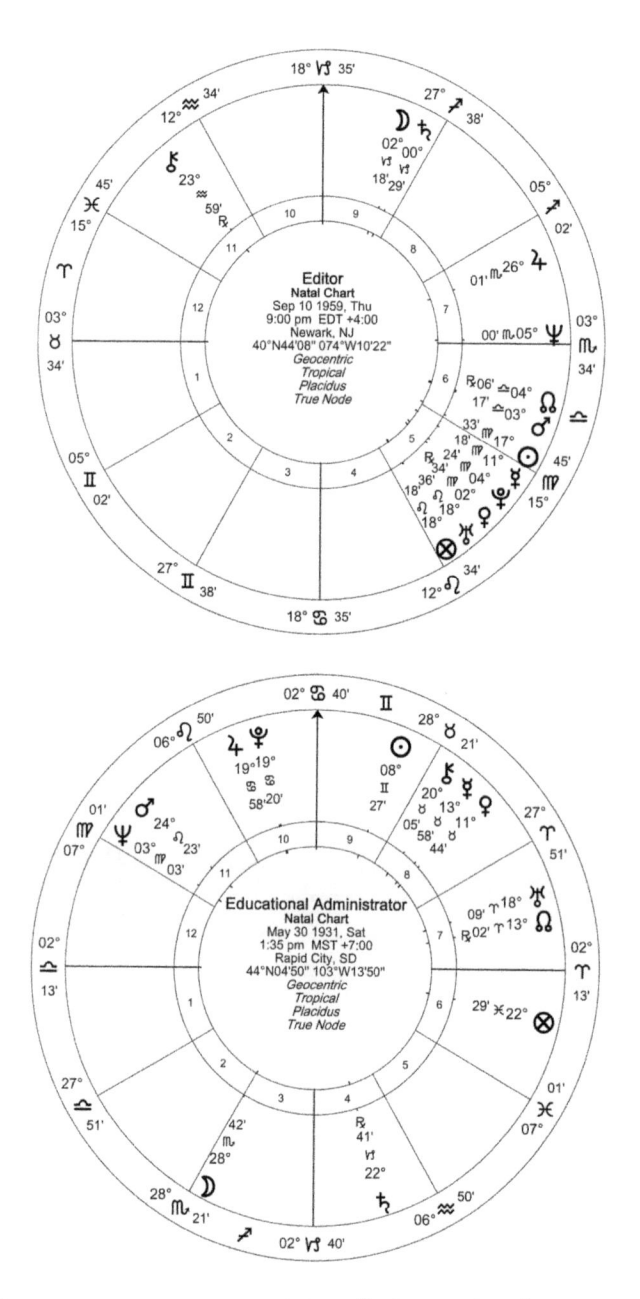

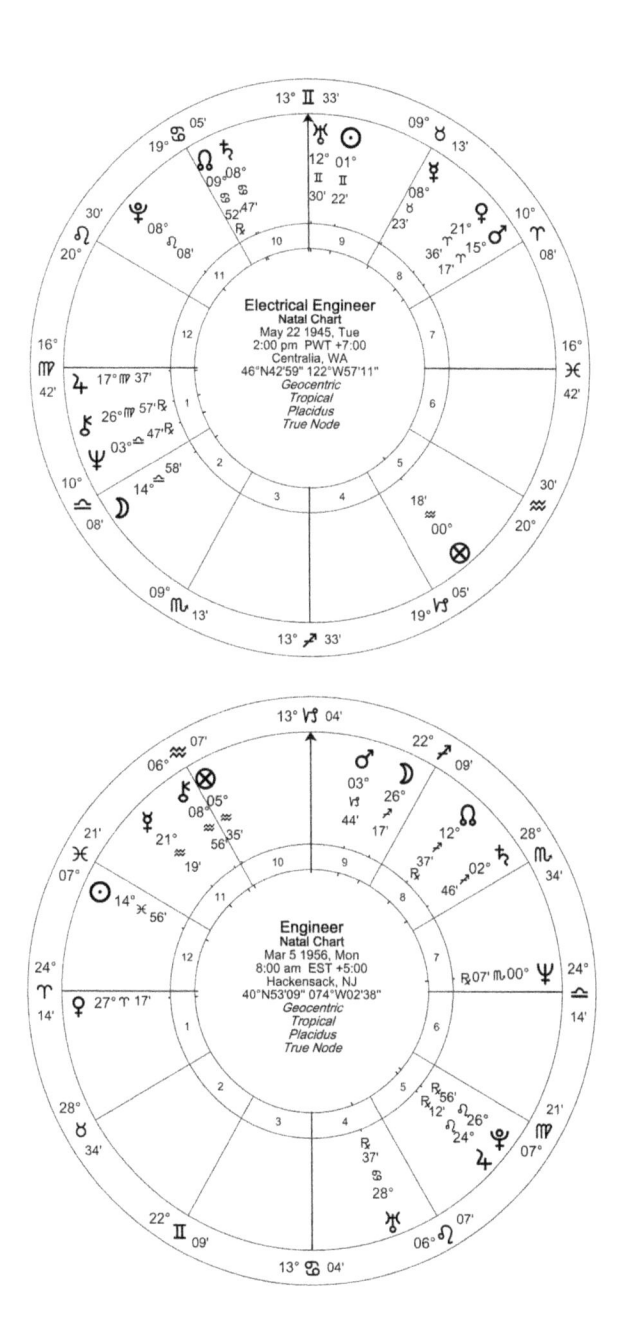

Vocational Astrology

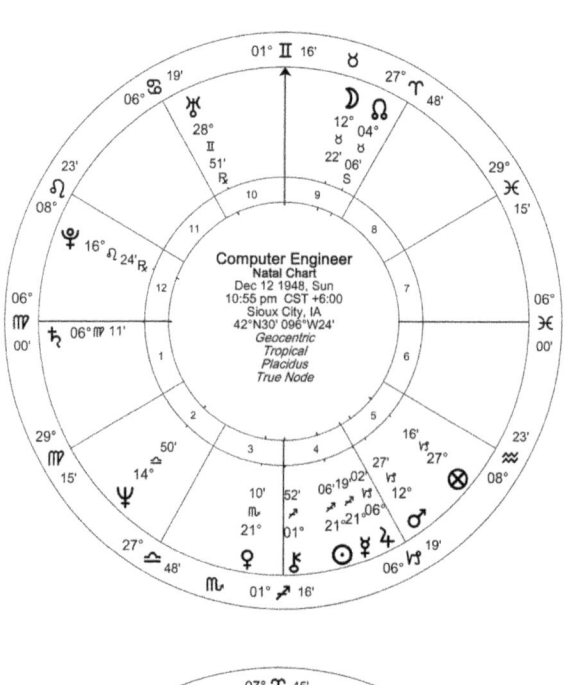

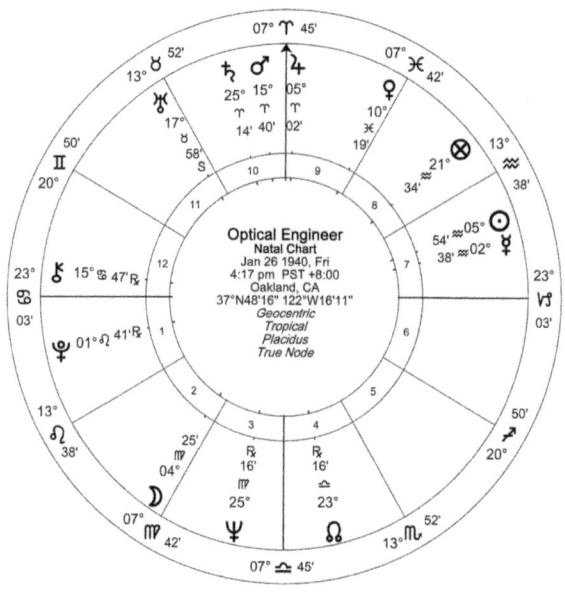

Appendix C: Vocational Horoscopes

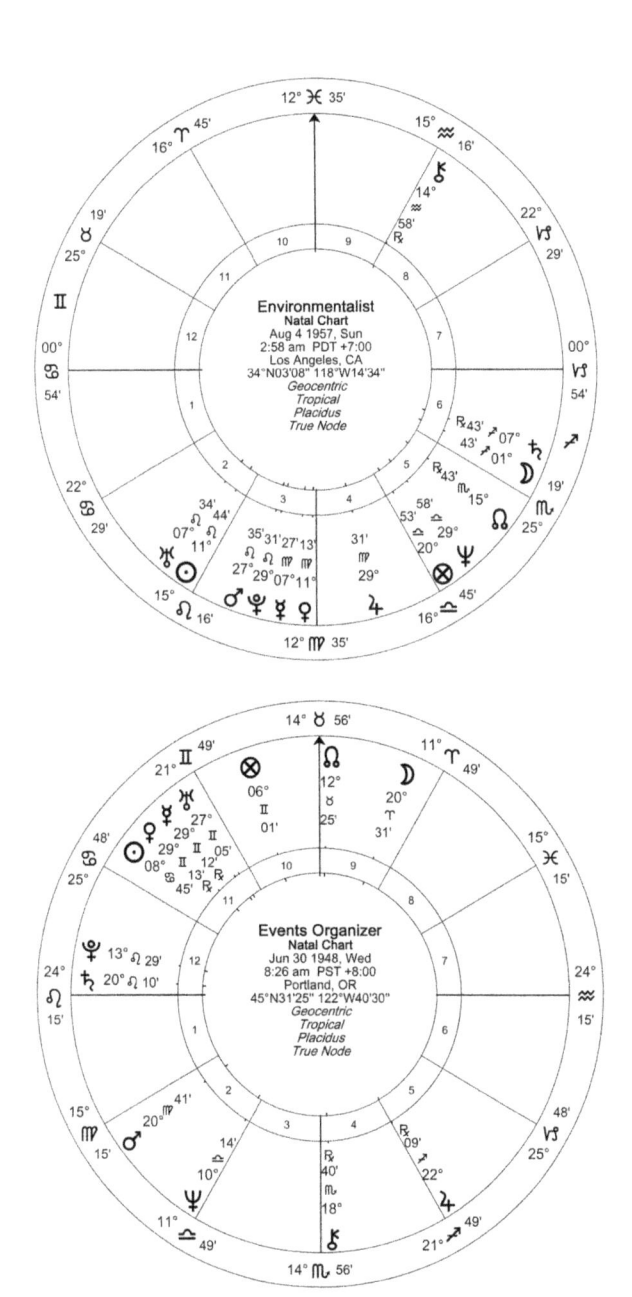

Vocational Astrology

168   Appendix C: Vocational Horoscopes

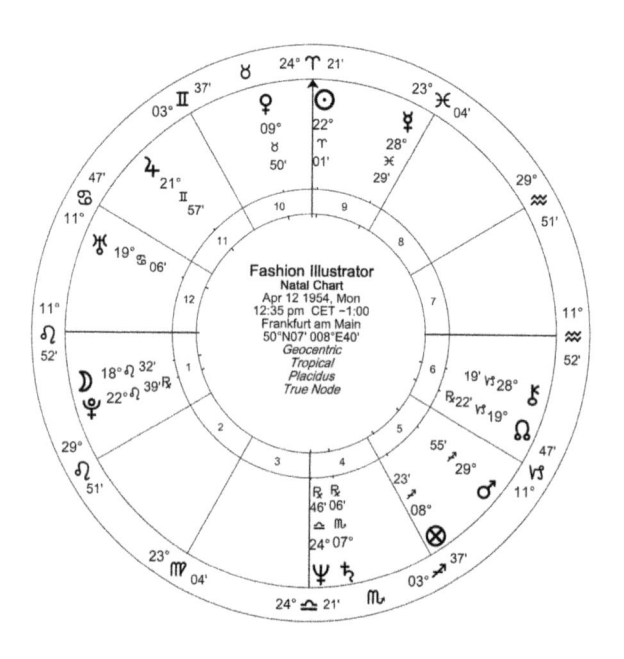

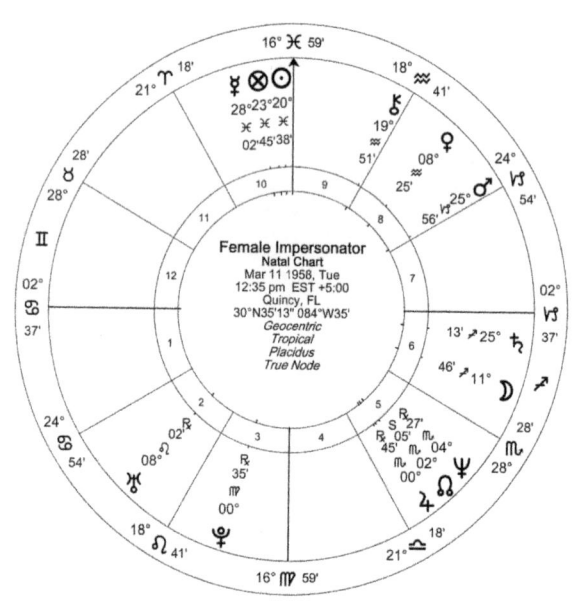

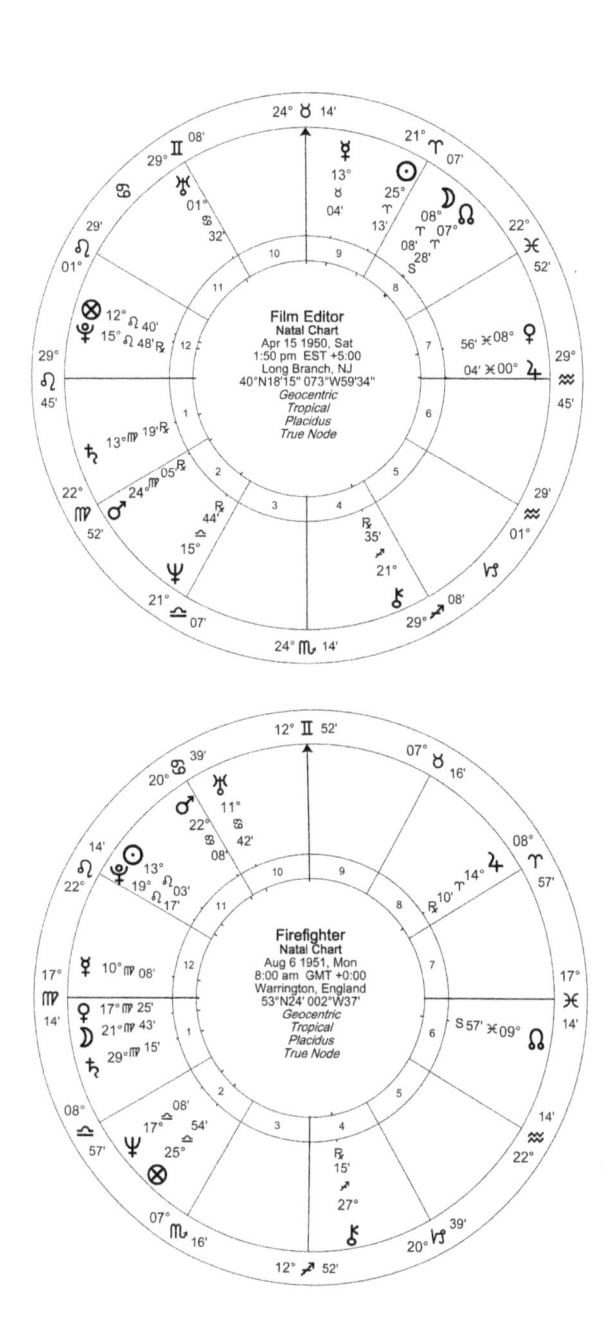

Vocational Astrology

Appendix C: Vocational Horoscopes

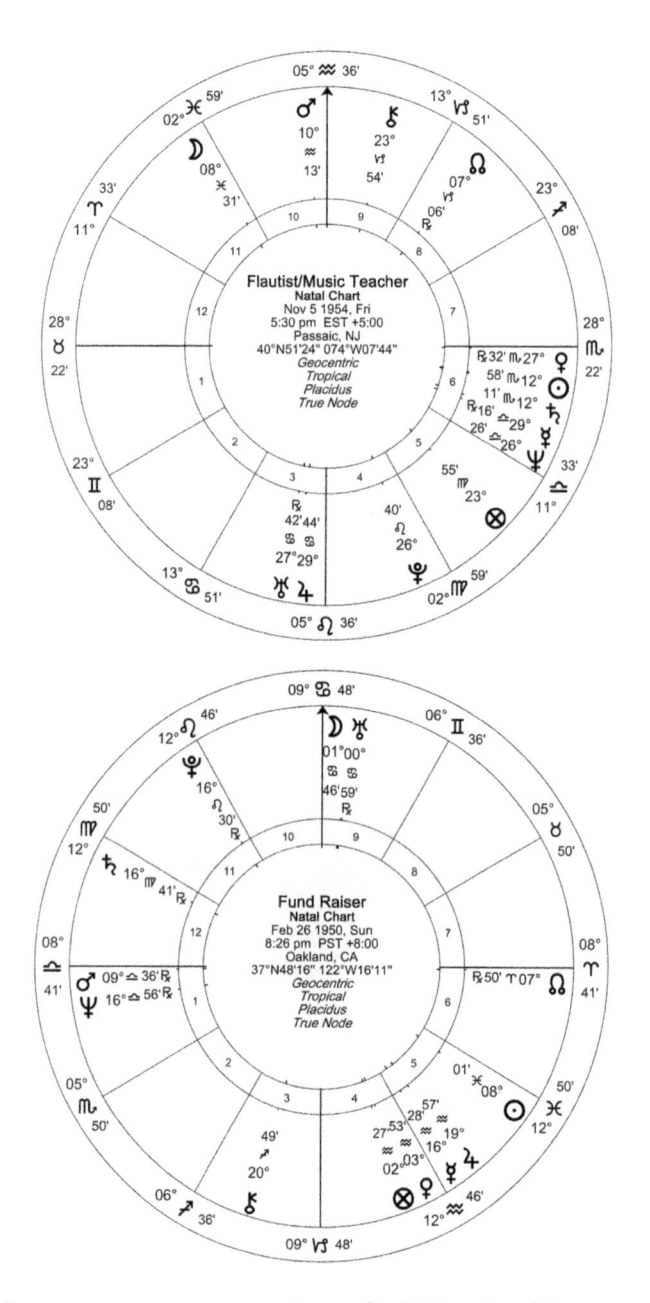

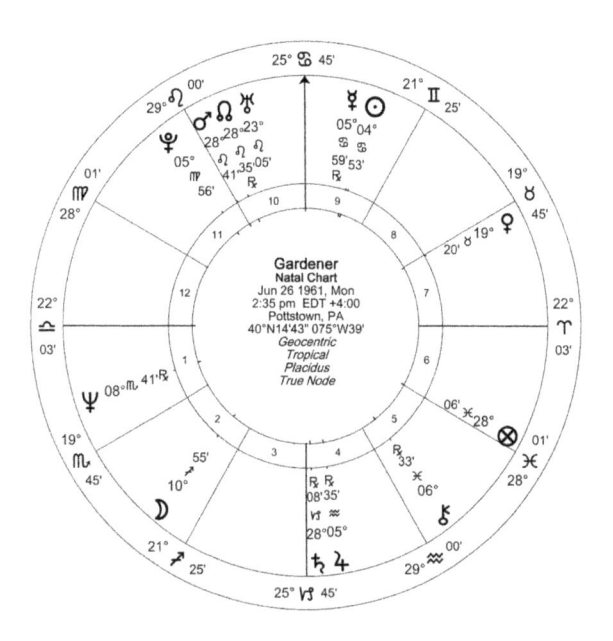

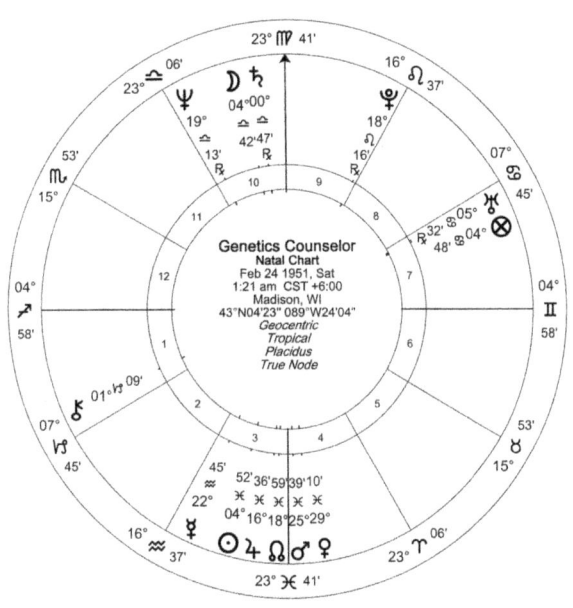

Vocational Astrology

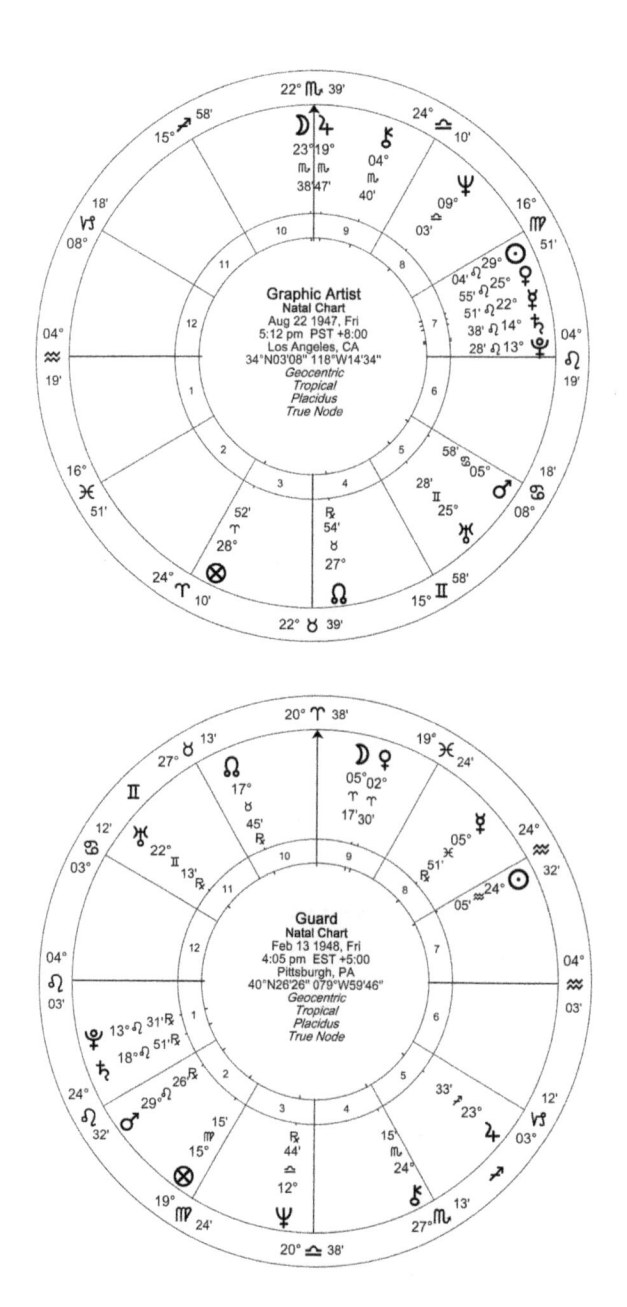

Appendix C: Vocational Horoscopes

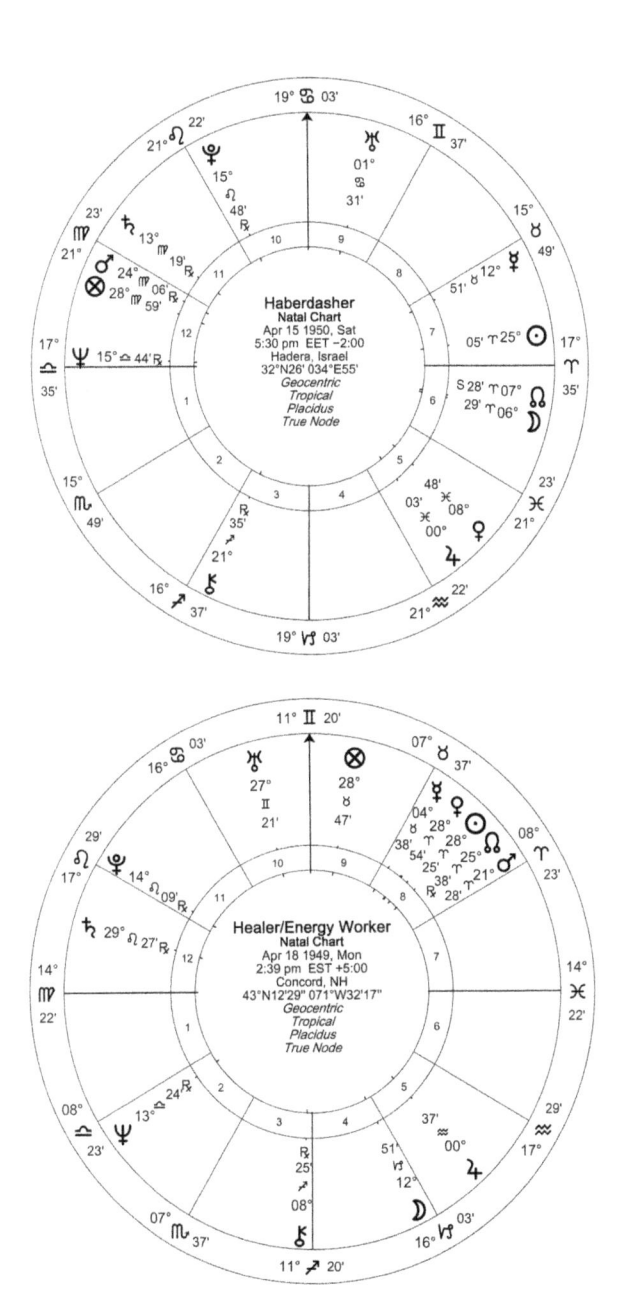

Vocational Astrology

Appendix C: Vocational Horoscopes

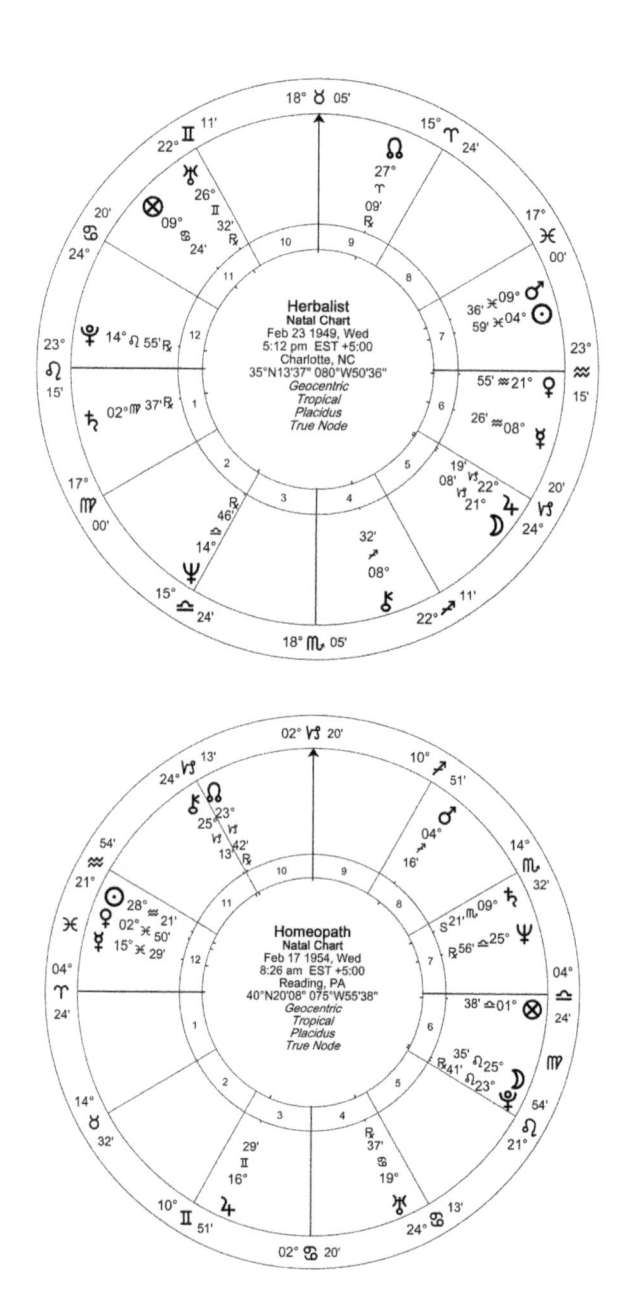

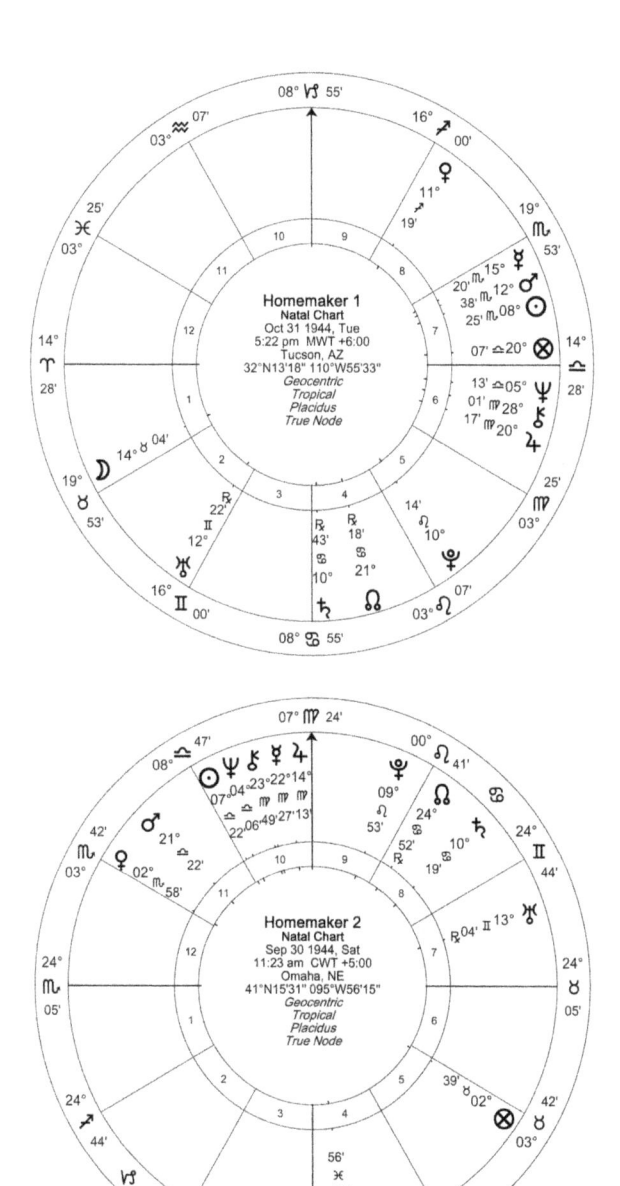

Vocational Astrology

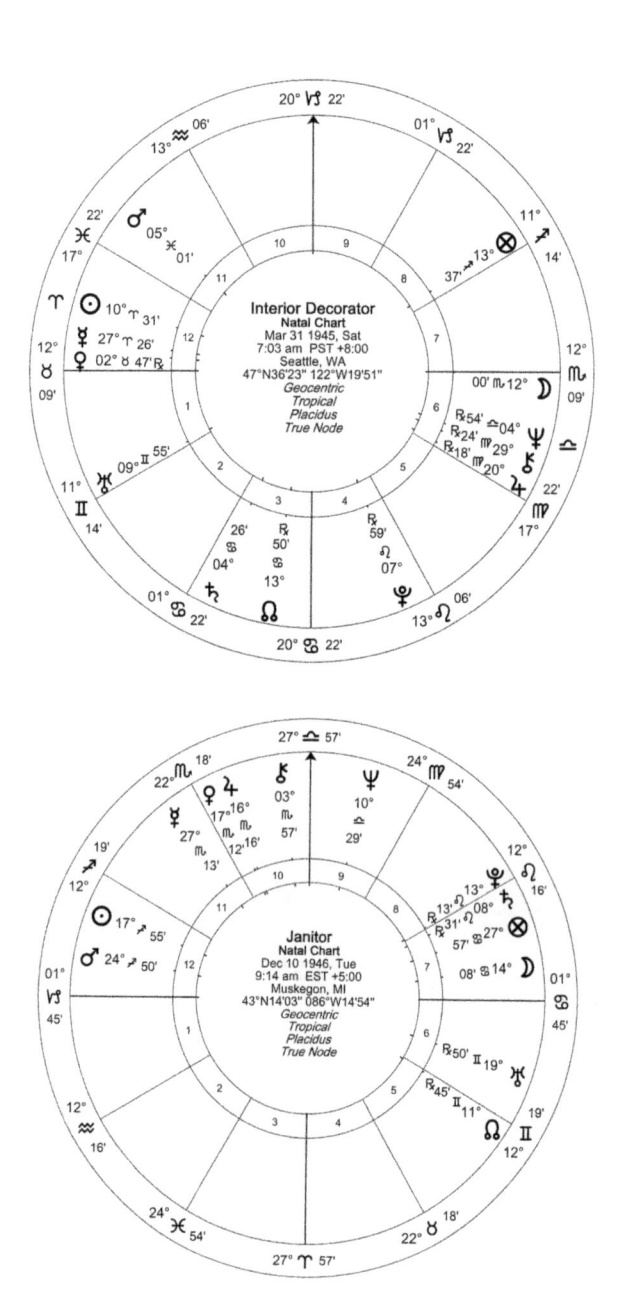

Appendix C: Vocational Horoscopes

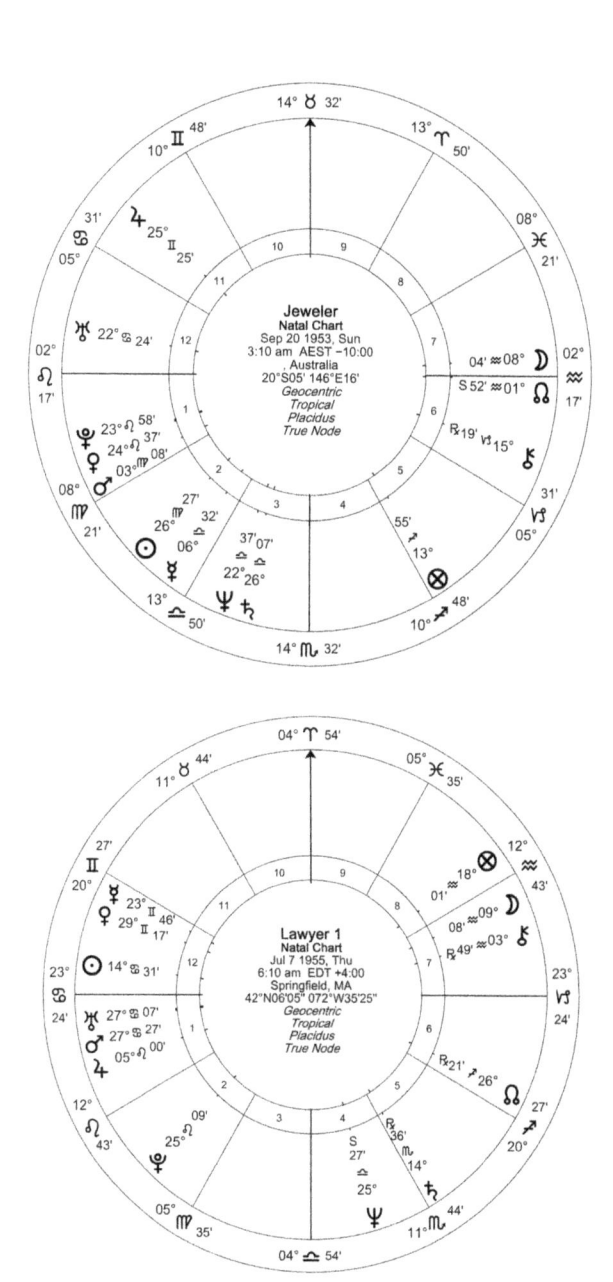

Vocational Astrology

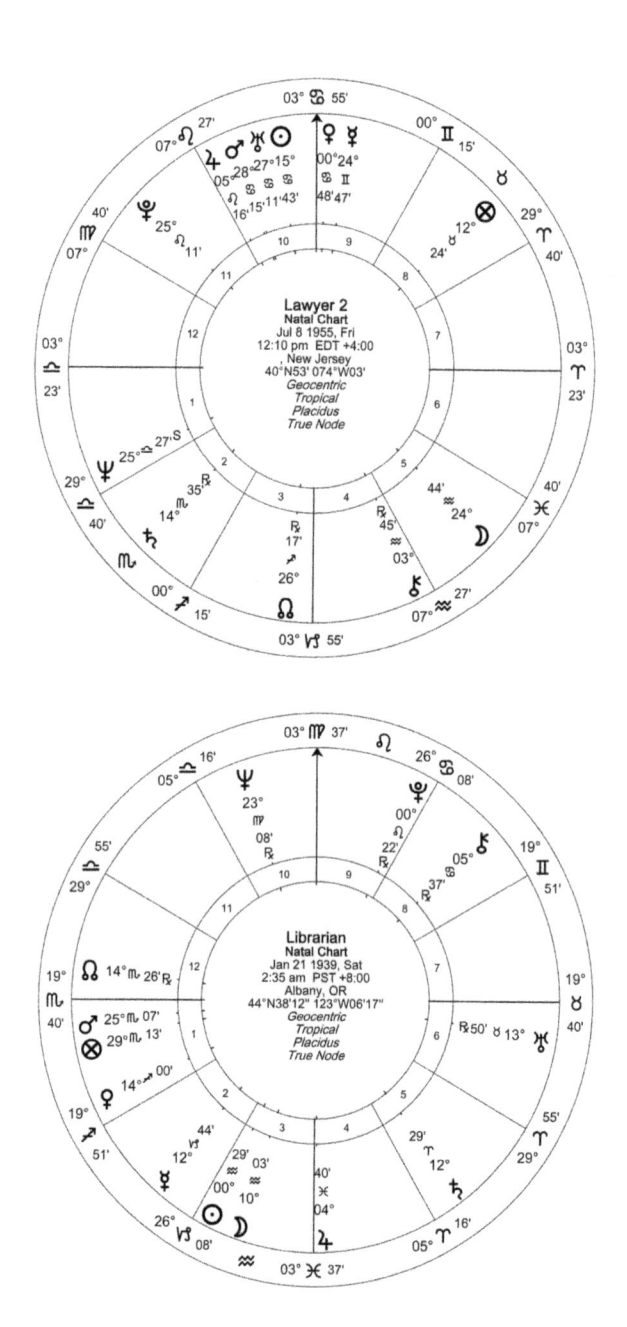

Appendix C: Vocational Horoscopes

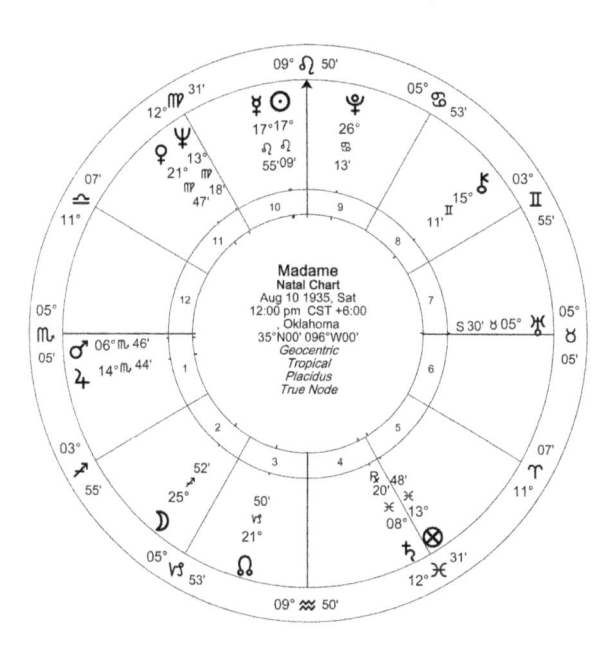

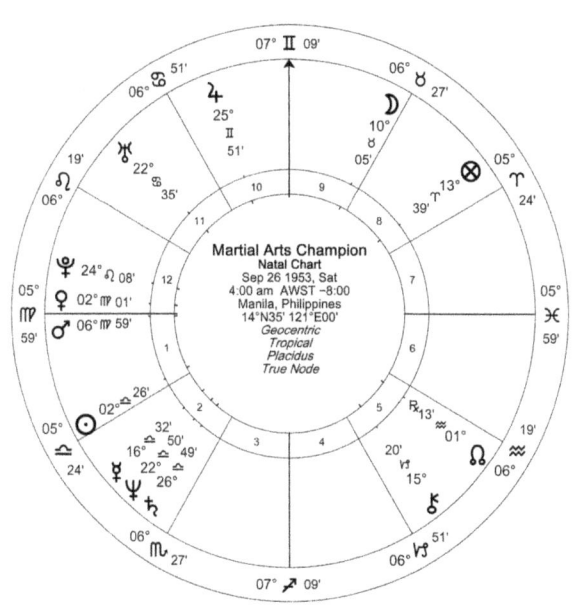

Vocational Astrology

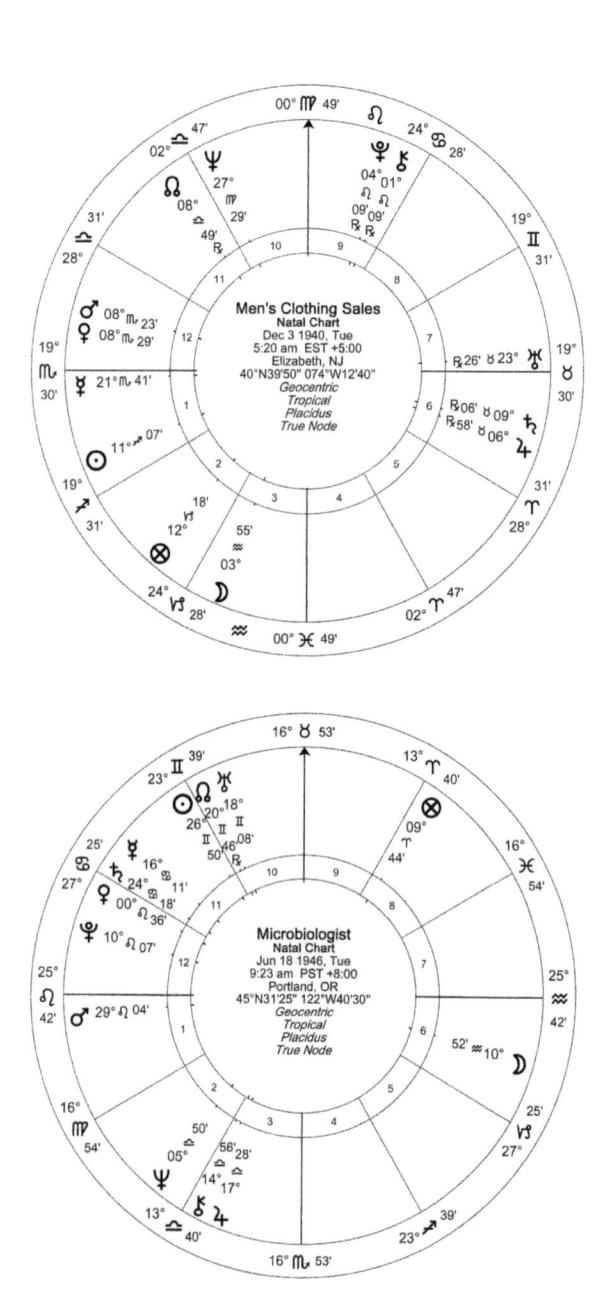

Appendix C: Vocational Horoscopes

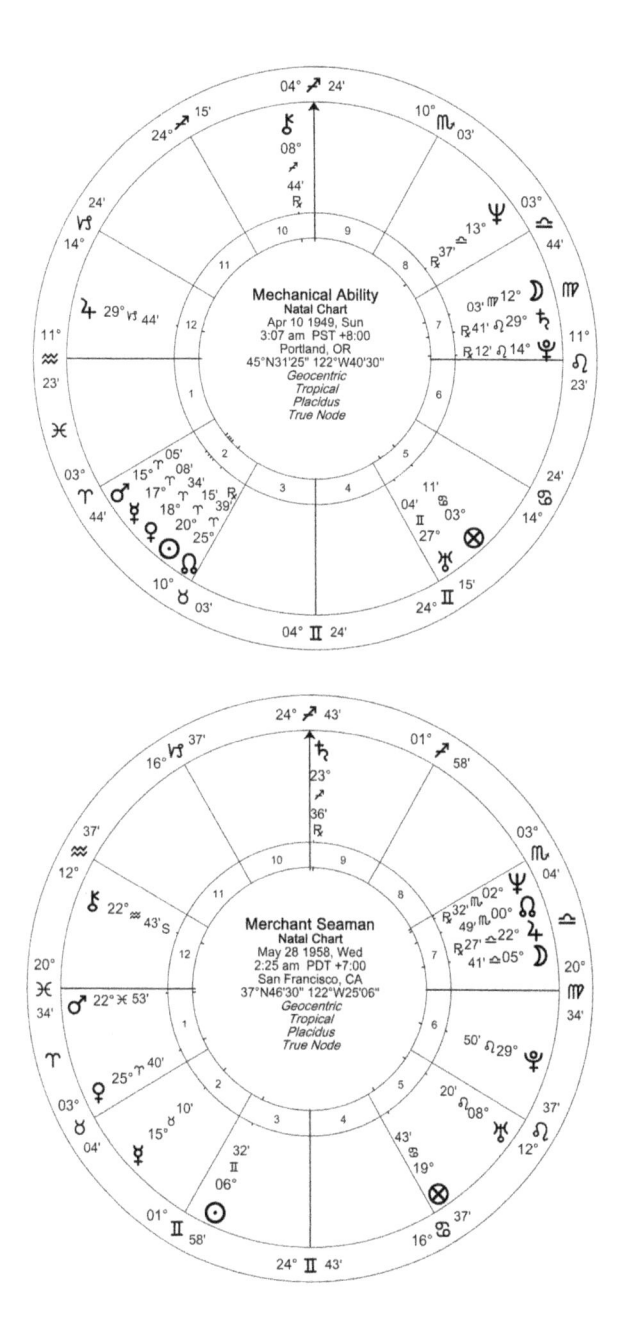

Mechanical Ability
Natal Chart
Apr 10 1949, Sun
3:07 am PST +8:00
Portland, OR
45°N31'25" 122°W40'30"
Geocentric
Tropical
Placidus
True Node

Merchant Seaman
Natal Chart
May 28 1958, Wed
2:25 am PDT +7:00
San Francisco, CA
37°N46'30" 122°W25'06"
Geocentric
Tropical
Placidus
True Node

Vocational Astrology 181

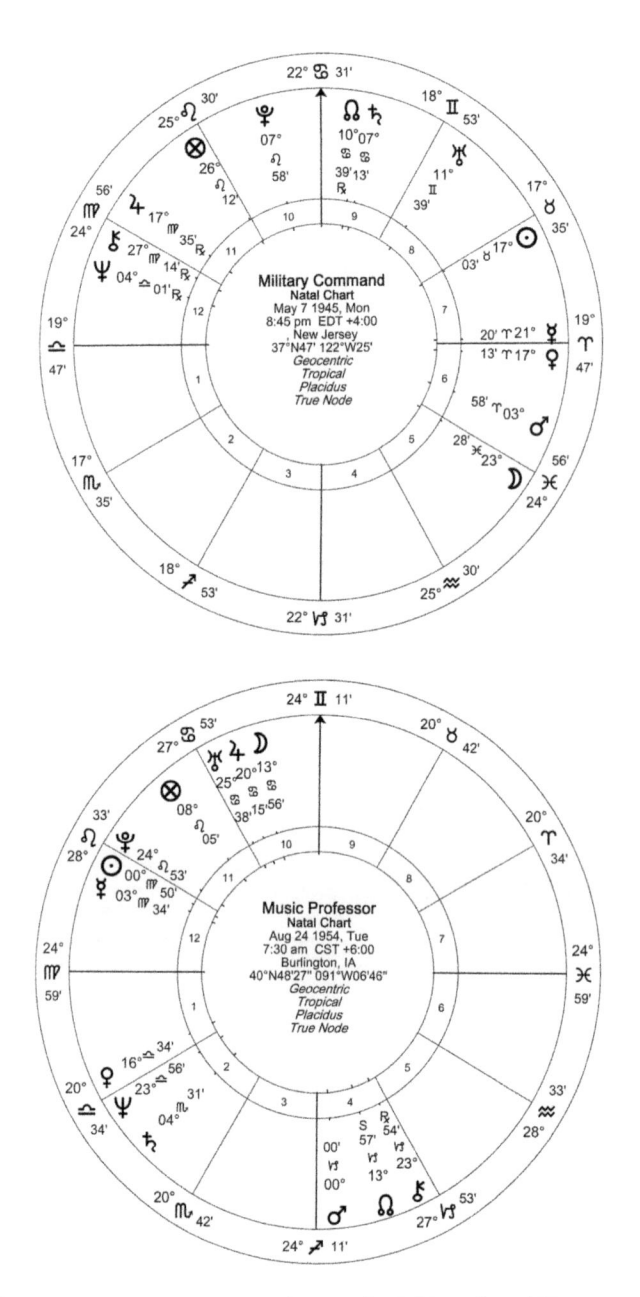

Appendix C: Vocational Horoscopes

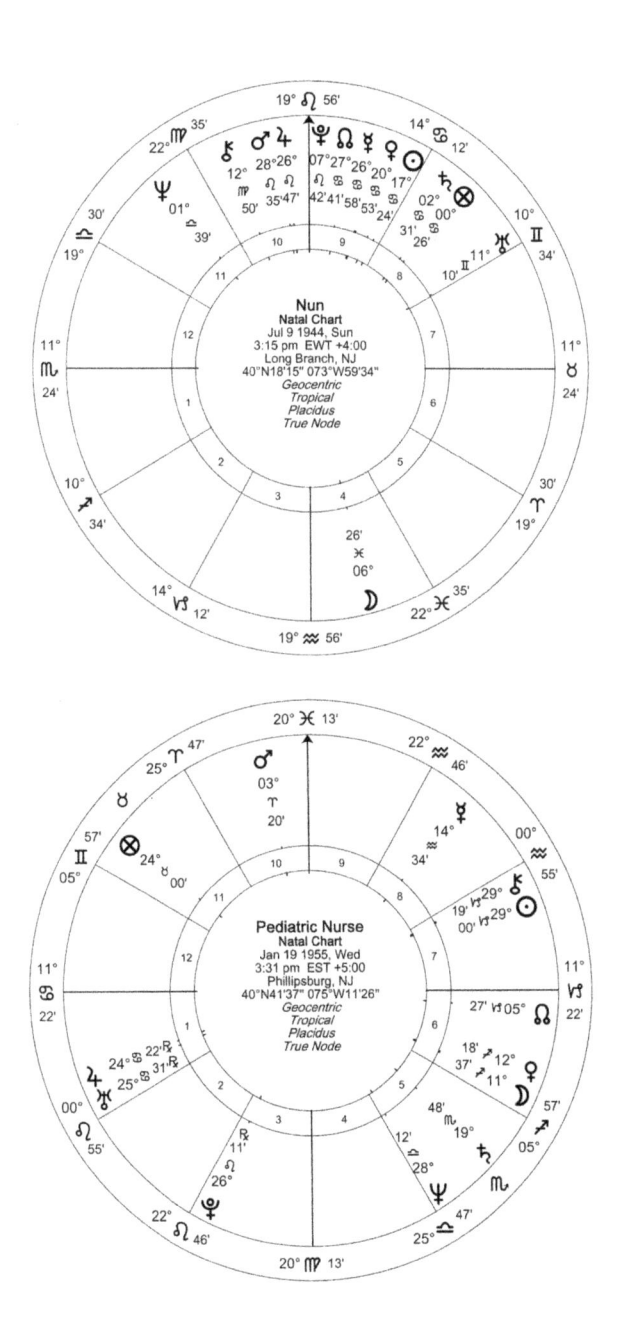

Nun
Natal Chart
Jul 9 1944, Sun
3:15 pm EWT +4:00
Long Branch, NJ
40°N18'15" 073°W59'34"
Geocentric
Tropical
Placidus
True Node

Pediatric Nurse
Natal Chart
Jan 19 1955, Wed
3:31 pm EST +5:00
Phillipsburg, NJ
40°N41'37" 075°W11'26"
Geocentric
Tropical
Placidus
True Node

Vocational Astrology

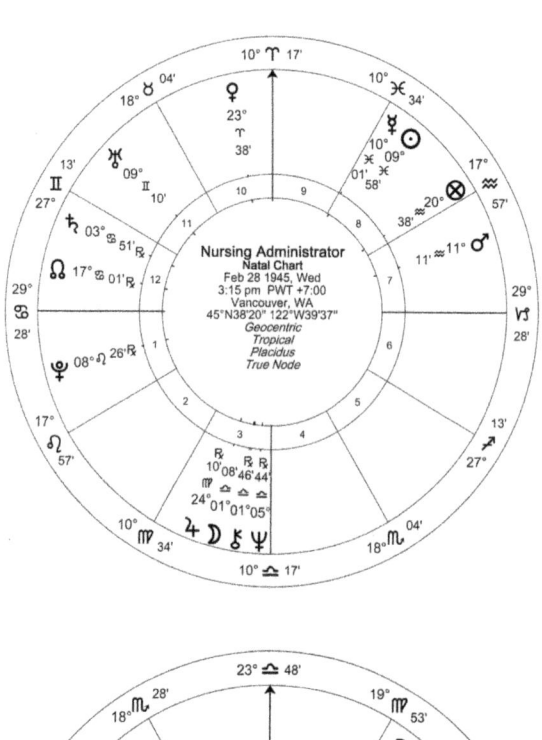

Appendix C: Vocational Horoscopes

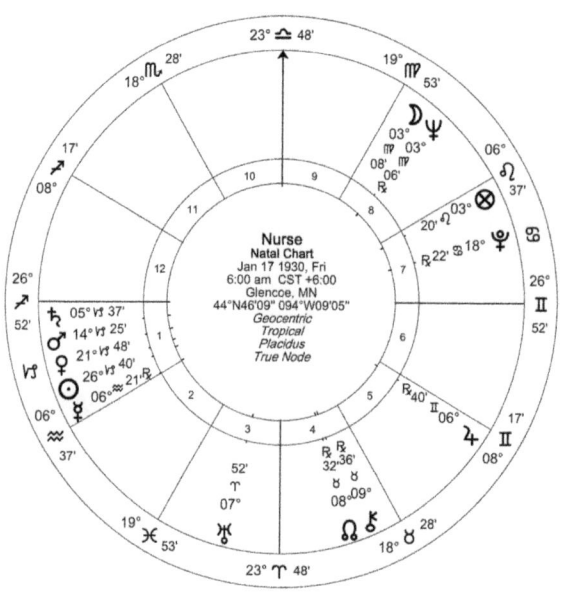

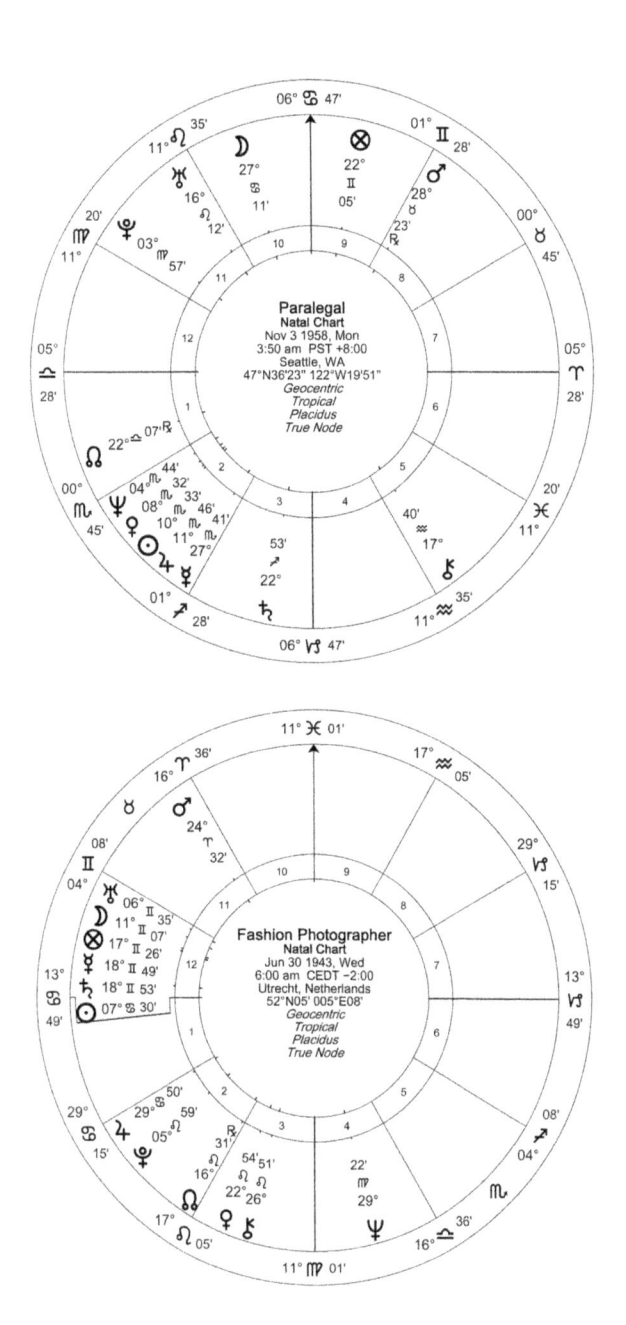

Paralegal
Natal Chart
Nov 3 1958, Mon
3:50 am PST +8:00
Seattle, WA
47°N36'23" 122°W19'51"
Geocentric
Tropical
Placidus
True Node

Fashion Photographer
Natal Chart
Jun 30 1943, Wed
6:00 am CEDT -2:00
Utrecht, Netherlands
52°N05' 005°E08'
Geocentric
Tropical
Placidus
True Node

Vocational Astrology 185

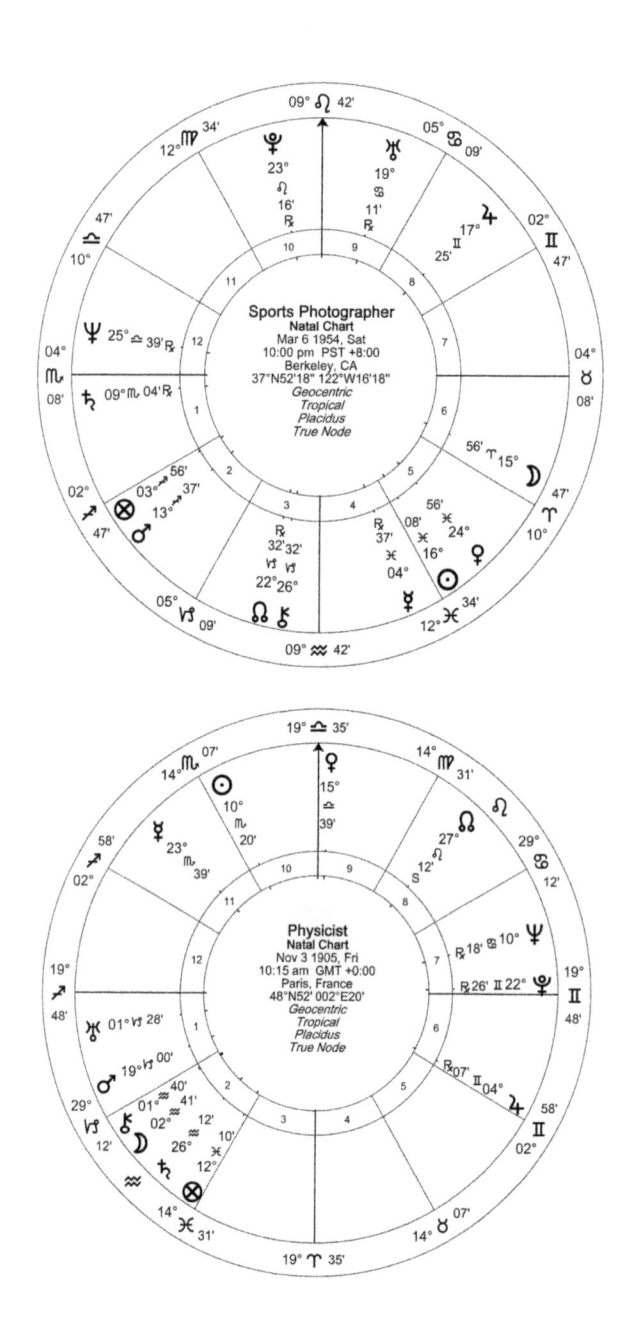

Appendix C: Vocational Horoscopes

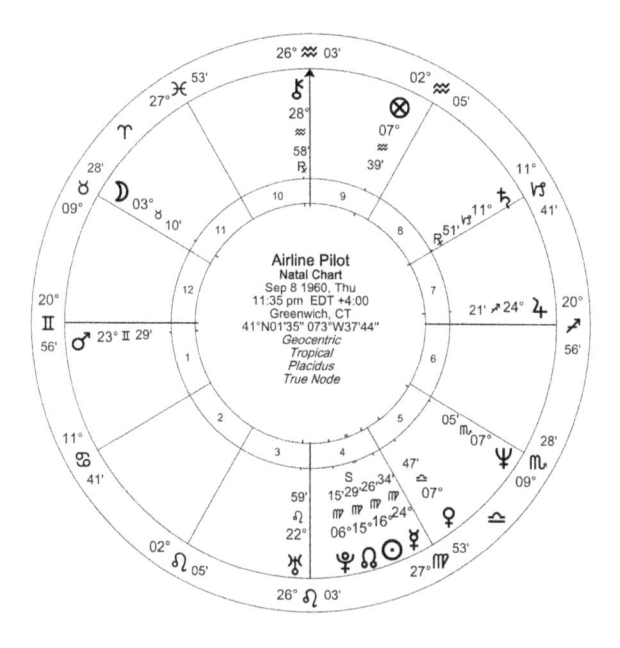

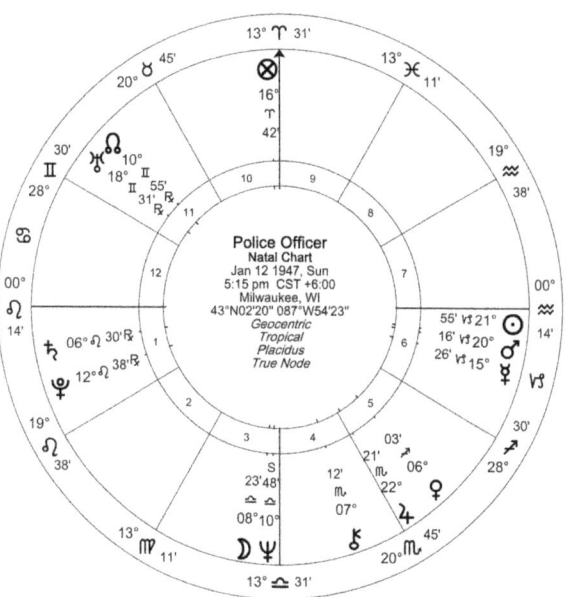

Vocational Astrology

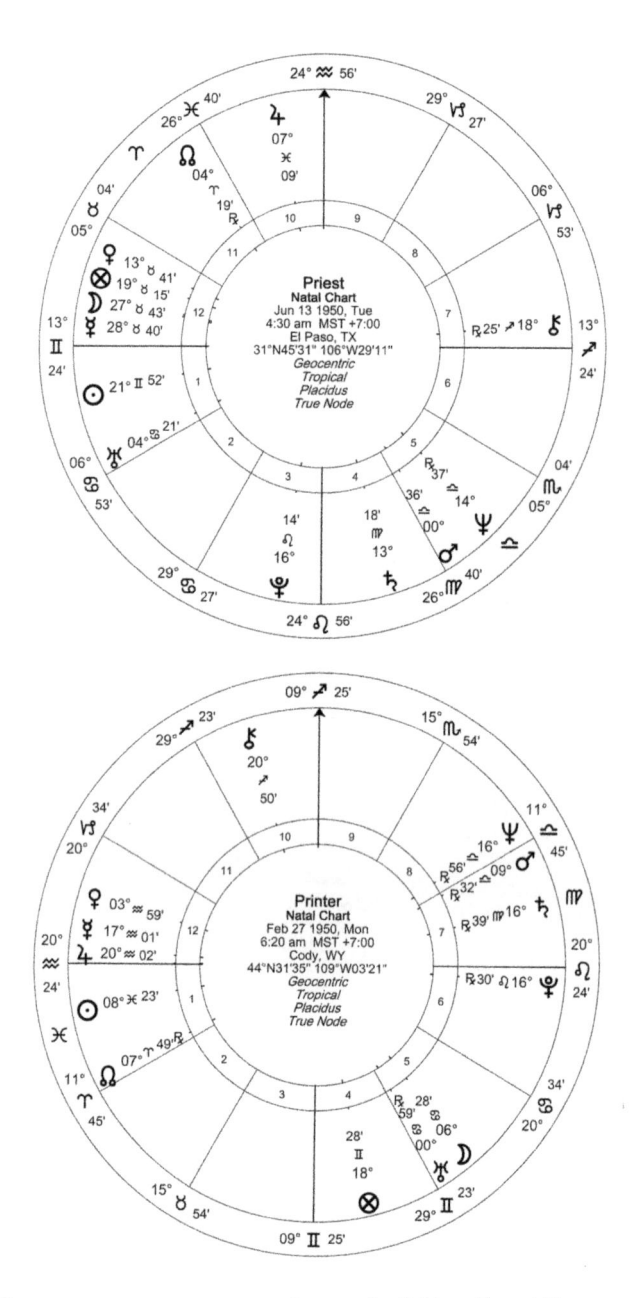

Appendix C: Vocational Horoscopes

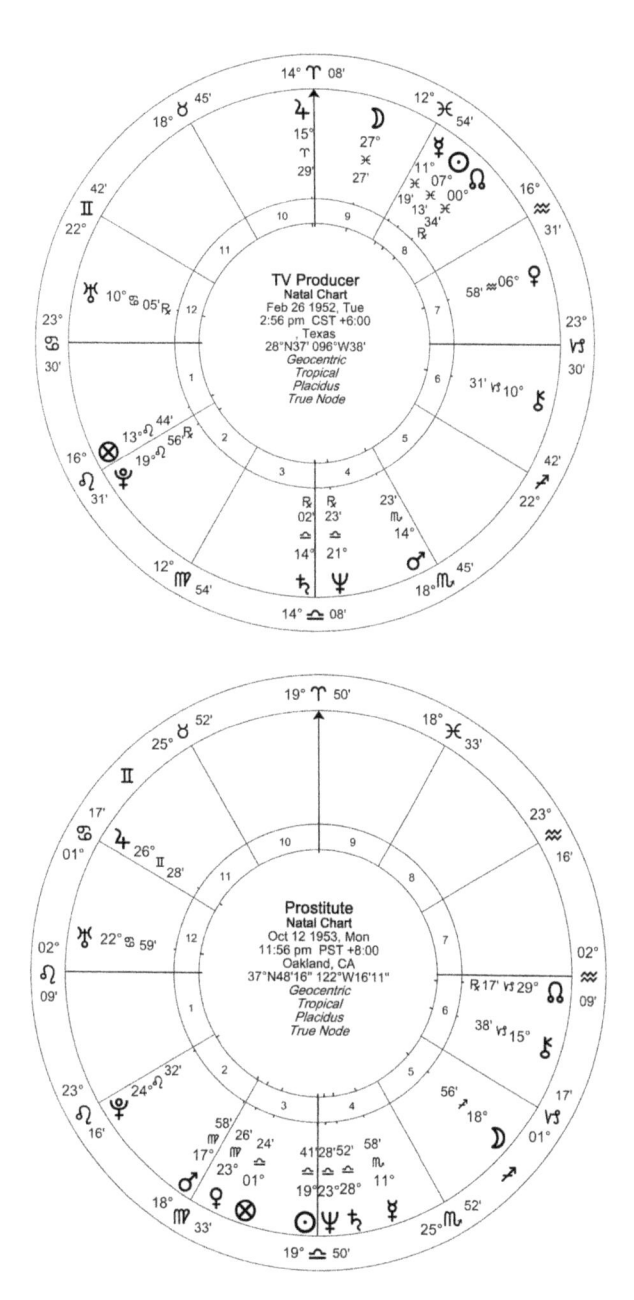

TV Producer
Natal Chart
Feb 26 1952, Tue
2:56 pm CST +6:00
Texas
28°N37' 096°W38'
Geocentric
Tropical
Placidus
True Node

Prostitute
Natal Chart
Oct 12 1953, Mon
11:56 pm PST +8:00
Oakland, CA
37°N48'16" 122°W16'11"
Geocentric
Tropical
Placidus
True Node

Vocational Astrology 189

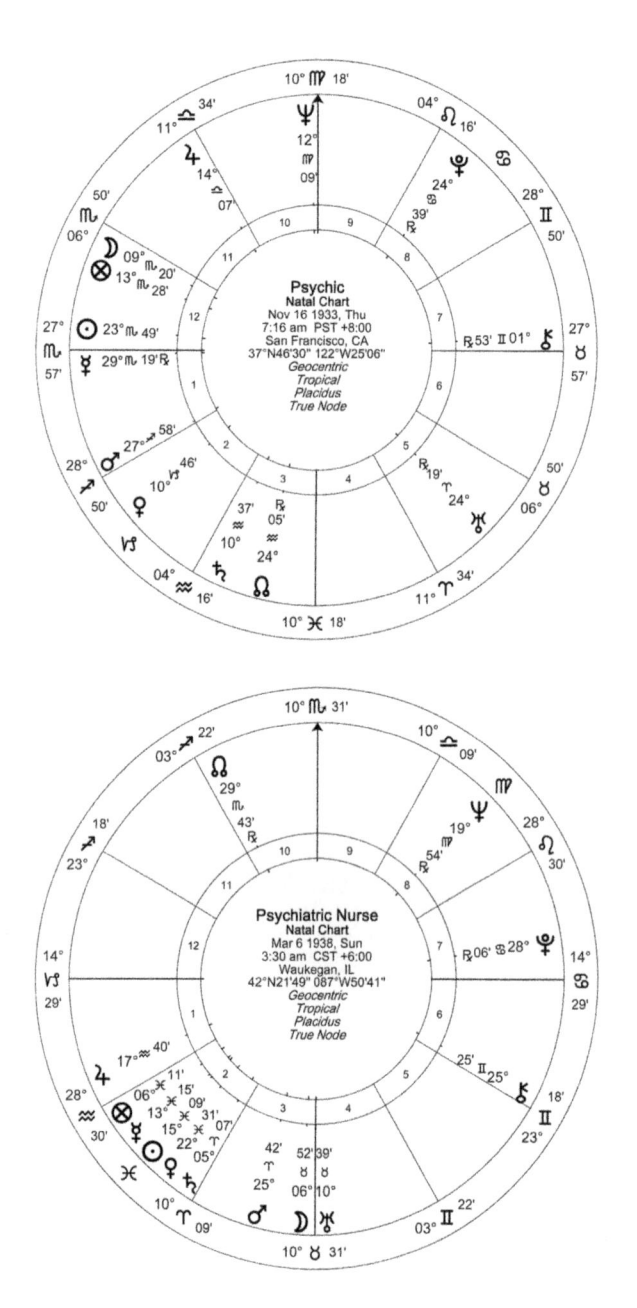

Appendix C: Vocational Horoscopes

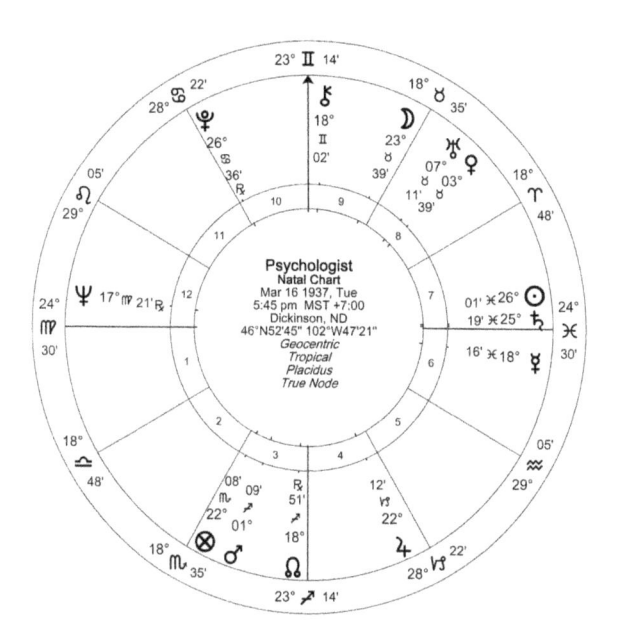

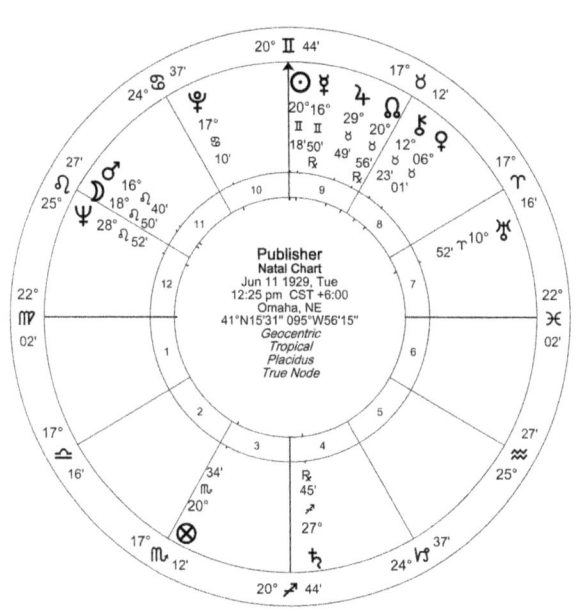

Vocational Astrology

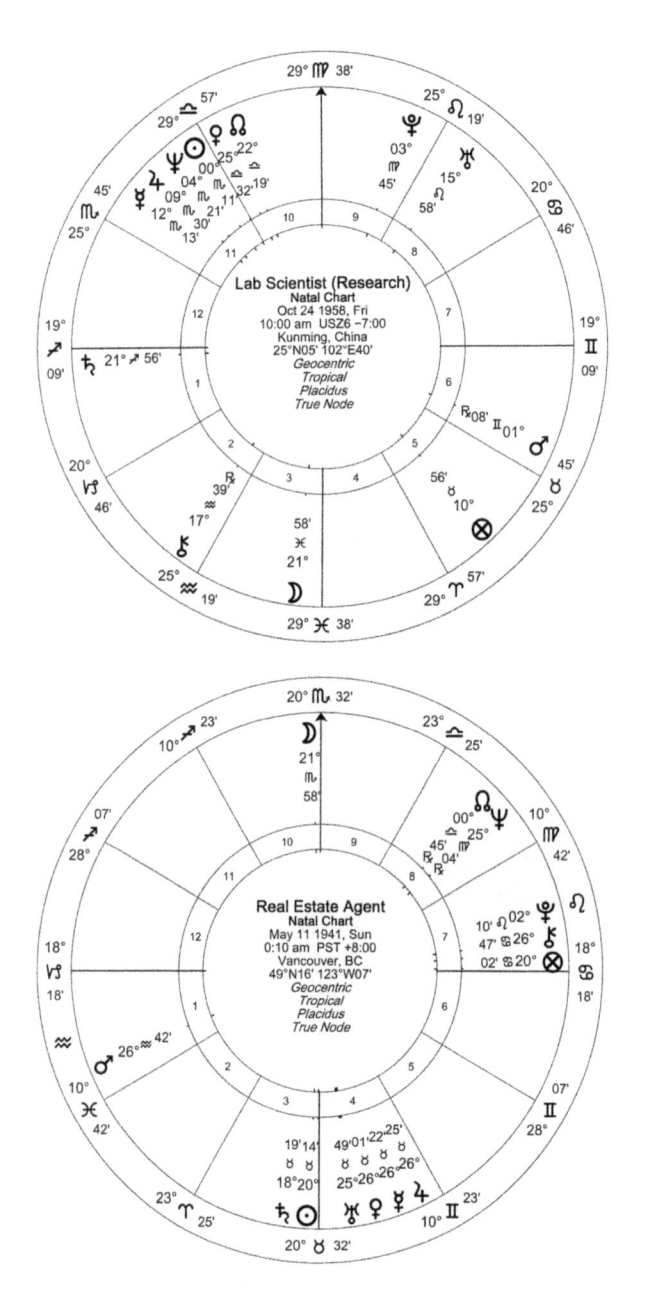

Appendix C: Vocational Horoscopes

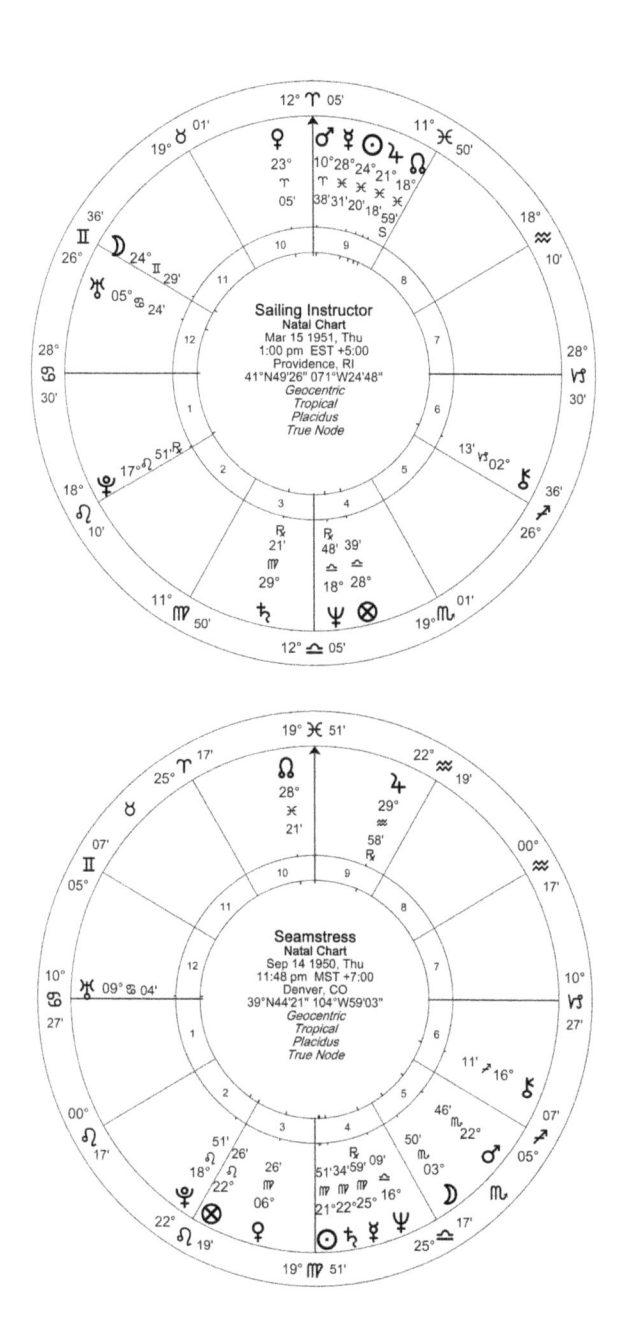

Sailing Instructor
Natal Chart
Mar 15 1951, Thu
1:00 pm EST +5:00
Providence, RI
41°N49'26" 071°W24'48"
Geocentric
Tropical
Placidus
True Node

Seamstress
Natal Chart
Sep 14 1950, Thu
11:48 pm MST +7:00
Denver, CO
39°N44'21" 104°W59'03"
Geocentric
Tropical
Placidus
True Node

Vocational Astrology

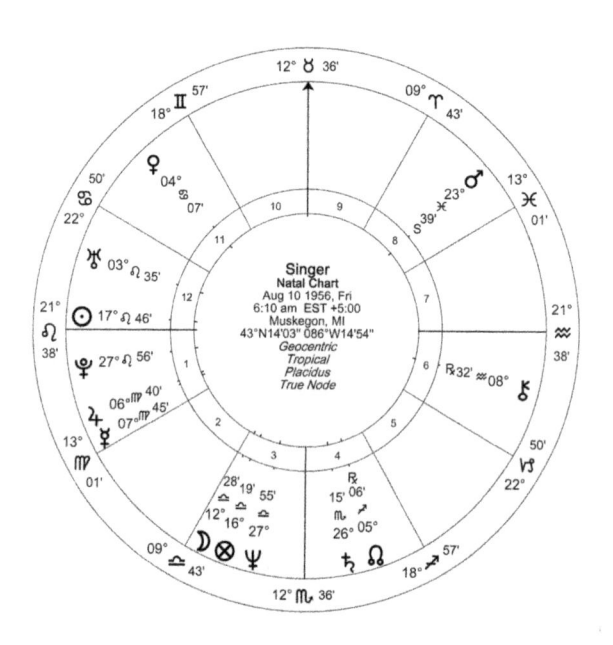

Singer
Natal Chart
Aug 10 1956, Fri
6:10 am EST +5:00
Muskegon, MI
43°N14'03" 086°W14'54"
Geocentric
Tropical
Placidus
True Node

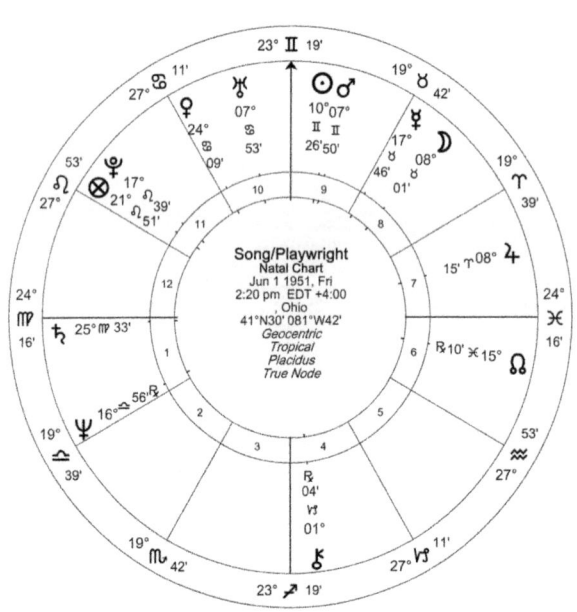

Song/Playwright
Natal Chart
Jun 1 1951, Fri
2:20 pm EDT +4:00
, Ohio
41°N30' 081°W42'
Geocentric
Tropical
Placidus
True Node

Appendix C: Vocational Horoscopes

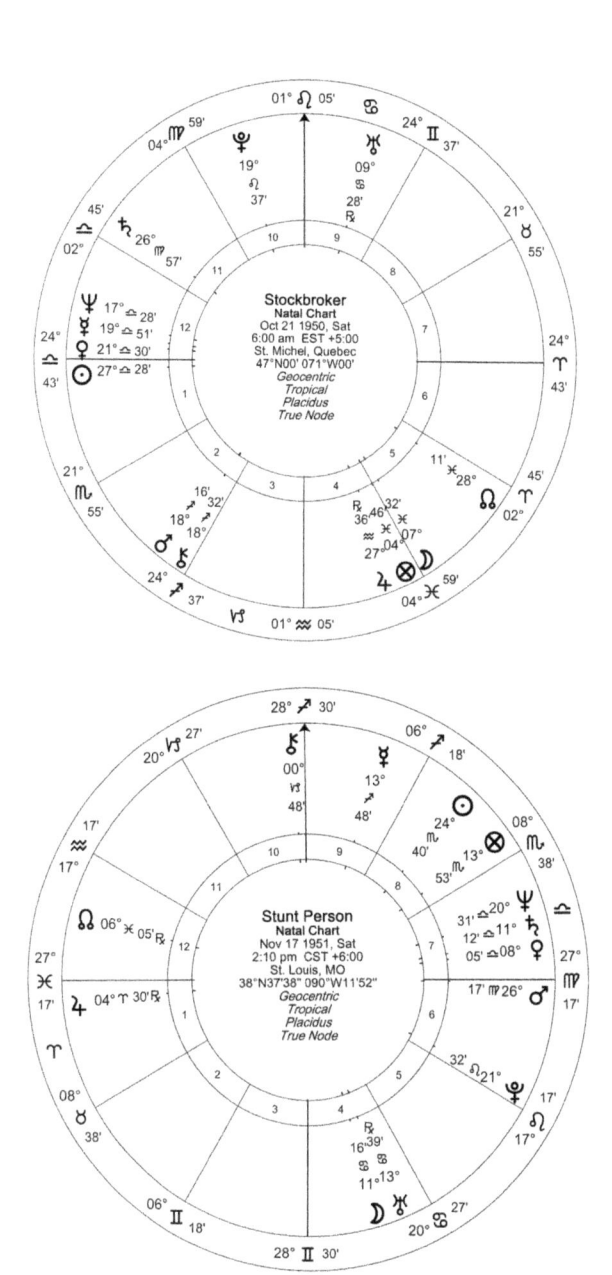

Vocational Astrology

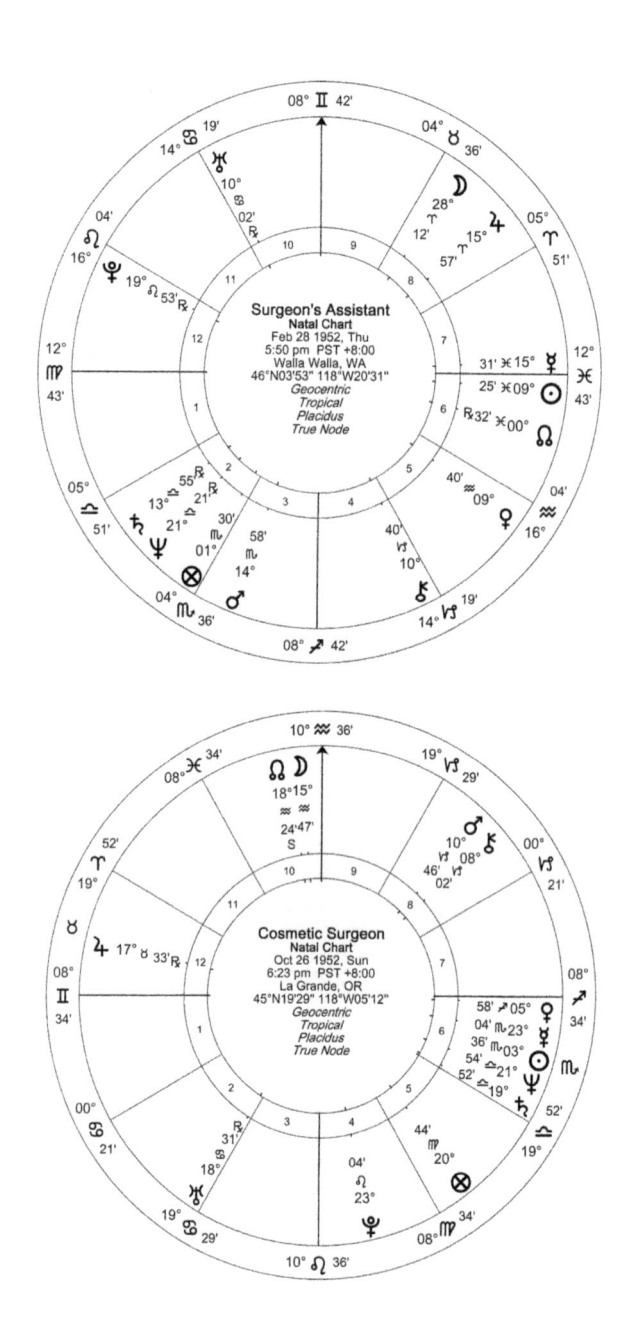

Appendix C: Vocational Horoscopes

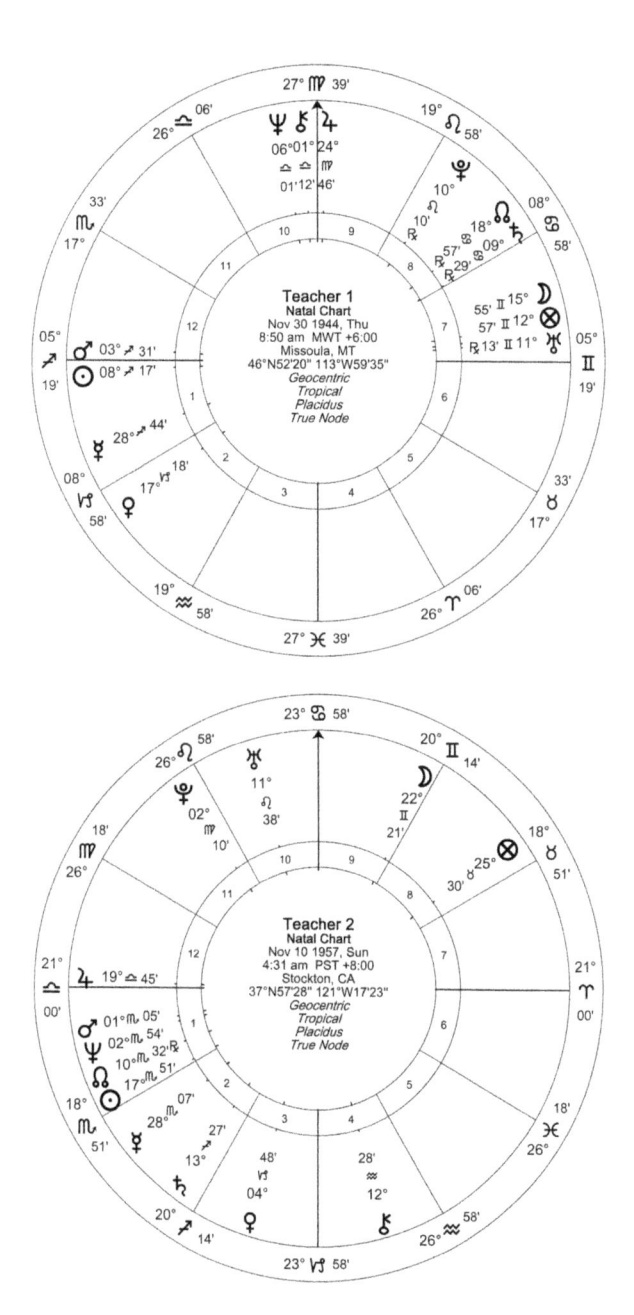

Vocational Astrology

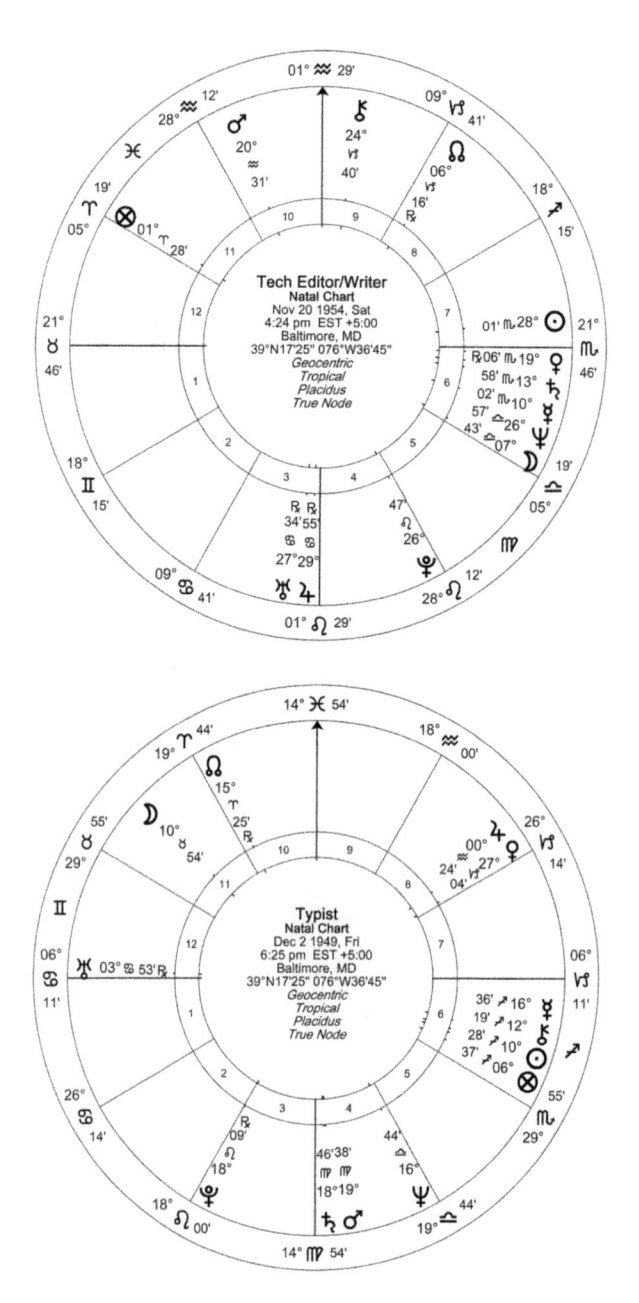

Appendix C: Vocational Horoscopes

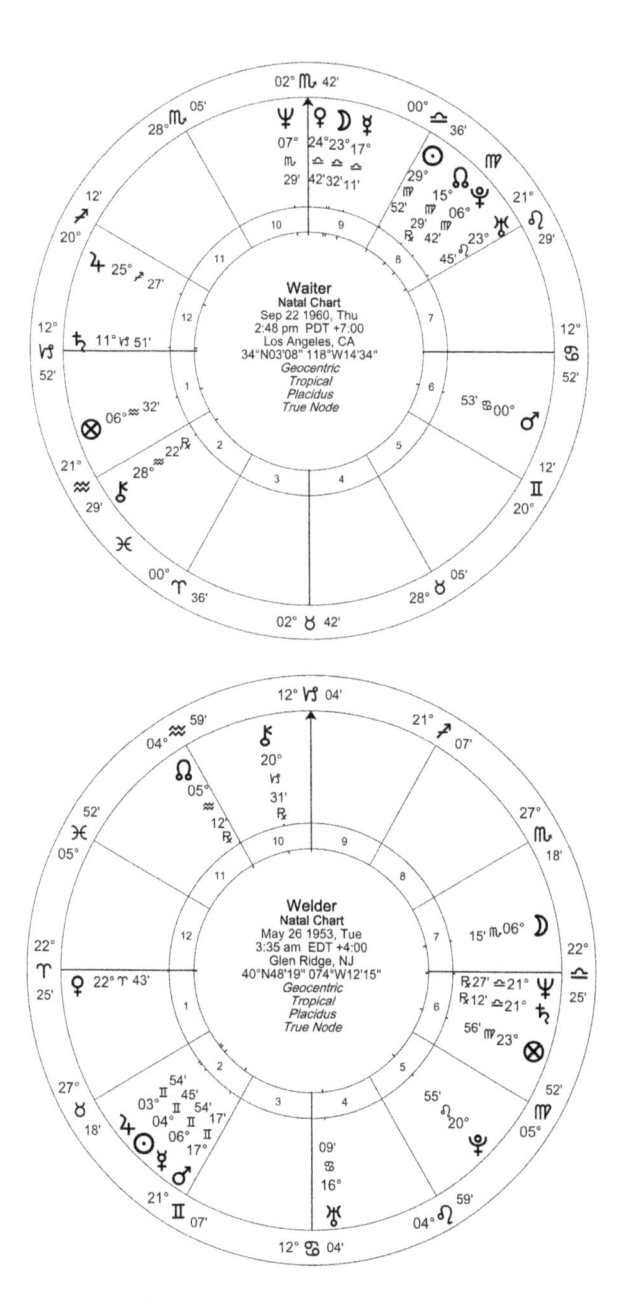

Vocational Astrology

Bibliography

Books

Llewellyn George, *The A to Z Horoscope Maker and Delineator*, Llewellyn Publications, St. Paul MN, 1970

William Lilly, *An Introduction to Astrology*, Newcastle Publishing, CA, 1972 (164 7)

Sepharial, *The Manual of Astrology*, Wholesale Books, NY, 1972

Carl E. Wagner, Jr., *Characterology*, Samuel Weiser, York Beach ME, 1986

Claudius Ptolemy, *Tetrabiblos*, 140, reprinted by The Aries Press, Chicago, 1936

Maharshi Parasara, *Brihat Parasara Hora Sastra*, Vol. I and II, Ranjan Publishers, New Delhi

Michel Gauquelin, *Birth Times*, Hill and Wang, NY, 1983 Michel Gauquelin, The Cosmic Clock, Avon, NY, 1969

Charles E. Luntz, *Vocational Guidance by Astrology*, Llewellyn Publications, St. Paul MN, 1962

Maude Haughton Champion, *The Science of Vocational Astrology*, Macoy Publishing Co., NY, 1933

William G. Benham, *The Laws of Scientific Hand Reading*, Hawthorn Books, NY, 1946

Hart De Fouw and Robert Svoboda, *Light on Life*, Penguin Books

Vivian Robson, *The Fixed Stars and Constellations in Astrology*, Samuel Weiser, The Aquarian Press, 1969

Percival and Fox, *Mundane Tables of Fixed Stars in Astrology*, Quick Specs, Blackwood Terrace NJ, 1975

Fred Gettings, *Dictionary of Astrology*, Routledge and Kegan Paul, London, 1985

James T. Braha, *Ancient Hindu Astrology for the Modern Western Astrologer*, Hermetician Press, Miami, 1986

Ralph William Holden, *The Elements of House Division*, L.N. Fowler and Co., Ltd., Essex, England

Nicholas Devore, *The Encyclopedia of Astrology*, Philosophical Library, NY

Robert Zoller, *The Arabic Parts in Astrology*, Inner Traditions Intl., Ltd.

Reinhold Ebertin, *The Combination of Stellar Influences*, AFA, Tempe AZ, 1940

George White, *The Moon's Nodes*, AFA, Tempe AZ, 2004

Project Hindsight, Recommended: Greek Track (tapes), Sect (pamphlet), Golden Hind Press, Berkeley Springs WV

Nick Kollerstrom, *The Metal-Planet Relationship*, Borderland Sciences Research Foundation, Bayside CA, 1991

Alison Davison, *Metal Power*, Borderland Sciences Research Foundation, Bayside CA, 1991

Georges Lakhovsky, *The Secret of Life: Cosmic Rays and Radiations of Living Beings*, 1939, reprinted by Borderland Sciences Research Foundation, Bayside CA, 1991

Penny Thornton, *The Forces of Destiny*, Weidenfield and Nickolson, Ltd., London, 1990

Arthur Young, *The Geometry of Meaning*, Robert Briggs & Assoc., 1976

Arthur Young, *The Reflexive Universe*, Robert Briggs & Assoc.

Books by the Author

Medical Astrology, a Guide to Planetary Pathology, Stellium Press, 2011

The Astrological Body Types: Face, Form and Expression, Stellium Press, 1993, 1997, 2013

The Lunar Nodes, Your Key to Excellent Chart Interpretation, Stellium Press, 2010

Eclipses and You, How to Align with Life's Hidden Tides, Stellium Press, 2013

A Wonderbook of True Astrological Case Files, Judith Hill and Andrea Gehrz, 2013

Mrs. Winkler's Cure, Stellium Press, Julia Holly aka Judith Hill, 2010

The Part of Fortune in Astrology, Stellium Press, 1998

Astroseismology: Earthquakes and Astrology, (compendium with Mark Polit) Stellium Press, 2000

The Mars-Redhead Files, (compendium with Jacalyn Thompson) Stellium Press, 2000

Journal Articles by the Author

Judith A. Hill and Jacalyn Thompson, "The Mars-Redhead Link," *NCGR Journal*, Winter 1988-89; also published by *Above & Below*, Canada, first publication *Linguace Astrale* (Italy), *AA Journal* (Great Britain, FAA Journal (Australia)

Judith A. Hill, "The Mars Redhead Link II: Mars Distribution Patterns in Redhead Populations," *Borderland Sciences Research Foundation Journal*, Vol. L1, No. 1 (part one) and Vol. L1, No. 2 (part two) Judith A. Hill, "Commentary on the John Addey Redhead Data," *NCGR Journal*, Winter 1988-89

Judith A. Hill, "Redheads and Mars," *The Mountain Astrologer*, May 1996

Judith A. Hill, "The Regional Factor in Planetary-Seismic Correlation," *Borderland Sciences Research Foundation Journal*, Vol. L1, No. 3, 1995 (reprint courtesy of American Astrology)

Judith A. Hill and Mark Polit, "Correlation of Earthquakes with Planetary Placement: The Regional Factor," *NCGR Journal*, 5 (1), 1987

Judith A. Hill, "American Redhead's Project Replication," *Correlation*, Vol. 13, No. 2, Winter 1994-95

Judith A. Hill, "Octaves of Time," *Borderland Sciences Research Foundation Journal*, Vol. LI, No. 4, Fourth Quarter, 1995

Judith A. Hill, "Gemstones, Antidotes for Planetary Weaknesses," *ISIS Journal*, 1994

Judith A. Hill, "Medical Astrology," *Borderland Sciences Research Foundation Journal*, Vol. LI I, No. I, First Quarter, 1996

Judith A. Hill, "Astrological Heredity," *Borderland Sciences Research Foundation Journal*, 1996

Judith A. Hill, "The Electional and Horary Branches," *Sufism*, IAS, Vol. 1, No. 2

Judith A. Hill, "Astrology: A Philosophy of Time and Space," *Sufism*, IAS, Vol. 1, No. 1

Judith A. Hill "Natal Astrology," *Sufism*, IAS, Vol. 1, No. 3

Judith A. Hill, "An Overview of Medical Astrology," *Sufism*, IAS, Vol. 1, No. 4

Judith A. Hill, "Predictive Astrology in Theory an Practice," *Sufism*, IAS, Vol. 11, No. 1

Judith A. Hill, "Esoteric Astrology," *Sufism*, IAS, Vol. 11, Nos. 2, 3

Judith A. Hill, "Mundane Astrology," *Sufism*, IAS, Vol. 11, No. 4

Judith A. Hill, "Vocational Astrology," *Sufism*, IAS, Part 1 and 2, Vol. 11, Nos. 1, 2

Judith A. Hill, "Astro-Psychology," *Sufism*, IAS, Vol. 11, Nos. 3, 4

Judith A. Hill, "The Planetary Time Clocks," *Sufism*, IAS, Vol. 4, Nos. 1, 2, 3, 4

Judith A. Hill, "Astrophysiognomy," *Sufism*, IAS, Vol. 4, Nos. 1, 2

Judith A. Hill, "Spiritual Signposts in the Birth Map," *Sufism*, IAS, Vol. 5, Nos. 2, 3

Judith A. Hill, "The Philosophical Questions Most Frequently Asked of the Astrologer," *Sufism*, IAS, Vol. 5, No. 4, Vol. 6, Nos. 1, 2

About the Author

Judith Hill is a second generation astrologer and has worked as an astrological consultant for more than thirty years. She has served as educational director for the San Francisco NCGR (National Council for Geocosmic Research) chapter and as a faculty member of ISIS (Institute for Stellar Influence Studies). Her specialty is vocational astrology. In 1999, she received the American Federation of Astrologers Paul R. Grell Best Book Award for *Vocational Astrology*.

Judith achieved 100 percent accuracy in the matching of five anonymous birth charts to biographies in a 1986 skeptic-designed NCGR-sponsored challenge.

Her two breakthrough research reports—"The Mars-Redhead Link" (with Jacalyn Thompson) and "The Regional Factor in Planetary-Seismic Correlation" (with Mark Polit)—have been internationally published. Strange Universe, a national television show, in 1997 produced a segment on Judith's astro-genetic work. She is the author of *The Astrological Body Types*, which has been translated into Russian and Lettish language editions (Judith is of Latvian-Jewish heritage), and *The Part of Fortune in Astrology*.

For more than four years she contributed her own section, "Astrology, A Philosophy of Time and Space," to Sufism, published by IAS. This historic column might represent the first time that serious commentary on astrology was continuously featured outside of astrological journals.

Judith was named "Best Astrologer in Portland, Oregon" by the *Willamette Week* in 1996. She has lectured widely and made guest appearance on many popular radio and television programs, and was featured as the weekly vocational astrologer on the New York-based "Job l" radio show in 1998. She was interviewed by Tony Howard for the December 2010 issue of *The*

Mountain Astrologer.

Judith strives to improve the public image of astrology through her informative lectures on several branches of astrology, including scientific research, medical, vocational, electional, seismic, genetic, horary, Vedic-Western comparison and Vedic gem antidotes. She is currently producing The Lost Secrets of Renaissance Medicine Conference: Herbs, Medical Astrology, Alchemy.